HISTORY OF INDIA

HISTORY OF INDIA

Edited by
A. V. WILLIAMS JACKSON, Ph. D., LL.D.

VOLUME II

From the Sixth Century B.C. to the Mohammedan Conquest, Including the Invasion of Alexander the Great

BY
VINCENT A. SMITH, M.A., M.R.A.S., F.R.N.S.

GYAN

Published by

Gyan Publishing House
5, Ansari Road
Daryaganj, New Delhi-110002
Phone: 011-47034999, 9811692060
E-mail: books@gyanbooks.com

Distribution Network
gyanbooks.com
India, USA, Canada, UK, Australia, France

ISBN : 978-81-212-6780-9 (Set)
978-81-212-4560-9 (HB)
First Published, 1906

2nd Impression 2022

Printed at: Gyan Press, Delhi.

HISTORY OF INDIA (VOL. II)
Author: Vincent A. Smith

HISTORY *of* INDIA

Edited by

A. V. WILLIAMS JACKSON, Ph. D., LL. D.

Professor of Indo-Iranian Languages in Columbia University

VOLUME II

From the Sixth Century B. C. to the Mohammedan Conquest, Including the Invasion of Alexander the Great

By

VINCENT A. SMITH, M.A., M.R.A.S., F.R.N.S.

Late of the Indian Civil Service, Author of "Asoka, the Buddhist Emperor of India"

PREFACE BY THE EDITOR

This volume covers the interesting period from the century in which Buddha appeared down to the first centuries after the Mohammedans entered India, or, roughly speaking, from 600 B.C. to 1200 A.D. During this long era India, now Aryanized, was brought into closer contact with the outer world. The invasion of Alexander the Great gave her at least a touch of the West; the spread of Buddhism and the growth of trade created new relations with China and Central Asia; and, toward the close of the period, the great movements which had their origin in Arabia brought her under the influences which affected the East historically after the rise of Islam.

In no previous work will the reader find so thorough and so comprehensive a description as Mr. Vincent Smith has given of Alexander's inroad into India and of his exploits which stirred, even if they did not deeply move, the soul of India; nor has there existed hitherto so full an account of the great rulers, Chandragupta, Asoka, and Harsha, each of whom made famous the age in which he lived. The value of the book is further enhanced by a historical sketch of the mediæval kingdoms of the North and the Deccan and by a brief outline of the history of Southern Hindustan, a section to which attention should be devoted by the historian who wishes fully to understand India's present condition as well as her past. Throughout the work the author has taken advantage of every available source, whether literary, traditional, archæological, monumental, epigraphic, or numismatic, including also the narratives of the early Chinese pilgrims who visited India and whose narratives yield important historic results.

The plan of the series has necessitated certain changes from the original edition of the author's work so as to bring the volume into closer accord with the others of this History; to these alterations Mr. Smith, like the other writers, has courteously consented, a concession which I, as editor, desire to acknowledge with appreciation. It was necessary, for example, to omit the foot-notes and marginal references, one or two maps, and some of the longer appendices that were of a strictly technical character, in order to bring the volume within the compass required. In no case, I believe, has anything been eliminated that was essential to the main theme, namely, the continuous story of India's development during the period indicated. The reader who may desire to pursue the subject further and devote attention more specifically to minute details will consult Mr. Smith's larger volume, which abounds in references.

In choosing the illustrations for the history of this period, as of the others, much care has been taken and an endeavour has been made to add to the existing material by including photographs from my own collection made in India. Other persons also have kindly aided in carrying out this part of the plan as designed, by granting permission to reproduce pictures which were their special property.

Among the obligations which both the publishers and myself most cordially recognize is an indebtedness to Mr. Holland Thompson, A. M., Instructor in History in the College of the City of New York, who rendered generous assistance in connection with the preparation of the text to conform with the needs of the series, and for aid in making the index.

With these words I present the volume, recalling the reader once more from the present to the past, to the early ages of India before and after the Christian era.

A. V. Williams Jackson.

CONTENTS

LIST OF ILLUSTRATIONS

FRIEZE FROM A BUDDHIST STUPA.

CHAPTER I

INTRODUCTION

THE researches of a multitude of scholars working in various fields have disclosed an unexpected wealth of materials for the reconstruction of ancient Indian history, and the necessary preliminary studies of a technical kind have been carried so far that the moment seems to have arrived for taking stock of the accumulated stores of knowledge. It now appears to be practicable to exhibit the results of antiquarian studies in the shape of a "connected relation" not less intelligible to the ordinary educated reader than Elphinstone's narrative of the transactions of the Mohammedan period.

The first attempt to present such a narrative of the leading events in Indian political history for eighteen centuries is made in this book, which is designedly confined almost exclusively to the relation of political vicissitudes. A sound framework of dynastic annals must be provided before the story of Indian literature and art can be told aright. Although literary and artistic problems are touched on very lightly in this volume, the references made will suffice, perhaps, to convince the reader that the key is often to be found in the accurate chronological presentation of dynastic facts.

European students, whose attention has been directed almost exclusively to the Græco-Roman foundation of modern civilization, may be disposed to agree with the German philosopher in the belief that "Chinese, Indian, and Egyptian antiquities are never more than curiosities;" but, however well founded that opinion may have been in Goethe's day, it can no longer command assent. The researches of Orientalists during the last hundred years have established many points of contact between the ancient East and the modern West, and no Hellenist can now afford to profess complete ignorance of the Babylonian and Egyptian culture which forms the bed-rock of European institutions. Even China has been brought into touch with Europe, while the languages, literature, art, and philosophy of the West have been proved to be connected by innumerable bonds with those of India. Although the names of even the greatest monarchs of ancient India are at present unfamiliar to the general reader, and awaken few echoes in the minds of any save specialists, it is not unreasonable to hope that an orderly presentation of the ascertained facts of ancient Indian history may be of interest to a larger circle than that of professed Orientalists, and that, as the subject becomes more familiar to the reading public, it will be found no less worthy of attention than more familiar departments of historical study. A recent Indian author justly observes that "India suffers to-day in the estimation of the world more through the world's ignorance of the achievements of the heroes of Indian history than through the absence or insignificance of such achievements." The following pages may serve to prove that the men of old time in India did deeds worthy of remembrance and deserving of rescue from the oblivion in which they have been buried for so many centuries.

The section of this work which deals with the invasion of Alexander the Great may claim to make a special appeal to the interest of readers trained in the ordinary course of classical studies, and the subject has been treated accordingly with much fulness of detail. The existing English accounts of Alexander's marvellous campaign treat the story rather as an appendix to the history of Greece than as part of that of India, and fail to make full use of the results of the labours of modern geographers and archæologists. In this volume the campaign is discussed as a memorable episode in the history of India, and an endeavour has been made to collect all the rays of light from recent investigation and to focus them upon the narratives of ancient authors.

The author's aim is to present the story of ancient India, so far as practicable, in the form of a connected narrative, based upon the most authentic evidence available; to relate facts, however established, with impartiality; and to discuss the problems of history in a judicial spirit. He has striven to realize, however imperfectly, the ideal expressed in the words of Goethe: —

"The historian's duty is to separate the true from the false, the certain from the uncertain, and the doubtful from that which cannot be accepted. . . . Every investigator must before all things look upon himself as one who is summoned to serve on a jury. He has only to consider how far the statement of the case is complete and clearly set forth by the evidence. Then he draws his conclusion and gives his vote, whether it be that his opinion coincides with that of the foreman or not."

The application of these principles necessarily involves the wholesale rejection of mere legend as distinguished from tradition, and the omission of many picturesque anecdotes, mostly folk-lore, which have clustered round the names of the mighty men of old in India.

The historian of the remote past of any nation must be content to rely much upon tradition as embodied in literature, and to acknowledge that the results of his researches, when based upon traditionary materials, are inferior in certainty to those obtainable for periods of which the facts are attested by contemporary evidence. In India, with very few exceptions, contemporary evidence of any kind is not available before the time of Alexander; but critical examination of records dated much later than the events referred to can extract from them testimony which may be regarded with a high degree of probability as traditionally transmitted from the sixth or perhaps the seventh century B.C.

Even contemporary evidence, when it is available for later periods, cannot be accepted without criticism. The flattery of courtiers, the vanity of kings, and many other clouds which obscure the absolute truth, must be recognized and allowed for. Nor is it possible for the writer of a history, however great may be his respect for the objective fact, to eliminate altogether his own personality. Every kind of evidence, even the most direct, must reach the reader, when in narrative form, as a reflection from the mirror of the writer's mind, with the liability to unconscious distortion. In the following pages the author has endeavoured to exclude the subjective element so far as possible, and to make no statement of fact without authority.

But no obligation to follow authority in the other sense of the word has been recognized, and the narrative often assumes a form which appears to be justified by the evidence, although opposed to the views stated in well-known books by authors of repute. Indian history has been too much the sport of credulity and hypothesis, inadequately checked by critical judgment of evidence or verification of fact, and "the opinion of the foreman," to use Goethe's phrase, cannot be implicitly followed.

Although this work purports to relate the early history of India, the title must be understood with certain limitations. India, encircled as she is by seas and mountains, is indisputably a geographical unit, and, as such, is rightly designated by one name. Her type of civilization, too, has many features which differentiate it from that of all other regions of the world, while they are common to the whole country, or rather continent, in a degree sufficient to justify its treatment as a unit

INDIA'S SACRED LOTUS.
From stereograph, copyright 1903, by Underwood & Underwood, New York.

in the history of human, social, and intellectual development.

But the complete political unity of India under the control of a paramount power, wielding unquestioned authority, is a thing of yesterday, barely a century old. The most notable of her rulers in the olden time cherished the ambition of universal Indian dominion, and severally attained it in a greater or less degree. But not one of them attained it completely, and this failure implies a lack of unity in political history which renders the task of the historian difficult.

The same difficulty besets the historian of Greece still more pressingly; but, in that case, with the attainment of unity, the interest of the history vanishes. In the case of India the converse proposition holds good, and the reader's interest varies directly with the degree of unity attained, the details of Indian annals being insufferably wearisome except when generalized by the application of a bond of political union.

A history of India, if it is to be read, must necessarily be the story of the predominant dynasties, and either ignore, or relegate to a very subordinate position, the annals of the minor states. Elphinstone acted upon this principle in his classic work, and practically confined his narrative to the transactions of the Sultans of Delhi and their Mogul successors. The same principle has been applied in this book, and attention has been concentrated upon the dominant dynasties which, from time to time, have attained or aspired to paramount power.

Twice in the long series of centuries dealt with in this history, the political unity of all India was nearly attained: first, in the third century B. C., when Asoka's empire extended to the latitude of Madras; and again, in the fourth century A. D., when Samudragupta carried his victorious arms from the Ganges to the extremity of the Peninsula. Other princes, although their conquests were less extensive, yet succeeded in establishing, and for a time maintaining, empires which might fairly claim to rank as paramount powers. With the history of such princes the following narrative is chiefly concerned, and the affairs of the minor states are either slightly noticed or altogether ignored.

The paramount power in early times, when it existed, invariably had its seat in Northern India — the region of the Ganges plain lying to the north of the great barrier of jungle-clad hills which shut off the Deccan from Hindustan. That barrier may be defined conveniently as consisting of the Vindhya ranges, or may be identified, still more compendiously, with the river Narmada, or Nerbudda, which falls into the Gulf of Cambay.

The ancient kingdoms of the south, although rich and populous, inhabited by Dravidian nations not inferior in culture to their Aryan rivals in the north, were ordinarily so secluded from the rest of the civilized world, including Northern India, that their affairs remained hidden from the eyes of other nations, and, native annalists being lacking, their history, previous to the year 1000 of the Christian era, has almost wholly perished. Except on the rare occasions when an unusually enterprising sovereign of the north either penetrated or turned the forest barrier, and for a moment lifted the veil of secrecy in which the southern potentates lived enwrapped, very little is known concerning political events in the south during the long period extending from 600 B.C. to 1000 A.D. To use the words of Elphinstone, no "connected relation of the national transactions" of Southern India in early times can be written, and an early history of India must, perforce, be concerned mainly with the north.

The time dealt with is that extending from the beginning of the historical period in 600 B.C. to the Mohammedan conquest, which may be dated in round numbers as having occurred in 1200 A.D. in the north, and a century later in the south. The earliest political event in India to which an approximately correct date can be assigned is the establishment of the Saisunaga dynasty of Magadha about 600 B.C.

The sources of, or original authorities for, the early history of India may be arranged in four classes. The first of these is tradition, chiefly as recorded in native literature; the second consists of those writings of foreign travellers and historians which contain observations on Indian subjects; the third is the evidence of archæology, which may be subdivided into the monumental, the epigraphic, and the numismatic; and the fourth comprises the few works of native contemporary literature which deal expressly with historical subjects.

For the period anterior to Alexander the Great, extending from 600 B.C. to 326 B.C., dependence must be placed almost wholly upon literary tradition, communicated through works composed in many different ages, and frequently recorded in scattered, incidental notices. The purely Indian traditions are supplemented by the notes of the Greek authors, Ktesias, Herodotus, the historians of Alexander, and Megasthenes.

The Kashmir chronicle, composed in the twelfth century, which is in form the nearest approach to a work of regular history in extant Sanskrit literature, contains a large body of confused ancient traditions, which can be used only with much caution. It is also of high value as a trustworthy record of local events for the period contemporary with, or slightly preceding, the author's lifetime.

The great Sanskrit epics, the Mahabharata and the Ramayana, while of value as traditional pictures of social life in the heroic age, do not seem to contain matter illustrating the political relations of states during the historical period.

Sanskrit specialists have extracted from the works of grammarians and other authors many incidental references to ancient tradition, which collectively amount to a considerable addition to historical knowledge. These passages from Sanskrit literature, so far as they have come to my notice, have been utilized in this work, but some references may have escaped attention.

The sacred books of the Jain sect, which are still very imperfectly known, also contain numerous historical statements and allusions of considerable value.

The Jatakas, or Birth stories, and other books of the Buddhist canon include many incidental references to the political condition of India in the fifth and sixth centuries B. C., which, although not exactly contemporary with the events alluded to, certainly transmit genuine historical tradition.

The chronicles of Ceylon in the Pali language, of which the *Dipavamsa*, dating probably from the fourth century A. D., and the *Mahavamsa* are the best known, offer several discrepant versions of early Indian traditions, chiefly concerning the Maurya dynasty. These Sinhalese stories, the value of which has been sometimes overestimated, demand cautious criticism at least as much as do other records of popular and ecclesiastical tradition.

The most systematic record of Indian historical tradition is that preserved in the dynastic lists of the Puranas. Five out of the eighteen works of this class, namely, the Vayu, Matsya, Vishnu, Brahmanda, and Bhagavata, contain such lists. The Brahmanda and Bhagavata Puranas being comparatively late works, the lists in them are corrupt, imperfect, and of slight value. But those in the oldest documents, the Vayu, Matsya, and Vishnu, are full, and evidently based upon good authorities. The latest of these three works, the Vishnu, is the best known, having been completely translated into English; but in some cases its evidence is not so good as that of the Vayu and Matsya. It was composed, probably, in the fifth or sixth century A. D., and corresponds most closely with the theoretical definition that a Purana should deal with "the five topics of primary creation, secondary creation, genealogies of gods and patriarchs, reigns of various Manus, and the histories of the old dynasties of kings." The Vayu seems to go back to the middle of the fourth century A.D., and the Matsya is probably intermediate in date between it and the Vishnu. The principal Puranas seem to have been edited in their present form before 500 A.D.

Modern European writers have been inclined to disparage unduly the authority of the Puranic lists, but closer study finds in them much genuine and valuable historical tradition. For instance, the Vishnu Purana gives the outline of the history of the Maurya dynasty with a near approach to accuracy, and the Radcliffe manuscript of the Matsya is equally trustworthy for Andhra history. Proof of the surprising extent to which coins and inscriptions confirm the Matsya list of the Andhra kings has recently been published.

STATUE OF BUDDHA AT SANCHI.
From a photograph.

The earliest foreign notice of India is that in the inscriptions of the Persian king Darius, son of Hystaspes, at Persepolis and Naksh-i-Rustam, the latter of which may be referred to the year 486 B.C. Herodotus, who wrote late in the fifth century, contributes valuable information concerning the relation between India and the Persian empire, which supplements the less detailed statements of the inscriptions. The fragments of the works of Ktesias of Knidos, who was physician to Artaxerxes Mnemon in 401 B.C., and amused himself by collecting travellers' tales about the wonders of the East, are of very slight value.

Europe was practically ignorant of India until the veil was lifted by Alexander's operations and the reports of his officers. Some twenty years after his death the Greek ambassadors, sent by the Kings of Syria and Egypt to the court of the Maurya emperors, recorded careful observations on the country to which they were accredited, which have been partially preserved in the works of many Greek and Roman authors. The fragments of Megasthenes are especially valuable.

Arrian, a Græco-Roman official of the second century A. D., wrote a capital description of India, as well as an admirable critical history of Alexander's invasion. Both these works, being based upon the reports of Ptolemy, son of Lagos, and other officers of Alexander, and the writings of the Greek ambassadors, are entitled to a large extent to the credit of contemporary documents, so far as the Indian history of the fourth century B. C. is concerned. The works of Quintus Curtius and other authors who essayed to tell the story of Alexander's Indian campaign are far inferior in value, but each has merits of its own.

The Chinese "Father of History," Ssu-ma-ch'ien, who completed his work about 100 B. C., is the first of a long series of Chinese historians whose writings throw much light upon the early annals of India. The accurate chronology of the Chinese authors gives their statements peculiar value.

The long series of Chinese Buddhist pilgrims who

continued for several centuries to visit India, which they regarded as their Holy Land, begins with Fa-hien (Fa-hsien), who started on his travels in 399 A. D. and returned to China fifteen years later. The book in which he recorded his journeys has been preserved complete, and has been translated once into French and four times into English. It includes a very interesting and valuable description of the government and social condition of the Ganges provinces during the reign of Chandragupta II, Vikramaditya. Several other pilgrims left behind them works which contribute something to the elucidation of Indian history, and their testimony will be cited in due course.

But the prince of pilgrims, the illustrious Hiuen Tsang, whose fame as Master of the Law still resounds through all Buddhist lands, deserves more particular notice. His travels, described in a work entitled *Records of the Western World*, which has been translated into French, English, and German, extended from 629 A. D. to 645 or 646, and covered an enormous area, including almost every part of India, except the extreme south. His book is a treasure-house of accurate information, indispensable to every student of Indian antiquity, and has done more than any archæological discovery to render possible the remarkable resuscitation of lost Indian history which has recently been effected. Although the chief historical value of Hiuen Tsang's work consists in its contemporary description of political and social institutions, the pilgrim has increased the debt of gratitude due to his memory by recording a considerable mass of ancient tradition, which would have been lost but for his care to preserve it. The *Life of Hiuen Tsang*, composed by his friend Hwui-li, contributes many details supplemental to the narrative in the Travels.

The learned mathematician and astronomer, Alberuni, almost the only Mohammedan scholar who has ever taken the trouble to learn Sanskrit, essentially a language of idolatrous unbelievers, when regarded from a Moslem point of view, entered India in the train of Mahmud of Ghazni. His work, descriptive of the country, and entitled "An Enquiry into India" (*Tahkik-i-Hind*), which was finished in 1031 A. D., is of high value as an account of Hindu manners, science, and literature, but contributes little information which can be utilized for the purposes of political history.

The visit of the Venetian traveller, Marco Polo, to Southern India in 1294-5 A. D. comes just within the limits of this volume.

The Mohammedan historians of India are valuable authorities for the history of the conquest by the armies of Islam.

The monumental class of archæological evidence, considered by itself and apart from the inscriptions on the walls of buildings, offers little direct contribution to the materials for political history, but is of high illustrative value and greatly helps the student in realizing the power and magnificence of some of the ancient dynasties.

Unquestionably the most copious and important

source of early Indian history is the epigraphic, and the accurate knowledge of many periods of the long-forgotten past which has now been attained is derived mainly from the patient study of inscriptions during the last seventy years. Inscriptions are of many kinds. Asoka's edicts, or sermons on stone, form a class by themselves, no other sovereign having imitated his practice of engraving ethical exhortations on the rocks. Equally peculiar is the record of two Sanskrit plays on tables of stone at Ajmir. But the great majority of inscriptions are commemorative, dedicatory, or donative. The former two classes comprise a vast variety of records, extending from the mere signature of a pilgrim's name to an elaborate panegyrical poem in the most artificial style of Sanskrit verse, and are for the most part incised on stone. The donative inscriptions, or grants, on the other hand, are mostly engraved on plates of copper, the favourite material used for permanent records of conveyances.

The south of India is peculiarly rich in inscriptions of almost all kinds, both on stone and copper, some of which attain extraordinary length. The known southern inscriptions are believed to number several thousands, and many must remain for future discovery. But these records, notwithstanding their abundance, are inferior in interest to the rarer northern documents, by reason of their comparatively recent date. No southern inscription earlier than the Christian era is known, except the Mysore edition of Asoka's Minor Rock Edicts and the brief dedications of the Bhattiprolu caskets; and the records prior to the seventh century A.D. are very few.

The oldest northern document is probably the Sakya dedication of the relics of Buddha at Piprawa, which may date back to about 450 B.C., and the number of inscriptions anterior to the Christian era is considerable. Records of the second and third centuries A.D., however, are rare.

PIPRAWA INSCRIBED VASE CONTAINING RELICS OF BUDDHA.

Supposed to be the oldest memorial of Buddha, probably about 450 B.C.

The numismatic evidence is more accessible as a whole than the epigraphic. Many classes of Indian coins have been discussed in special treatises, and compelled to yield their contributions to history. From the time of Alexander's invasion coins afford invaluable aid to the researches of the historian in every period, and for the Bactrian, Indo-Greek, and Indo-Parthian dynasties they constitute almost the sole evidence.

The fourth class of materials for, or sources of, early Indian history, namely, contemporary native literature of a historical kind, is of very limited extent, comprising only two works in Sanskrit and a few poems in Tamil. None of these works is pure history:

they are all of a romantic character, and present the facts with much embellishment.

The best known composition of this class is that entitled the "Deeds of Harsha" (*Harsha-Charita*), written by Bana, about 620 A. D., in praise of his master and patron, King Harsha of Thanesar and Kanauj, which is of high value, both as a depository of ancient tradition, and as a record of contemporary history, in spite of obvious faults. A similar work called "The Deeds of Vikramanka," by Bilhana, a poet of the twelfth century, is devoted to the eulogy of a powerful king who ruled a large territory in the south and west between 1076 and 1126 A. D. The earliest of the Tamil poems alluded to is believed to date from the sixth or seventh century A. D. These compositions, which are panegyrics on famous kings of the south, appear to contain a good deal of historical matter.

The obstacles which have hitherto prevented the construction of a continuous narrative of early Indian history are due not so much to the deficiency of material as to the lack of definite chronology. The rough material is not so scanty as has been supposed. The data for the reconstruction of the early history of all nations are very meagre, largely consisting of bare lists of names, supplemented by vague and often contradictory traditions which pass insensibly into popular mythology. The historian of ancient India is fairly well provided with a supply of such lists, traditions, and mythology, which, of course, require to be treated on the strict critical principles applied by modern students to the early histories of both Western and Eastern nations. The application of those principles is not more difficult in the case of India than it is in that of Babylonia, Egypt, Greece, or Rome. The real difficulty is the determination of fixed chronological points. A body of history must be supported upon a skeleton of chronology, and without chronology history is impossible.

The Indian nations, in so far as they maintained a record of political events, kept it by methods of their own, which are difficult to understand, and until recently were not at all understood. The eras used to date evênts not only differ from those used by other nations, but are very numerous and obscure in their origin and application. Cunningham's *Book of Indian Eras* enumerates more than a score of systems which have been employed at different times and places in India for the computation of dates, and his list might be considerably extended. The successful efforts of several generations of scholars to recover the forgotten history of ancient India have been largely devoted to a study of the local modes of chronological computation, and have resulted in the attainment of accurate knowledge concerning most of the eras used in inscriptions and other documents. Armed with these results, it is now possible for a writer on Indian history to compile a narrative arranged in orderly chronological sequence, which could not have been thought of forty years ago.

At that time the only approximately certain date in the early history of India was that of the accession of Chandragupta Maurya, as determined by his identification with Sandrakottos, the contemporary of Seleukos Nikator, according to Greek authors. By the subsequent establishment of the synchronism of Chandragupta's grandson, Asoka, with Antiochos Theos, grandson of Seleukos, and four other Hellenistic princes, the chronology of the Maurya dynasty was placed upon a firm basis, and it is no longer open to doubt in its main outlines.

A great step in advance was gained by Doctor Fleet's determination of the Gupta era, which had been the subject of much wild conjecture. His demonstration that the year 1 of that era is 319-20 A. D. fixed the chronological position of a most important dynasty, and reduced chaos to order. Fa-hien's account of the civil administration of the Ganges provinces at the beginning of the fourth century thus became an important historical document illustrating the reign of Chandragupta II, Vikramaditya, one of the greatest of Indian kings. Most of the difficulties which continued to embarrass the chronology of the Gupta period, even after the announcement of Doctor Fleet's discovery in 1887, have been removed by M. Sylvain Lévi's publication of the synchronism of Samudragupta with King Meghavarna of Ceylon (304 to 332 A. D.).

A connected history of the Andhra dynasty has been rendered possible by the establishment of synchronisms between the Andhra kings and the western satraps.

In short, the labours of many scholars have succeeded in tracing in firm lines the outline of the history of Northern India from the beginning of the historical period to the Mohammedan conquest, with one important exception, that of the Kushan, or Indo-Scythian, period, the date of which is still open to discussion. The system of Kushan chronology adopted in this volume has much to recommend it, and is sufficiently supported to serve as a good working hypothesis. If it should ultimately commend itself to general acceptance, the whole scheme of North Indian chronology may be considered as settled, although many details will remain to be filled in.

Much progress has been made in the determination of the chronology of the southern dynasties, and the dates of the Pallavas, a dynasty the very existence of which was unknown until 1840, have been worked out with special success.

CHAPTER II

THE DYNASTIES BEFORE ALEXANDER

600 B. C. TO 326 B. C.

THE political history of India begins for an orthodox Hindu more than three thousand years before the Christian era with the famous war waged on the banks of the Jumna, between the sons of Kuru and the sons of Pandu, as related in the vast epic known as the Mahabharata. But the modern critic fails to find sober history in bardic tales, and is constrained to travel much farther before he comes to an anchorage of solid fact.

That line which separates the dated from the undated, in the case of India, may be drawn through the middle of the seventh century B. C., a period of progress, marked by the development of maritime commerce and the diffusion of a knowledge of the art of writing. Up to about that time the inhabitants of India, even the most intellectual races, seem to have been generally ignorant of the art of writing, and to have been obliged to trust to highly trained memory for the transmission of knowledge.

In those days vast territories were still covered by forest, the home of countless wild beasts and scanty tribes of savage men; but regions of great extent in Northern India had been occupied for untold centuries by more or less civilized communities of the higher races who, from time to time, during the unrecorded past, had pierced the mountain barriers of the northwestern frontier. Practically nothing is known concerning the early history of the possibly equally advanced Dravidian races who entered India, perhaps from the valley of the lower Indus, spread over the plateau of the Deccan, and penetrated to the extremity of the Peninsula. Our slender stock of knowledge is limited to the fortunes of the vigorous races, speaking an Aryan tongue, who poured down from the mountains of the Hindu Kush and Pamirs, filling the plains of the Panjab and the upper basin of the Ganges with a sturdy and quick-witted population, unquestionably superior to the aboriginal races. The settled country between the Himalaya Mountains and the Narmada River was divided into a multitude of independent states, some monarchies, and some tribal republics, owning no allegiance to any paramount power, secluded from the outer world, and free to fight among themselves. The most ancient literary traditions, compiled probably in the fourth or fifth century B. C., but looking back to an older time, enumerate sixteen of such states or powers, extending from Gandhara, on the extreme northwest of the Panjab, the modern districts of Peshawar and Rawalpindi, to Avanti or Malwa, with its capital Ujjain, which still retains its ancient name unchanged.

The works of ancient Indian writers from which our historical data are extracted do not profess to be histories, and are mostly religious treatises of various kinds. In such compositions the religious element necessarily takes the foremost place, and the secular

BUDDHIST TOPE AND JAIN TEMPLE AT SARNATH NEAR BENARES.
From a photograph.

affairs of the world occupy a very subordinate position. The particulars of political history incidentally recorded refer in consequence chiefly to the countries most prominent in the development of Indian religion.

The systems which we call Jainism and Buddhism had their roots in the forgotten philosophies of the prehistoric past, but, as we know them, were founded respectively by Vardhamana Mahavira and Gautama

The Jain Temple, Mount Abu, Dilwara

At Dilwara on Mount Abu in Western India there are two of the oldest and finest specimens of temples consecrated to the Jain religion that are to be found anywhere in Hindustan. They date from the eleventh and twelfth centuries of our era, and fabulous sums of money were spent in erecting and adorning them. They are remarkable not only for their beauty and wonderful carving, but also for the picturesque scenery amid which they stand on a mountain-top five thousand feet above the level of the sea.

Buddha. Both these philosophers, who were for many years contemporary, were born, lived, and died in or near the kingdom of Magadha, the modern Bihar. Mahavira, the son of a nobleman of Vaisali, the famous city north of the Ganges, was nearly related to the royal family of Magadha, and died at Pawa, in the modern district of Patna, within the territory of that kingdom.

Gautama Buddha, although born farther north, in the Sakya territory at the foot of the Nepal hills, underwent his most memorable spiritual experiences at Bodh Gaya in Magadha, and spent many years of his ministry within the limits of that state. The Buddhist and Jain books, therefore, tell us much about the Vrijjian confederacy, of which Vaisali was the capital, and about Magadha, with its subordinate kingdom of Anga.

The neighbouring realm of Kosala, the modern kingdom of Oudh, was closely connected with Magadha by many ties, and its capital Sravasti (Savatthi), situated on the upper course of the Rapti at the foot of the hills, was the reputed scene of many of Buddha's most striking discourses.

In the sixth century B. C. Kosala appears to have occupied the rank afterward attained by Magadha, and to have enjoyed precedence as the premier state of Upper India. It is therefore as often mentioned as the rival power. At the beginning of the historical period, the smaller kingdom of Kasi, or Benares, had lost its independence and had been annexed by Kosala, with which its fortunes were indissolubly bound up. This little kingdom owes its fame in the ancient books not only to its connection with its powerful neighbour, but also to its being one of the most sacred spots in Buddhist church history, the scene of Buddha's earliest public preaching, where he first "turned the wheel of the Law."

TEMPLE OF THE SACRED BO-TREE AT BODH GAYA, WHERE BUDDHA RECEIVED THE REVELATION.
From a photograph.

The reputation for special sanctity enjoyed by both Benares and Gaya in Magadha among orthodox Brahmanical Hindus adds little to the detailed information available, which is mainly derived from the writings of Jains and Buddhists, who were esteemed as heretics by the worshippers of the old gods. But the Brahmanical Puranas, compiled centuries later in honour of the orthodox deities, happily include lists of the Kings of Magadha, which had become, before the time of their compilation, the recognized centre, both religious and political, of India; and so it happens that the Jain, Buddhist, and Brahmanical books combined tell us much about the history of Magadha, Anga, Kosala, Kasi, and Vaisali, while they leave us in the dark concerning the fortunes of most other parts of India.

In the Puranic lists the earliest dynasty which can claim historical reality is that known as the Saisunaga, from the name of its founder, Sisunaga.

He was, apparently, the king, or raja, of a petty state corresponding roughly with the present Patna and Gaya Districts, his capital being Rajagriha (Rajgir), among the hills near Gaya. Nothing is known about his history, and the second, third, and fourth kings are likewise mere names.

The first monarch about whom anything substantial is known is Bimbisara, or Srenika, the fifth of his line. He is credited with the building of New Rajagriha, the lower town at the base of the hill crowned by the ancient fort, and with the annexation of Anga, the small kingdom to the east, corresponding with the modern District of Bhagalpur, and probably including Monghyr (Mungir). The annexation of Anga was the first step taken by the kingdom of Magadha in its advance to greatness and the position of supremacy which it attained in the following century, and Bimbisara may be regarded as the real founder of the Magadha imperial power. He strengthened his position by matrimonial alliances with the more powerful of the neighbouring states, taking one consort from the royal family of Kosala, and another from the influential Lichchhavi clan at Vaisali. The latter lady was the mother of Ajatasatru, also called Kunika, or Kuniya, the son who was selected as heir apparent and crown prince. If tradition may be believed, the reign of Bimbisara lasted for twenty-eight years, and it is said that, toward its close, he resigned the royal power into the hands of this favourite son, and retired into

GREAT CHAITYA OR TOPE OF SANCHI.

private life. But the young prince was impatient, and could not bear to await the slow process of nature. Well-attested tradition brands him as a parricide and accuses him of having done his father to death by the agonies of starvation.

Orthodox Buddhist tradition affirms that this hideous crime was instigated by Devadatta, Buddha's cousin, who figures in the legends as a malignant plotter and wicked schismatic, but ecclesiastical rancour may be suspected of the responsibility for this accusation. Devadatta certainly refused to accept the teaching of Gautama, and, preferring that of "the former Buddhas," became the founder and head of a rival sect, which still survived in the seventh century A. D.

Schism has always been esteemed by the orthodox a deadly sin, and in all ages the unsuccessful heretic has been branded as a villain by the winning sect. Such, probably, is the origin of the numerous tales concerning the villainies of the Devadatta, including the supposed incitement of his princely patron to commit the crime of parricide.

There seems to be no doubt that both Vardhamana Mahavira, the founder of the system known as Jainism, and Gautama, the last Buddha, the founder of Buddhism as known to later ages, were preaching in Magadha during the reign of Bimbisara.

The Jain saint, who was a near relative of Bimbisara's queen, the mother of Ajatasatru, probably passed away very soon after the close of Bimbisara's reign, and early in that of Ajatasatru, while the death of Gautama Buddha occurred not much later. There is reason to believe that the latter event took place in or about the year 487 B. C.

Gautama Buddha was certainly an old man when Ajatasatru, or Kunika, as the Jains call him, came to the throne about 495 or 490 B. C., and he had at least one interview with that king.

One of the earliest Buddhist documents narrates in detail the story of a visit paid to Buddha by Ajatasatru, who is alleged to have expressed remorse for his crime, and to have professed his faith in Buddha, who accepted his confession of sin. The concluding passage of the tale may be quoted as an illustration of an ancient Buddhist view of the relations between Church and State.

KING AJATASATRU COMES TO CONFESSION TO BUDDHA.
From the Bharahat Stupa, probably about 200 B. C.
(After Cunningham.)

"And when he had thus spoken, Ajatasatru the king said to the Blessed One: 'Most excellent, Lord, most excellent! Just as if a man were to set up that which has been thrown down, or were to reveal that which is hidden away, or were to point out the right road to him who has gone astray, or were to bring a lamp into the darkness so that those who have eyes could see external forms — just even so, Lord, has the truth been made known to me, in many a figure, by the Blessed One. And now I betake myself, Lord, to the Blessed One as my refuge, to the Truth, and to the Order. May the Blessed One accept me as a disciple, as one who, from this day forth, as long as life endures, has taken his refuge in them. Sin has overcome me, Lord, weak and foolish and wrong that I am, in that for the sake of sovereignty, I put to death my father, that righteous man, that righteous king! May the Blessed One accept it of me, Lord, that I do so acknowledge it as a sin, to the end that in future I may restrain myself.'

"'Verily, O king, it was sin that overcame you in acting thus. But inasmuch as you look upon it as sin, and confess it according to what is right, we accept your confession as to that. For that, O king, is custom in the discipline of the noble ones, that whosoever looks upon his fault as a fault, and rightfully confesses it, shall attain to self-restraint in future.'

"When he had thus spoken, Ajatasatru the king said to the Blessed One, 'Now, Lord, we would fain go. We are busy, and there is much to do.'

"'Do, O king, whatever seemeth to thee fit.'

"Then Ajatasatru the king, pleased and delighted with the words of the Blessed One, arose from his seat, and bowed to the Blessed One, and, keeping him on the right hand as he passed him, departed thence.

"Now the Blessed One, not long after Ajatasatru the king had gone, addressed the brethren, and said: 'This king, brethren, was deeply affected, he was touched in heart. If, brethren, the king had not put to death his father, that righteous man, and righteous king, then would the clear and spotless eye for the truth have arisen in him, even as he sat here.'

"Thus spake the Blessed One. The brethren were pleased and delighted at his words."

PORTION OF RAIL AT BHARAHAT, AS FIRST UNCOVERED.

It is difficult to sympathize with the pleasure and delight of the brethren. The stern and fearless reprobation of a deed of exceptional atrocity which we should expect from a great moral teacher is wholly wanting in Buddha's words, and is poorly compensated for by the politeness of a courtier. Whatever be the reader's judgment concerning the sincerity of the royal penitent or the moral courage of his father confessor, it is clear from the unanimity of tradition that the crime on which the story is based really occurred, and that Ajatasatru slew his father to gain a throne. But when the Ceylonese chronicler asks us to believe that he was followed in due course by four other parricide kings, of whom the last was dethroned by his minister, with the approval of a justly indignant people, too great a demand is made upon the reader's credulity.

The crime by which he gained the throne naturally involved Ajatasatru in war with the aged King of Kosala, whose sister, the queen of the murdered Bimbisara, is alleged to have died from grief. Fortune in the contest inclined now to one side and now to another, and on one occasion, it is said, Ajatasatru was carried away as a prisoner in chains to his opponent's capital. Ultimately peace was concluded, and a princess of Kosala was given in marriage to the King of Magadha. The facts of the struggle are obscure, being wrapped up in legendary matter from which it is impossible to disentangle them, but the probability is that Ajatasatru won for Magadha a decided preponderance over its neighbour of Kosala. It is certain that the latter kingdom is not again mentioned as an independent power, and that in the fourth century B.C. it formed an integral part of the Magadha empire.

The ambition of Ajatasatru, not satisfied with the humiliation of Kosala, next induced him to undertake the conquest of the country to the north of the Ganges, now known as Tirhut, in which the Lichchhavi clan, famous in Buddhist legend, then occupied a prominent position. The invasion was successful; the Lichchhavi capital, Vaisali, was occupied, and Ajatasatru became master of his maternal grandfather's territory. It is probable that the invader carried his victorious arms to their natural limit, the foot of the mountains, and that from this time the whole region between the Ganges and the Himalaya became subject, more or less directly, to the suzerainty of Magadha.

The victor erected a fortress at the village of Patali on the bank of the Ganges to curb his Lichchhavi opponents. The foundations of a city nestling under the shelter of the fortress were laid by his grandson Udaya. The city so founded was known variously as Kusumapura, Pushpapura, or Pataliputra, and rapidly developed in size and magnificence, until, under the Maurya dynasty, it became the capital, not only of Magadha, but of India.

Buddha, as has been mentioned above, died early in the reign of Ajatasatru. Shortly before his death, Kapilavastu, his ancestral home, was captured by Virudhaka, King of Kosala, who is alleged to have perpetrated a ferocious massacre of the Sakya clan to which Buddha belonged. The story is so thickly encrusted with miraculous legend that the details of the event cannot be ascertained, but the coating of miracle was probably deposited upon a basis of fact, and we may believe that the Sakyas suffered much at the hands of Virudhaka.

If the chronology adopted in this chapter be even approximately correct, Bimbisara and Ajatasatru must be regarded as the contemporaries of Darius, the son of Hystaspes, autocrat of the Persian empire from 521 to 485 B. C. Darius, who was a very capable ruler, employed his officers in the exploration of a great part of Asia by means of various expeditions.

One of these expeditions was despatched at some date later than 516 B. C. to prove the feasibility of a passage by sea from the mouth of the Indus to Persia. The commander, Skylax of Karyanda in Karia, managed somehow to equip a squadron on the waters of the Panjab rivers in the Gandhara country, to make his way down to the ocean, and ultimately to reach the Red Sea. The particulars of his adventurous voyage have been lost, but we know that the information collected was of such value that, by utilizing it, Darius was enabled to annex the Indus valley, and to send his fleets into the Indian Ocean. The archers from India formed a valuable element in the army of Xerxes, and shared the defeat of Mardonius at Platæa.

The conquered provinces were formed into a separate satrapy, the twentieth, which was considered the richest and most populous province of the empire. It paid the enormous tribute of 360 Euboic talents of gold-dust, or 185 hundredweights, worth fully a million sterling, and constituting about one-third of the total bullion revenue of the Asiatic provinces. Although the exact limits of the Indian satrapy cannot be determined, we know that it was distinct from Aria (Herat), Arachosia (Kandahar), and Gandaria (Northwestern Panjab). It must have comprised, therefore, the course of the Indus from Kalabagh to the sea, including the whole of Sind, and perhaps included a considerable portion of the Panjab east of the Indus. But when Alexander invaded the country, nearly two centuries later, the Indus was the boundary between the Persian empire and India, and both the Panjab and Sind were governed by numerous native princes. In ancient times the courses of the rivers were quite different from what they now are, and vast tracts in Sind and the Panjab, now desolate, were then rich and prosperous. This fact largely explains the surprising value of the tribute paid by the twentieth satrapy.

When Ajatasatru's blood-stained life ended (*cir.* 459 B. C.), he was succeeded, according to the Puranas, by a son named Darsaka or Harshaka, who was in turn succeeded by his son Udaya. The Buddhist books omit the intermediate name, and represent Udaya as the son and immediate successor of Ajatasatru. It is difficult to decide which version is correct, but on the whole the authority of the Puranas seems to be preferable in this case. If Darsaka, or Harshaka, was a reality, nothing is known about him.

The reign of Udaya may be assumed to have begun about 434 B. C. The tradition that he built Pataliputra is all that is known about him. His successors, Nandi-

Low Caste Hindu Woman — Bhil Type.
From a Photograph.

vardhana and Mahanandin, according to the Puranic lists, are still more shadowy, mere *nominis umbræ*. Mahanandin, the last of the dynasty, is said to have had by a Sudra, or low-caste, woman a son named Mahapadma Nanda, who usurped the throne, and so established the Nanda family or dynasty. This event may be dated in or about 361 B. C.

At this point all our authorities become unintelligible and incredible. The Puranas treat the Nanda dynasty as consisting of two generations only, Mahapadma and his eight sons, of whom one was named Sumalya. These two generations are supposed to have reigned for a century, which cannot possibly be true. The Jains, doing still greater violence to reason, extend the duration of the dynasty to 155 years, while the Buddhist Mahavamsa, Dipavamsa, and Asokavadana deepen the confusion by hopelessly muddled and contradictory stories not worth repeating. Some powerful motive must have existed for the distortion of the history of the so-called "Nine Nandas" in all forms of the tradition, but it is not easy to make even a plausible guess at the nature of that motive.

The Greek and Roman historians, who derived their information either from Megasthenes or the companions of Alexander, and thus rank as contemporary witnesses reported at second hand, throw a little light on the real history. When Alexander was stopped in his advance at the Hyphasis in 326 B. C., he was informed by a native chieftain named Bhagala or Bhagela, whose statements were confirmed by Poros, that the King of the Gangaridai and Prasii nations on the banks of the Ganges was named, as nearly as the Greeks could catch the unfamiliar sounds, Xandrames or Agrammes. This monarch was said to command a force of twenty thousand horse, two hundred thousand foot, two thousand chariots, and three or four thousand elephants. Inasmuch as the capital of the Prasii nation was undoubtedly Pataliputra, the reports made to Alexander can have referred only to the King of Magadha, who must have been one of the Nandas mentioned in native tradition. The reigning king was alleged to be extremely unpopular, owing to his wickedness and base origin. He was, it is said, the son of a barber, who, having become the paramour of the queen of the last legitimate sovereign, contrived the king's death, and, under pretence of acting as guardian to his sons, got them into his power and exterminated the royal family. After their extermination he begot the son who was reigning at the time of Alexander's campaign and who, "more worthy of his father's condition than his own, was odious and contemptible to his subjects."

This story confirms the statements of the Puranas that the Nanda dynasty was of ambiguous origin and comprised only two generations. The Vishnu Purana brands the first Nanda, Mahapadma, as an avaricious person, whose reign marked the end of the Kshatriya, or high-born, princes, and the beginning of the rule of those of low degree, ranking as Sudras. The Mahavamsa, when it dubs the last Nanda by the name of Dhana, or "Riches," seems to hint at the imputation of avariciousness made against the first Nanda by the Puranic writer, and the Chinese pilgrim Hiuen Tsang also refers to the Nanda raja as the reputed possessor of great wealth.

By putting all the hints together we may conclude with tolerable certainty that the Nanda family was

PILGRIMS AND BEGGARS AT THE WELL OF KNOWLEDGE, BENARES.

From a photograph.

really of base origin, that it acquired power by the assassination of the legitimate king, and that it retained possession of the throne for two generations only. The great military power of the usurpers, as attested by Greek testimony, was the result of the conquests effected by Bimbisara and Ajatasatru, and presumably continued by their successors; but the limits of the Nanda dominions cannot be defined, nor can the dates of the dynasty be determined with accuracy. It is quite certain that the two generations did not last for a hundred and fifty-five, or even for a hundred, years; but it is impossible to determine the actual duration, and the period of forty years has been assumed as reasonable and probably not far from the truth.

However mysterious the Nine Nandas may be — if, indeed, there really were nine — there is no doubt that the last of them was deposed and slain by Chandragupta Maurya, who seems to have been an illegitimate scion of the family. There is no difficulty in believing the tradition that the revolution involved the extermination of all related to the fallen monarch, for revolutions in the East are not effected without much shedding of blood. Nor is there any reason to discredit the statements that the usurper was attacked by a confederacy of the northern powers, including Kashmir, and that the attack failed owing to the Machiavellian intrigues of Chandragupta's Brahman adviser, who is variously named Chanakya, Kautilya, and Vishnugupta.

His accession to the throne of Magadha may be dated with practical certainty in 321 B.C. The dominions of the Magadha crown were then extensive, certainly including the territories of the nations called Prasii and Gangaridai by the Greeks, and probably comprising at least the kingdoms of Kosala and Benares, as well as Anga and Magadha proper. Four years before the revolution at Pataliputra, Alexander had swept like a hurricane through the Panjab and Sind, and it is said that Chandragupta, then a youth, met the mighty Macedonian. Whether that anecdote be true or not, it is certain that the troubles consequent upon the death of Alexander in the summer of 323 B. C. gave young Chandragupta his opportunity. He assumed the command of the native revolt against the foreigner, and destroyed most of the Macedonian garrisons. He had thus become the master of North-western India before he attempted the revolution in Magadha, and when that enterprise was accomplished, he was undoubtedly the paramount power in India. But before the story of the deeds of Chandragupta Maurya and the descendants who succeeded him on the throne of Magadha can be told, we must pause to unfold the wondrous tale of the Indian adventure of "Philip's warlike son."

CHAPTER III

ALEXANDER'S INDIAN CAMPAIGN

The Advance

ALEXANDER THE GREAT, having completed the subjugation of Bactria, resolved to execute his cherished purpose of emulating and surpassing the mythical exploits of Dionysos, Herakles, and Semiramis by effecting the conquest of India. Toward the close of spring in the year 327 B. C., when the sun had sufficiently melted the snows, he led his army, including perhaps fifty or sixty thousand Europeans, across the lofty Khawak and Kaoshan passes of the Hindu Kush, or Indian Caucasus, and after ten days' toil amidst the mountains emerged in the rich valley now known as the Koh-i-Daman.

Here, two years earlier, before the Bactrian campaign, he had founded a town, named as usual, Alexandria, as a strategical outpost to secure his intended advance. The governor of this town, whose administration had been a failure, was replaced by Nikanor, son of Parmenion, the king's intimate friend; the population was recruited by fresh settlers from the surrounding districts; and the garrison was strengthened by a reinforcement of veterans discharged from the ranks of the expeditionary force as being unequal to the arduous labours of the coming campaign.

The important position of Alexandria, which commanded the roads over three passes, having been thus secured, in accordance with Alexander's customary caution, the civil administration of the country between the passes and the Kophen, or Kabul, River was provided for by the appointment of Tyriaspes as satrap. Alexander, when assured that his communications were safe, advanced with his army to a city named Nikaia, situated to the west of the modern Jalalabad, on the road from Kabul to India.

Here the king divided his forces. Generals Hephaistion and Perdikkas were ordered to proceed in advance with three brigades of infantry, half of the horse-guards, and the whole of the mercenary cavalry by the direct road to India through the valley of the Kabul River, and to occupy Peukelaotis, now the Yusufzi country, up to the Indus. Their instructions were couched in the spirit of the Roman maxim, – "*Parcere subiectis et debellare superbos.*"

Most of the tribal chiefs preferred the alternative of submission, but one named Hasti (Astes) ventured to resist. His stronghold, which held out for thirty days, was taken and destroyed. During this march eastward, Hephaistion and Perdikkas were accompanied by the King of Taxila, a great city beyond the Indus, who had lost no time in obeying Alexander's summons and in placing his services at the disposal of the invader. Other chiefs on the western side of the Indus adopted the same course, and, with the help of these native potentates, the Macedonian generals were enabled to make satisfactory progress in the task of bridging the Indus, which had been committed to them by their sovereign.

Alexander in person assumed the command of the second corps, or division, consisting of the infantry known as hypaspists, the foot-guards, the Agrianian or Thracian light infantry, the archers, the mounted lancers, and the rest of the horse-guards. With this force he undertook a flanking movement through the difficult hill country north of the Kabul River, in order to subdue the fierce tribes which inhabited, as they still inhabit, that region, and thus to secure his communications, and protect his army from attacks on the flank and rear. The difficulties of the operation due to the ruggedness of the country, the fierce heat of summer, the bitter cold of winter, and the martial spirit of the hill-men, were enormous, but no difficulties could daunt the courage or defeat the skill of Alexander.

Although it is absolutely impossible to trace his movements with precision, or to identify with even approximate certainty the tribes which he encountered, or the strongholds which he captured and destroyed in the course of some five months' laborious marching, it is certain that he ascended the valley of the Kunar River for a considerable distance. At a nameless town in the hills, Alexander was wounded in the shoulder by a dart, and the incident so enraged his troops that all the prisoners taken there were massacred, and the town was razed to the ground.

Soon after this tragedy, Alexander again divided his forces, leaving Krateros, "the man most faithful to him, and whom he valued equally with himself," to complete the reduction of the tribesmen of the Kunar valley, while the king in person led a body of picked troops against the Aspasians, who were defeated with great slaughter.

He then crossed the mountains and entered the valley now called Bajaur, where he found a town named Arigaion, which had been burnt and abandoned by the inhabitants. Krateros, having completely executed his task in the Kunar valley, now rejoined his master, and measures were concerted for the reduction of the tribes farther east, whose subjugation was indispensable before an advance into India could be made with safety.

The Aspasians were finally routed in a second great battle, losing, it is said, more than forty thousand prisoners and 230,000 oxen. The perfection of the arrangements by which Alexander maintained communication with his remote European base is strikingly illustrated by the fact that he selected the best and handsomest of the captured cattle, and sent them to Macedonia for use in agriculture.

A fancied connection with Dionysos and the sacred Mount Nysa of Greek legend gave special interest to the town and hill-state called Nysa, which was among the places next attacked. An attempt to take the town by assault having failed by reason of the depth of the protecting river, Alexander was preparing to reduce it by blockade when the speedy submission of the inhabitants rendered further operations unnecessary. They are alleged to have craved his clemency on the ground that they were akin to Dionysos and the Greeks, because the ivy and vine grew in their country, and the triple-peaked mountain which overshadowed their town was no other than Mount Meros. Alexander, who found such fancies useful as a stimulant to his home-sick troops, did not examine the evidence for the kinship with Dionysos in too critical a spirit, but was glad to accept the Nysaian appeals and to exercise a gracious clemency.

In order to gratify his own curiosity, and to give some of his best troops a pleasant holiday, he paid a visit to the mountain, now known as the Koh-i-Mor, accompanied by an adequate escort of the companion cavalry and foot-guards. The chants and dances of the natives, the ancestors of the Kafirs of the present day, bore sufficient resemblance to the Bacchanalian rites of Hellas to justify the claims made by the Nysaians, and to encourage the soldiers in their belief that, although far from home, they had at last found a people who shared their religion and might be regarded as kinsmen. Alexander humoured the convenient delusion and allowed his troops to enjoy with the help of their native friends a ten days' revel in the jungles. The Nysaians, on their part, showed their gratitude for the clemency which they had experienced, by contributing a contingent of three hundred horsemen, who remained with Alexander throughout the whole period of his advance, and were not sent home until October, 326 B. C., when he was about to start on his voyage down the rivers to the sea.

Alexander now undertook in person the reduction of the formidable nation called the Assakenoi, who were reported to await him with an army of twenty thousand cavalry, more than thirty thousand infantry, and thirty elephants. Quitting the Bajaur territory, Alexander crossed the Gouraios (Panjkora) River, with a body of picked regiments, including, as usual, a large proportion of mounted troops, and entered the Assakenian territory, in order to attack Massaga, the greatest city of those parts and the seat of the sovereign power.

This formidable fortress, probably to be identified with Minglaur, or Manglawar, the ancient capital of Suwat, was strongly fortified both by nature and art. On the east, an impetuous mountain stream, the Suwat River, flowing between steep banks, barred access, while on the south and west gigantic rocks, deep chasms, and treacherous morasses impeded the approach of an assailing force. Where nature failed to give adequate protection, art had stepped in, and had girdled the city with a mighty rampart, built of brick, stone, and timber, about four miles (35 *stadia*) in circumference, and guarded by a deep moat. While reconnoitring these formidable defences, and considering his plan of attack, Alexander was again wounded by an arrow. The wound was not very serious, and did not prevent him from continuing the active supervision of the siege operations, which were designed and controlled throughout by his master mind.

Commanded by such a general the meanest soldier becomes a hero. The troops laboured with such zeal that within nine days they had raised a mole level with the ground sufficient to bridge the moat, and to allow the movable towers and other engines to approach the walls. The garrison was disheartened by the death of their chief, who was killed by a blow from a missile discharged by an engine, and the place was taken by storm. Kleophis, the consort of the slain chieftain, and her infant son were captured, and it is said that she subsequently bore a son to Alexander.

The garrison of Massaga had included a body of seven thousand mercenary troops from the plains of India. Alexander, by a special agreement, had granted these men their lives on condition that they should change sides and take service in his ranks. In pursuance of this agreement, they were allowed to retire and encamp on a small hill facing, and about nine miles (80 *stadia*) distant from, the Macedonian camp. The mercenaries being unwilling to aid the foreigner in the subjugation of their countrymen, desired to evade the unwelcome obligation which they had incurred, and proposed to slip away by night and return to their homes. Alexander, having received information of their design, suddenly attacked the Indians while they reposed in fancied security, and inflicted severe loss upon them. Recovering from their surprise, the mercenaries formed themselves into a hollow circle, with the women and children in the centre, and offered a desperate resistance, in which the women took an active part. At last the gallant defenders were overpowered by superior numbers, and, in the words of an ancient historian, "met a glorious death which they would have disdained to exchange for a life with dishonour." The unarmed camp-followers and the women were spared.

This incident, which has been severely condemned by various writers, ancient and modern, as a disgraceful breach of faith by Alexander, does not seem to have been, as supposed by Diodorus, the outcome of implacable enmity felt by the king against the mercenaries. The slaughter of the contingent was rather, as represented by Arrian, the tremendous penalty for a meditated breach of faith on the part of the Indians, and, if this explanation be true, the penalty cannot be regarded as altogether undeserved. While the accession of seven thousand brave and disciplined troops would have been a welcome addition to Alexander's small army, the addition of such a force to the enemy in the plains would have been a serious impediment to his advance; and he was, perhaps, justified in protecting himself against such a formidable increase of the enemy's strength.

Alexander next captured a town called Ora or Nora, and occupied an important place named Bazira, the inhabitants of which, with those of other towns, had retired to the stronghold of Aornos near the Indus, the great mountain now known as Mahaban. The desire of Alexander to capture this position, believed to be impregnable, was based upon military exigencies, and fired by a legend that the demigod Herakles, whom he claimed as an ancestor, had been baffled by the defences.

The mountain, which is at least twelve miles in circumference, and rises to a height of more than seven thousand feet above the sea, or five thousand above the Indus, is washed on its southern face by that river, which at this point is of great depth, and enclosed by rugged and precipitous rocks, forbidding approach from that side. On the other sides, as at Massaga, ravines, cliffs, and swamps presented obstacles sufficient to daunt the bravest assailant. A single path gave access to the summit, which was well supplied with water, and comprised arable land requiring the labour of a thousand men for its cultivation. The summit was crowned by a steeply scarped mass of rock, which formed a natural citadel, and was doubtless further protected by art.

Before undertaking the siege of this formidable stronghold, Alexander, with his habitual foresight, secured his rear by placing garrisons in the towns of Ora, Massaga, Bazira, and Orobatis, in the hills of Suwat and Buner.

He further isolated the fortress by personally marching down into the plains, probably through the Shahkot pass, and receiving the submission of the important city of Peukelaotis (Charsadda) and the surrounding territory, now known as the Yusufzi country. During this operation he was assisted by two local chiefs. He then made his way somehow to Embolima, the modern Amb, a small town on the Indus, at the foot of Aornos, and there established a depôt under the command of Krateros. In case the assault should fail, and the siege be converted into a blockade, this depot was intended to serve as a base for protracted operations, should such prove to be necessary.

Having thus deliberately made his dispositions for the siege, Alexander spent two days in careful personal reconnaissance of the position with the aid of a small force, chiefly consisting of light-armed troops. Assisted by local guides, whose services were secured by liberal reward, Ptolemy, the son of Lagos, secured a valuable foothold on the eastern spur of the mountain, where he entrenched his men. An attempt made by the king to support him having been frustrated, this failure led to a vigorous attack by the Indians on Ptolemy's entrenchments, which was repulsed after a hard fight.

A second effort made by Alexander to effect a junction with his lieutenant, although stoutly opposed by the besieged, was successful, and the Macedonians were now in secure possession of the vantage-ground from which an assault on the natural citadel could be delivered.

The task before the assailants was a formidable one,

for the crowning mass of rock did not, like most eminences, slope gradually to the summit, but rose abruptly in the form of a steep cone. Examination of the ground showed that a direct attack was impossible until some of the surrounding ravines should be filled up. Plenty of timber was available in the adjoining forests, and Alexander resolved to use this material to form a pathway. He himself threw the first trunk into the ravine, and his act was greeted with a loud cheer signifying the keenness of the troops, who could not shrink from any labour, however severe, to which their king was the first to put his hand.

Within the brief space of four days Alexander succeeded in gaining possession of a small hill on a level with the rock, and in thus securing a dominant position. The success of this operation convinced the garrison that the capture of the citadel was merely a question of time, and the negotiations for capitulation on terms were begun.

The besieged, being more anxious to gain time for escape than to conclude a treaty, evacuated the rock during the night, and attempted to slip away unobserved in the darkness. But the unsleeping vigilance of Alexander detected the movement, and partially defeated their plans. Placing himself at the head of seven hundred picked men, he clambered up the cliff the moment the garrison began to retire, and slew many.

In this way the virgin fortress, which even Herakles had failed to win, became the prize of Alexander. The king, justly proud of his success, offered sacrifice and worship to the gods, dedicated altars to Athene and Nike, and built a fort for the accommodation of the garrison which he quartered on the mountain. The command of this important post was entrusted to Sisi-

THE INDUS NEAR ATTOCK.

kottos (Sasigupta), a Hindu, who long before had deserted from the Indian contingent attached to the army of Bessus, the rebel satrap of Bactria, and had since proved himself a faithful officer in the Macedonian service.

Alexander then proceeded to complete the subjugation of the Assakenians by another raid into their country, and occupied a town named Dyrta, which probably lay to the north of Aornos. This town and the surrounding district were abandoned by the inhabitants, who had crossed the Indus, and taken refuge in the Abhisara country, in the hills between the Hydaspes (Jihlam) and Akesines (Chinab) Rivers. He then slowly forced his way through the forests down to the bridge-head at Ohind. Although the direct distance is not great, the work of clearing a road passable for an army was so arduous that fifteen or sixteen marches were required to reach Hephaistion's camp.

Opinions have differed concerning the location of the bridge over the Indus, and most writers have been inclined to place it at Attock (Atak), where the river is narrowest. But the recent investigations of M. Foucher have clearly established the fact that the bridge, probably constructed of boats, must have been at Ohind, or Und, sixteen miles above Attock. Having arrived at the bridge-head, Alexander sacrificed to the gods on a magnificent scale, and gave his army thirty days of much needed rest, amusing them with games and gymnastic contests.

At Ohind Alexander was met by an embassy from Ambhi (Omphis), who had recently succeeded to the throne of Taxila, the great city three marches beyond the Indus. The lately deceased king had met the invader in the previous year at Nikaia and tendered the submission of his kingdom. This tender was now renewed on behalf of his son by the embassy, and was supported by a contingent of seven hundred horse and the gift of valuable supplies, comprising thirty elephants, three thousand fat oxen, more than ten thousand sheep, and two hundred talents of silver.

The ready submission of the rulers of Taxila is explained by the fact that they desired Alexander's help against their enemies in the neighbouring states. Taxila was then at war both with the hill kingdom of Abhisara and with the more powerful state governed by the king whom the Greeks called Poros, which corresponded with the modern districts of Jihlam, Gujarat, and Shahpur.

Spring had now begun, and as the omens were favourable, the refreshed army began the passage of the river one morning at daybreak, and, with the help of the Taxilan king, safely effected entrance on the soil of India, which no European traveller or invader had ever before trodden.

A curious incident marked the last day's march to Taxila. When four or five miles from the city Alexander was startled to see a complete army in order of battle advancing to meet him. He supposed that treacherous opposition was about to be offered, and had begun to make arrangements to attack the Indians, when Ámbhi galloped forward with a few attendants and explained that the display of force was intended as an honour, and that his entire army was at Alexander's disposal. When the misunderstanding had been removed, the Macedonian force continued its advance and was entertained at the city with royal magnificence.

Taxila, now represented by miles of ruins to the

northwest of Rawalpindi and the southeast of Hasan Abdal, was then one of the greatest cities of the East, and was especially famous as the principal seat of Hindu learning in Northern India, to which scholars of all classes flocked for instruction.

Ambhi recognized Alexander as his lord, and received from him investiture as lawful successor of his deceased father, the King of Taxila. In return for the favour shown to him by the invader, he provided

AN OLD HINDU FORT.

the Macedonian army with liberal supplies, and presented Alexander with eighty talents of coined silver and golden crowns for himself and all his friends. Alexander, not to be outdone in generosity, returned the presents, and bestowed on the donor a thousand talents from the spoils of war, along with many banqueting vessels of gold and silver, a vast quantity of Persian drapery, and thirty chargers caparisoned as when ridden by himself. This lavish generosity, although displeasing to Alexander's Macedonian officers, was probably prompted more by policy than by sentiment. It purchased a contingent of five thousand men, and secured the fidelity of a most useful ally.

While Alexander was at Taxila, the hill chieftain of Abhisara, who really intended to join Poros in repelling the invader, sent envoys who professed to surrender to Alexander all that their master possessed. This mission was favourably received, and Alexander hoped that Poros would display complaisance equal to that of his ally. But a summons sent requiring him to do homage and pay tribute was met with the proud answer that he would indeed come to his frontier to meet the invader, but at the head of an army ready for battle.

Having stayed in his comfortable quarters at Taxila for sufficient time to rest his army, Alexander led his forces, now strengthened by the Taxilan contingent and a small number of elephants, eastward to meet Poros, who was known to be awaiting him on the farther bank of the Hydaspes (Jihlam) River. The march from Taxila to Jihlam on the Hydaspes, in a south-easterly direction, a distance of about a hundred or a hundred and ten miles, according to the route followed, brought the army over difficult ground and probably occupied a fortnight. The hot season was at its height, but to Alexander all seasons were equally fit for campaigning, and he led his soldiers on and on from conquest to conquest, regardless of the snows of the mountains and the scorching heat of the plains. He arrived at Jihlam early in May, and found the river already flooded by the melting of the snow on the hills.

The boats which had served for the passage of the Indus were cut into sections and transported on wagons to be rebuilt on the bank of the Hydaspes, where they were again utilized for the crossing of that river.

In spite of the most elaborate preparations, the

ROPE BRIDGE ACROSS THE FLOODED JIHLAM.
From stereograph, copyright 1903, by Underwood & Underwood, New York.

problem of the passage of the Hydaspes in the face of a superior force could not be solved without minute local knowledge, and Alexander was compelled to defer his decision as to the best feasible solution until he should have acquired the necessary acquaintance with all the local conditions. On his arrival, he found the army of Poros, fifty thousand strong, drawn up on the opposite bank. It was obvious that the horses of the cavalry, the arm upon which the Macedonian commander placed his reliance, could not be induced to clamber up the bank of a flooded river in the face of a host of elephants, and that some device for evading this difficulty must be sought.

Alexander, therefore, resolved, in the words of Arrian, to "steal a passage." The easiest plan would have been for the invader to wait patiently in his lines until October or November, when the waters would subside and the river might become fordable. Although such dilatory tactics did not commend themselves to the impetuous spirit of Alexander, he endeavoured to lull the vigilance of the enemy by the public announcement that he intended to await the change of season, and gave a colour of truth to the declaration by employing his troops in foraging expeditions and the collection of a great store of provisions. At the same time his flotilla of boats continually moved up and down the river, and frequent reconnaissances were made in search of a ford. "All this," as Arrian observes, "prevented Poros from resting and concentrating his preparations at any one point selected in preference to any other as the best for defending the passage."

Rafts, galleys, and smaller boats were secretly prepared and hidden away among the woods and islands in the upper reaches of the river where it escapes from the mountains. These preliminaries occupied six or seven weeks, during which time the rains had broken, and the violence of the flood had increased. Careful study of the ground had convinced Alexander that the best chance of crossing in safety was to be found near a sharp bend in the river about sixteen miles marching distance above his camp, at a point where his embarkation would be concealed by a bluff and an island covered with forest. Having arrived at this decision, Alexander acted upon it, not only, as Arrian justly remarks, with "marvellous audacity," but with consummate prudence and precaution.

He left Krateros with a considerable force, including the Taxilan contingent of five thousand men, to guard the camp near Jihlam, and supplied him with precise instructions as to the manner in which he should use this reserve force to support the main attack. Half-way between the standing camp and the chosen crossing-place three generals were stationed with the mercenary cavalry and infantry, and had orders to cross the river as soon as they should perceive the Indians to be fairly engaged in action. All sections of the army were kept in touch by a chain of sentries posted along the bank.

When all these precautionary arrangements had been completed, Alexander in person took command of a picked force of about eleven or twelve thousand men, including the foot-guards, hypaspist infantry, mounted archers, and five thousand cavalry of various kinds, with which to effect the passage. In order to escape observation, he marched by night at some distance from the bank, and his movements were further concealed by a violent storm of rain and thunder which broke during the march. He arrived unperceived at the appointed place, and found the fleet of galleys, boats, and rafts in readiness.

The enemy had no suspicion of what was happening until the fleet appeared in the open river beyond the wooded island, and Alexander disembarked his force at daybreak without opposition. But when he had landed, he was disappointed to find that yet another deep channel lay in front, which must be crossed. With much difficulty a ford was found, and the infantry struggled through, breast-deep in the stream, while the horses swam with only their heads above water. The sole practicable road from the camp of Poros involved a wide detour, which rendered prompt opposition impossible, and Alexander was able to deploy his dripping troops on the mainland before any attempt could be made to stop him.

Then, when it was too late, the son of the Indian king came hurrying up with two thousand horse and 120 chariots. This inadequate force was speedily routed with the loss of four hundred killed and of all the chariots. Fugitives carried the disastrous news to the camp of Poros, who moved out with the bulk of his army to give battle, leaving a guard to protect his baggage against Krateros, who lay in wait on the opposite bank. The Indian army deployed on the only ground available, the plain now known as Karri, girdled on the north and east by low hills, and about five miles in width at its broadest part. The surface was a firm sandy soil, well adapted for military movements even in the rainy season.

A stately force it was with which the Indian monarch moved forth to defend his country against the audacious invader from the west. Two hundred huge elephants, stationed at intervals of not less than a hundred feet from one another, and probably in eight ranks, formed the front in the centre. The chief reli-

INDIAN SHIELDS.
From the Ajanta Cave Paintings. (After Griffiths.)

ance of Poros was on these monsters, who would, it was calculated, terrify the foreign soldiers and render the dreaded cavalry unmanageable. Behind the elephants stood a compact force of thirty thousand infantry with projections on the wings, and files of the infantry were pushed forward in the intervals between the elephants, so that the Indian army presented "very much the appearance of a city, — the elephants as they stood resembling its towers, and the men-at-arms placed between them resembling the lines of wall intervening between tower and tower." Both flanks were protected by cavalry with chariots in front. The cavalry numbered four thousand and the chariots three hundred. Each chariot was drawn by four horses, and carried six men, two of whom were archers, stationed one on each side of the vehicle, two were shield-bearers, and two were charioteers, who in the stress of battle were wont to drop the reins and ply the enemy with darts.

The infantry were all armed with a broad and heavy two-handed sword, and a long buckler of undressed ox-hide. In addition to these arms each man carried either javelins or a bow. The bow is described by Arrian as being "made of equal length with the man who bears it. This they rest upon the ground, and, pressing against it with their left foot, thus discharge the arrow, having drawn the string backwards; for the shaft they use is little short of being three yards long, and there is nothing which can resist an Indian archer's shot—neither shield nor breastplate, nor any stronger defence, if such there be."

But great as was the power of the Indian bow, it was too cumbrous to meet the attack of the mobile Macedonian cavalry. The slippery state of the surface prevented the archers from resting the end of their weapons firmly on the ground, and Alexander's horse were able to deliver their charge before the bowmen had completed their adjustments. The Indian horsemen, each of whom carried two javelins and a buckler, were far inferior in personal strength and military discipline to Alexander's men. With such force and such equipment Poros awaited the attack of the greatest military genius whom the world has seen.

Alexander clearly perceived that his small force would have no chance of success in a direct attack upon the enemy's centre, and resolved to rely on the effect of a vigorous cavalry charge against the Indian left wing. The generals in command of the six thousand infantry at his disposal were ordered to play a waiting game, and to take no part in the action until they should see the Indian foot and horse thrown into confusion by the charge of cavalry under Alexander's personal command.

He opened the action by sending his mounted archers, a thousand strong, against the left wing of the Indian army, which must have extended close to the bank of the river. The archers discharged a storm of arrows and made furious charges. They were quickly followed by the Guards led by Alexander himself. The Indian cavalry on the right wing hurried round by the rear to support their hard-pressed comrades on the left. But meantime two regiments of horse commanded by Koinos, which had been detached by Alexander for the purpose, swept past the front of the immobile host of Poros, galloped round its right wing, and threatened the rear of the Indian cavalry and chariots. While the Indian squadrons were endeavouring to effect a partial change of front to meet the impending onset from the rear, they necessarily fell into a certain amount of confusion. Alexander, seeing his opportunity, seized the very moment when the enemy's horse were changing front, and pressed home his attack. The Indian ranks on both wings broke and "fled for shelter to the elephants as to a friendly wall." Thus ended the first act in the drama.

The elephant drivers tried to retrieve the disaster by urging their mounts against the Macedonian horse, but the phalanx, which had now advanced, began to take its deferred share in the conflict. The Macedonian soldiers hurled showers of darts at the elephants and their riders. The maddened beasts charged and crushed through the closed ranks of the phalanx, impenetrable to merely human attack. The Indian horsemen seized the critical moment, and, seeking to revenge the defeat which they had suffered in the first stage of the action, wheeled round and attacked Alexander's cavalry. But the Indians were not equal to the task which they attempted, and, being repulsed, were again cooped up among the elephants. The second act of the drama was now finished.

The third and last began with a charge by the Macedonian massed cavalry, which crashed into the broken Indian ranks and effected an awful carnage. The battle ended at the eighth hour of the day in a scene of murderous confusion, which is best described in the words of Arrian, whose account is based on that of men who shared in the fight.

"The elephants," he writes, "being now cooped up within a narrow space, did no less damage to their friends than to their foes, trampling them under their feet as they wheeled and pushed about. There resulted in consequence a great slaughter of the cavalry, cooped up as it was within a narrow space around the elephants. Many of the elephant drivers, moreover, had been shot down, and of the elephants themselves some had been wounded, while others, both from exhaustion and the loss of their mahouts, no longer kept to their own side of the conflict, but, as if driven frantic by their sufferings, attacked friend and foe quite indiscriminately, pushed them, trampled them down, and killed them in all manner of ways. But the Macedonians, who had a wide and open field, and could therefore operate as they thought best, gave way when the elephants charged, and when they retreated followed at their heels and plied them with darts, whereas the Indians, who were in the midst of the animals, suffered far more from the effects of their rage.

" When the elephants, however, became quite exhausted, and their attacks were no longer made with vigour, they fell back like ships backing water, and merely kept trumpeting as they retreated with their faces to the enemy. Then did Alexander surround with his cavalry the whole of the enemy's line, and signal that the infantry, with their shields linked together so as to give the utmost compactness to their ranks, should advance in phalanx. By this means the cavalry of the Indians was, with a few exceptions, cut to pieces in the action. Such also was the fate of the infantry, since the Macedonians were now pressing them from every side. Upon this, all turned to flight wherever a gap could be found in the cordon of Alexander's cavalry."

Meanwhile, Krateros and the other officers left on the opposite bank of the river had crossed over, and with their fresh troops fell upon the fugitives, and wrought terrible slaughter. The Indian army was annihilated, all the elephants were either killed or captured, and the chariots destroyed. Three thousand horsemen, and not less than twelve thousand foot-soldiers were killed, and nine thousand taken prisoners. The Macedonian loss, according to the highest estimate, did not exceed a thousand.

Poros himself, a magnificent giant, six and a half feet in height, fought to the end, but at last succumbed to nine wounds, and was taken prisoner in a fainting condition.

Alexander had the magnanimity to respect his gallant adversary, and willingly responded to his proud request to be "treated as a king." The victor not only confirmed the vanquished prince in the government of his ancestral territory, but added to it other lands of still greater extent, and by this politic generosity secured for the brief period of his stay in the country a grateful and faithful friend.

The victory was commemorated by the foundation of two towns, one named Nikaia, situated on the battlefield, and the other, named Boukephala, situated at the point whence Alexander had started to cross the Hydaspes. The latter was dedicated to the memory of Alexander's famous charger, which had carried him safely through so many perils, and had now at last succumbed to weariness and old age. Boukephala, by reason of its position at a ferry on the high road from the west to the Indian interior, became a place of such fame and importance as to be reckoned by Plutarch among the greatest of Alexander's foundations. It was practically identical with the modern town of Jihlam (Jhelum), and its position is more closely marked by the extensive elevated mound to the west of the existing town.

The position of Nikaia, which never attained fame, is less certain, but should probably be sought at the village of Sukhchainpur to the south of the Karri plain, the scene of the battle.

Alexander, after performing with fitting splendour the obsequies of the slain, offered the customary sacrifices, celebrated games, and left Krateros behind with a portion of the army and orders to fortify posts and maintain communications. The king himself, taking a force of picked troops, largely composed of cavalry, invaded the country of a nation called Glausai or Glaukanikoi, adjacent to the dominions of Poros. Thirty-seven considerable towns and a multitude of villages, having readily submitted, were added to the extensive territory administered by Poros. The king of the lower hills, who is called Abisares by the Greek writers, finding resistance hopeless, again tendered his submission. Another Poros, nephew of the defeated monarch, who ruled a tract called Gandaris, probably that between the Chinab and Ravi Rivers now known as Gondal Bar,

Burial of Alexander's Favourite Horse Bucephalus.
From a Fifteenth Century MS. in the British Museum. (After McCrindle.)

sent envoys promising allegiance to the invincible invader, and sundry independent tribes followed the example of these princes.

Alexander, moving in a direction more easterly than before, crossed the Akesines (Chinab) at a point not specified, but certainly near the foot of the hills. The passage of the river, although unopposed, was difficult by reason of the rapid current of the flooded stream, which was three thousand yards (15 *stadia*) in width, and of the large and jagged rocks with which the channel was bestrewn, and on which many of the boats were wrecked.

The king, having made adequate arrangements for supplies, reinforcements, and the maintenance of communications, continued his advance eastwards, probably passing close to the ancient fortress of Sialkot. The Hydraotes (Ravi) River was crossed without difficulty and Hephaistion was sent back in order to reduce to obedience the younger Poros, who had revolted owing to feelings of resentment at the excessive favour shown to his uncle and enemy.

Alexander selected as the adversaries worthy of his steel the more important confederacy of independent tribes which was headed by the Kathaioi, who dwelt upon the left or eastern side of the Hydraotes, and enjoyed the highest reputation for skill in the art of war. Their neighbours, the Oxydrakai, who occupied the basin of the Hyphasis, and the Malloi, who were settled along the lower course of the Hydraotes below Lahore and were also famous as brave warriors, intended to join the tribal league, but had not actually done so at this time. The Kathaioi were now supported only by minor clans, their immediate neighbours, and the terrible fate which awaited the Malloi was postponed for a brief space.

On the second day after the passage of the Hydraotes, Alexander received the capitulation of a town named Pimprama, belonging to a clan called Adraïstai by Arrian, and, after a day's rest, proceeded to invest Sangala, which the Kathaioi and the allied tribes had selected as their main stronghold. The tribes protected their camp, which lay under the shelter of a low hill, by a triple row of wagons, and offered a determined resistance.

Meantime, the elder Poros arrived with a reinforcement for the besiegers of five thousand troops, elephants, and a siege-train, but before any breach in the city wall had been effected, the Macedonians stormed the place by escalade, and routed the allies, who lost many thousands killed. Alexander's loss in killed was less than a hundred, but twelve hundred of his men were wounded – an unusually large proportion. Sangala was razed to the ground, as a punishment for the stout resistance of its defenders.

Yet another river, the Hyphasis (Bias), lay in the path of the royal adventurer, who advanced to its bank and prepared to cross, being determined to subdue the nations beyond. These were reputed to be clans of brave agriculturists, enjoying an admirable system of aristocratic government, and occupying a fertile territory well supplied with elephants of superior size and courage.

Alexander, having noticed that his troops no longer followed him with their wonted alacrity, and were indisposed to proceed to more distant adventures, sought to rouse their enthusiasm by an eloquent address, in which he recited the glories of their wondrous conquests from the Hellespont to the Hyphasis, and promised them the dominion and riches of all Asia. But his glowing words fell on unwilling ears, and were received with painful silence, which remained unbroken for a long time.

At last Koinos, the trusted cavalry general, who had led the charge in the battle with Poros, summoned up courage to reply, and argued the expediency of fixing some limit to the toils and dangers of the army. He urged his sovereign to remember that out of the Greeks and Macedonians who had crossed the Hellespont eight years earlier, some had been invalided home, some were unwilling exiles in newly founded cities far from their own land, some were disabled by wounds, and others, the most numerous, had perished by the sword or by disease.

Few indeed were those left to follow the standards, and they were weary wretches, shattered in health, ragged, ill-armed, and despondent. He concluded his oration by saying: —

"Moderation in the midst of success, O king! is the noblest of virtues, for, although, being at the head of so brave an army, you have naught to dread from mortal foes, yet the visitations of the Deity cannot be foreseen or guarded against by man."

The words of Koinos were greeted with loud applause, which left no doubt about the temper of the men. Alexander, deeply mortified and unwilling to yield, retired within his tent, but emerged on the third day, convinced that farther advance was impracticable. The soothsayers judiciously discovered that the omens were unfavourable for the passage of the river, and Alexander, with a heavy heart, gave orders for retreat, in September, 326 B. C.

To mark the farthest point of his advance, he erected twelve huge altars, built of squared stone, and each fifty cubits in height, dedicated to the twelve great gods. Although the army had not passed the river, these massive memorials were erected on the farther bank, where they long remained to excite the wonder and veneration of both natives and foreigners. Traces of them may still exist, and should be looked for along the oldest bed of the Bias, near the hills, in one or other of the three districts — Gurdaspur, Hoshyarpur, or Kangra — where nobody has yet sought them.

The judicious Arrian simply records: —

" Alexander divided the army into brigades, which he ordered to prepare twelve altars equal in height to the loftiest military towers, while exceeding them in breadth, to serve both as thank-offerings to the gods who had led him so far on the path of conquest, and as a memorial of his achievements. When the altars had been constructed, he offered sacrifice upon them with the customary rites, and celebrated gymnastic and equestrian games."

The structures thus solemnly dedicated were well designed to serve their double purpose, and constituted a dignified and worthy monument of the piety and labours of the world's greatest general. Their significance was fully appreciated by the Indian powers which had been compelled to bend before the Macedonian storm. We are told that Chandragupta Maurya, the first Emperor of India who succeeded to the lordship of Alexander's conquests, and his successors for centuries afterward, continued to venerate the altars, and were in the habit of crossing the river to offer sacrifice upon them.

But, if Curtius and Diodorus are to be believed, the noble simplicity of the monumental altars was marred by a ridiculous addition designed to gratify the king's childish vanity. The tale is given in its fullest form by Diodorus, who gravely informs us that, after the completion of the altars, Alexander caused an encampment to be made thrice the size of that actually occupied by his army, encircled by a trench fifty feet wide and forty feet deep, as well as by a rampart of extraordinary dimensions. "He further," the story continues, "ordered quarters to be constructed as for foot-soldiers, each containing two beds four cubits in length for each man, and besides this, two stalls of twice the ordinary size for each horseman. Whatever else was to be left behind was directed to be likewise proportionately increased in size." We are asked to believe that these silly proceedings were intended to convince the country people that the invaders had been men of more than ordinary strength and stature.

It is incredible that Alexander could have been guilty of such senseless folly, and the legend may be rejected without hesitation as probably based on distorted versions of tales told by travellers who had seen the altars.

FROM AN AJANTA CAVE PAINTING.

CHAPTER IV

ALEXANDER'S INDIAN CAMPAIGN

The Retreat

THE retreating army retraced its steps, and arrived again without further adventure on the bank of the Akesines (Chinab), where Hephaistion had completed the building of a fortified town. Voluntary settlers from the neighbouring country and such of the mercenary troops as seemed unfit for active service were left to occupy and garrison this post, and Alexander began to prepare for his voyage down the rivers to the Great Sea.

Envoys bearing tribute from the kings of the lower hills, now known as the chieftainships of Rajauri and Bhimbhar and the British District of Hazàra, were received at this time. Alexander, who regarded his Indian conquests as permanent additions to the empire, and evidently cherished hopes of a return to the country, having accepted the tenders of submission, solemnly appointed the King of Abhisara (Bhimbhar and Rajauri) to the office of satrap, and invested him with authority over the King of Urasa (Hazara), who is called Arsakes by Arrian.

About the same time a welcome reinforcement of five thousand cavalry from Thrace, and seven thousand infantry, sent by the king's cousin, Harpalos, Satrap of Babylon, arrived, bringing no less than twenty-five thousand suits of armour inlaid with gold and silver. The new accoutrements were at once distributed to the ragged troops, and the old suits were burned.

Alexander then advanced to the Hydaspes (Jihlam), and encamped on the bank, probably on the site of the camp formerly occupied by Poros. Several weeks were now devoted to the final preparations for the voyage down the rivers. All available country boats plying on the river were impressed for the service, and deficiencies were supplied by the construction of new vessels, for which the forests at the base of the hills afforded ample facilities. Crews were provided from the contingents of seafaring nations, Phœnicians, Cyprians, Karians, and Egyptians, who accompanied the army, and by the end of October, 326 B. C., all was ready. The fleet, which included eighty galleys of thirty oars each, and a multitude of horse transports and small craft of all kinds, probably numbered nearly two thousand vessels.

Before the voyage began, Alexander convoked an assembly of his officers and the ambassadors of the Indian powers, and in their presence appointed Poros to be king of all the conquered territories lying between the Hydaspes and the Hyphasis. These territories are said to have been occupied by seven nations, the Glausai, Kathaioi, and others, and to have comprised no less than two thousand towns. The opportunity was seized to effect a reconciliation between Poros and his old enemy, the King of Taxila, and the friendship between the two monarchs was cemented by a matrimonial alliance. The King of Taxila, who had vied with his rival in zealous service to the invader, was formally confirmed in his sovereignty of the country between the Indus and the Hydaspes.

Alexander, who never neglected to make provision for the protection of his flank and rear, and for the uninterrupted maintenance of communications with his distant base in Europe, instructed Generals Hephaistion and Krateros to march with all possible speed to secure the capital of King Saubhuti (Sophytes, or Sopeithes), lord of the fastnesses of the Salt Range stretching from Jihlam to the Indus, who submitted without resistance.

The fleet was to be protected by an army of 120,000 men marching along the banks, under the generals above named. Krateros had the command on the right, or western, bank of the river, while the larger portion of the army, accompanied by two hundred elephants, was led by Hephaistion along the left, or eastern, bank. Philippos, satrap of the countries west of the Indus, had orders to follow three days later with the rear-guard.

Thus escorted the vast fleet began its memorable voyage. At daybreak one morning toward the end of

October, Alexander, having offered libations from a golden bowl to the river gods, his ancestor Herakles, Ammon, and any other god whom he was accustomed to reverence, gave the signal for starting by sound of trumpet. In stately procession, without confusion or disorder, the ships quitted their anchorage and moved down-stream to the astonishment of the crowds of

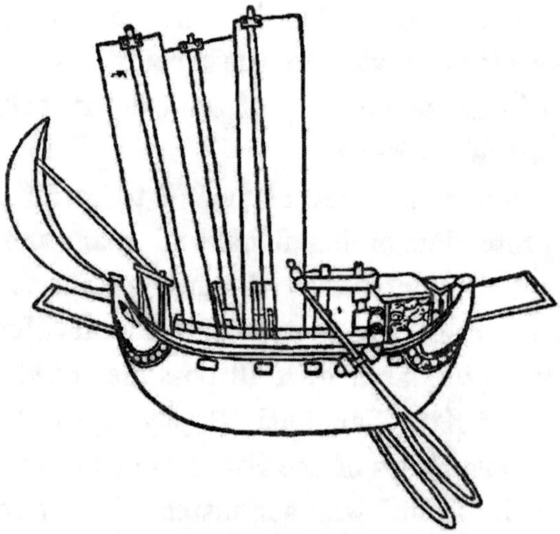

ANCIENT HINDU SHIP.
From an Ajanta Cave Painting. (After Griffiths.)

natives lining the banks, who had never before seen horses on board ship. The plash of thousands of oars, the words of command, and the chants of the rowers wakened the echoes, which reverberated from bank to bank, and enhanced the amazement of the gaping throngs of spectators. On the third day the fleet reached the place, perhaps Bhira, where Hephaistion and Krateros had been ordered to pitch their camps facing each other on opposite sides of the river. Here a halt was made for two days to allow the rear-guard under the command of Philippos to come up, and that general, on his arrival, was directed to convert his force into an advance-guard and proceed along the bank of the river.

On the fifth day after leaving the halting-place, the fleet arrived at the first river confluence, where the Hydaspes met the greater stream of the Akesines. The channel where the waters of the two rivers then met was so very narrow that dangerous whirlpools were formed, and much disorder was occasioned in the fleet. Two of the war-ships were sunk with the greater part of their crews, and the vessel which carried Alexander was in imminent danger of sharing the same fate. By dint of great exertion on the part of the king and all concerned, the bulk of the fleet was ultimately brought to a safe anchorage under the shelter of a headland, and the necessary steps were taken to repair the damage suffered.

It is impossible to determine the spot where these exciting incidents occurred. The confluence of the two rivers at Timmu (N. lat. 31° 10′) now takes place quietly, and presents none of the peculiarities to which Arrian and Curtius devote so much vivid description. All that can be said is that in Alexander's time the confluence must have been situated much farther to the north.

Our exact knowledge of the courses of the rivers in the Panjab and Sind begins only from the date of the Arab invasion in 712 A.D., more than a thousand years subsequent to the expedition of Alexander. Concerning the changes which happened during that millennium absolutely nothing is known. But during the twelve hundred years that have elapsed since the Arab conquests changes on a stupendous scale are known to have occurred, and it is certain that similar effects must have been produced by the ever operating causes during the thousand years which intervened between Alexander and Muhammad bin Kasim. During the known period, earthquakes, floods, changes of level, denudation, accretion, and alterations of climate have all contributed to transform the face of the country. The delta of the Indus has advanced more than fifty miles, and has thus lengthened the courses of the rivers, while diminishing their gradients and velocity. One huge river, the Hakra or Wahindah, which formerly gave life and wealth to the desert wastes of Bikanir, Bahawalpur, and Sind, has ceased to exist; the Bias (Hyphasis) has forsaken its ancient independent bed and become a tributary of the Sutlaj; and the other rivers, the Indus, Jihlam (Hydaspes), Chinab (Akesines), and Ravi (Hydraotes), have all repeatedly changed their courses and points of junction.

These facts, although indisputably true, have been ignored generally in practice by the historians of Alexander, who have pretended to trace the line of his river voyage on modern maps, and to "identify" town after town on the banks of the several rivers. All such identifications are vain. No man can tell in which of the ancient beds the Chinab or any of the other rivers named flowed in the time of Alexander, and, when the positions of the rivers are not ascertainable, it is clear that we cannot reasonably expect to identify places on their banks. The most that is possible is to give general indications of the course of the voyage and of the location of the principal nations encountered by Alexander. The sites of the towns and the precise positions of the confluences and crossing-places mentioned by the ancient historians cannot be precisely determined. Inasmuch as the courses of all the rivers were then much shorter than they now are, all the confluences must have been situated considerably farther north than at present, and this *a priori* inference appears to be fully supported by observation of the most ancient beds of the streams. The confluence of the Akesines and Hydaspes, the first of the four confluences described by Arrian, was probably situated not very far from the modern town of Jhang, and approximately in N. lat. 31°.

Alexander here landed his troops in order to subjugate the adjoining tribes, called Siboi and Agalassoi by Curtius, and to prevent them from joining the powerful nation of the Malloi (Sanskrit Malava or Malaya), who dwelt lower down the river, and were known to be preparing for strenuous resistance. The Siboi, who are described as rude folk clad in the skins of wild beasts and armed with clubs, submitted, and were allowed to retain their freedom. Their neighbours, the Agalassoi, who were able to muster a force estimated at forty thousand foot and three thousand horse, ventured to resist, and met with a terrible fate. Multitudes were put to the sword, and multitudes sold into slavery. Alexander advanced some thirty miles into their country, and captured their principal town. At a second town he met with an obstinate defence, which cost the lives of many Macedonians. The inhabitants, said to number twenty thousand, despairing of ultimate success, set fire to the town and cast themselves with their wives and children into the flames. The citadel escaped the fire, and was garrisoned by a detachment left behind for the purpose. The lives of three thousand of its gallant defenders were spared.

Information was received that a confederacy of the Malloi, Oxydrakai, and other independent tribes occupying the river valleys was being formed with the intention of offering strenuous resistance to the invasion. Alexander hastened the movements of his fleet and army with the object of attacking the confederates severally in detail, before they could mature their plans and combine their forces. The fleet and the bulk of the army received orders to assemble at the next confluence, that of the Hydraotes (Ravi) with the Akesines (Chinab, including the Hydaspes, or Jihlam).

Alexander in person landed with a picked force, largely composed, as usual, of mounted troops, to operate against the Malloi, the most formidable of the allied tribes, who occupied the fertile valley of the Hydraotes, on both banks of the river. Their neighbours, the Oxydrakai, who dwelt on the banks of the upper course of the Hyphasis, although ordinarily at war with the Malloi, had resolved to forget old enmities and to make common cause against the invader. The rival nations cemented the alliance by wholesale intermarriage, each giving and taking ten thousand young women for wives. But personal jealousies, such as in all ages have reduced to futility political combinations in India, prevented the alliance from taking effect. While the allies were discussing the claims of rival generals to command, Alexander acted, and with masterly strategy sweeping down upon the Malloi, extinguished their military power before the Oxydrakai could come to their aid. The forces at the command of the confederacy should have sufficed, if properly handled, to annihilate the small flying column at Alexander's disposal, for they are said to have comprised eighty or ninety thousand fully equipped infantry, ten thousand cavalry, and from seven to nine hundred chariots.

The exact strength of the Macedonian field force is not stated, but it must have been very small, not exceeding a few thousands. But what it lacked in numbers was compensated for by its perfect mobility and the genius of its general. The Macedonians were alarmed at the magnitude of the opposing forces, and a repetition of the mutiny of the Hyphasis was with difficulty prevented by a stirring address delivered by the king. By two forced marches across the waterless uplands, now known as the *Bār*, which separate the valleys of the Akesines and Hydraotes, Alexander completely surprised the Malloi, most of whom were working unarmed in the fields. Many of the helpless wretches were ruthlessly cut down, "without their even turning to offer resistance," and those who escaped the sword were shut up in the fortified towns.

One of these towns, with a citadel situated on a commanding height, was stormed under Alexander's personal direction, and two thousand of the garrison were slain. Another town, against which Perdikkas had been sent, was found to be deserted. The inhabitants fled to the marshes in the river valley, but, even among the reeds and rushes, they could not escape the weapons of the Macedonian cavalry. Alexander then pushed on to the Hydraotes, and overtook the retreating Malloi at the ford, inflicting severe loss upon them. He pursued them to the east of the river into the country now known as the Montgomery District, and took by mining and escalade a town inhabited by Brahmans. The king, with his customary disregard of danger, was the first man to scale the wall. The place was gallantly defended, but in vain. "About five thousand in all were killed, and as they were men of spirit, very few were taken prisoners."

The Malloi, being hard pressed, recrossed the Hydraotes, the passage of which they attempted to defend with fifty thousand men; but they were no match for the Europeans, and fled "with headlong speed" to the strongest fortified town in the neighbourhood. This small town, which cannot be identified precisely, and was situated somewhere near the boundary of the Jhang and Montgomery Districts, eighty or ninety miles to the northeast of Multan, was the scene of one of the most memorable incidents in Alexander's adventurous career, admirably described by Arrian from materials supplied by Ptolemy, who did not, however, himself take part in Alexander's defence, as has been erroneously asserted by some authors.

The Macedonians, already masters of the town, were endeavouring to scale the walls of the citadel, when

INDIAN ARCHER.
From the Ajanta Cave Paintings. (After Griffiths.)

Alexander, thinking that the men bearing the ladders loitered too long, snatched one from the man carrying it, and mounted the wall, followed by only three companions, Peukestas, Leonnatos, and Abreas. Standing on the wall in his gleaming armour, the king was a mark for every missile, and, feeling that he could effect nothing where he was without support, boldly leaped down into the citadel, followed by his three comrades. Abreas soon fell dead. Alexander, standing with his back to a tree that grew near the wall, slew the Indian governor and defended himself against all comers until his breast was pierced by an arrow, and he fell. Peukestas bestrode him as he lay, covering him with the sacred shield brought from Ilion, while Leonnatos, although severely wounded like his surviving comrade, protected him from side attacks. The ladders having broken, the maddened Macedonians were for a time powerless to help their king, but at last a few managed to scramble up the earthen wall, while others broke in a gate, and so saved Alexander, who had fainted.

The barbed arrow was withdrawn by a bold operation which involved much bleeding and threatened immediate death, but gradually Alexander's strong constitution triumphed, and the dangerous wound was healed. The infuriated troops fell upon the unfortunate inhabitants, and slew them all — sparing neither man, woman, nor child. When convalescent, Alexander was carried to the Hydraotes, and conveyed by boat to the junction with the Akesines, where he met his fleet and army, under the command respectively of Nearchos and Hephaistion.

The survivors of the Malloi, whose nation had felt the full weight of Alexander's hand, now tendered their humble submission, and the Oxydrakai, whom fortunate procrastination had saved, feeling that resistance would be hopeless, purchased the conqueror's clemency by offers of tribute and the delivery of valuable gifts. Alexander, stern and even cruel to those who opposed him, but always courteous and generous to the submissive, readily accepted the proposals, presents, and excuses of the tribal envoys. The presents are said to have included 1030 four-horse chariots, one thousand bucklers of native manufacture, one hundred talents of steel, a great store of cotton goods, a quantity of tortoise-shells, the skins of large lizards, with tame lions and tigers, in addition to a contingent of three hundred horsemen.

Philippos was then appointed satrap of the conquered nations, and the fleet, passing the third confluence, where the Hyphasis contributed its waters to the stream, continued its voyage to the fourth confluence, that of the Akesines (Chinab), including the Hydaspes (Jihlam), Hydraotes (Ravi), and Hyphasis (Bias), with the river which the ancient writers call the Indus. But it is probable that the "lost river of Sind," the Hakra, or Wahindah, then existed, and that all the Panjab rivers, including the Indus, joined it, and formed one great stream, afterward known as the Mihran of Sind.

It is absolutely impossible to determine the position of any of the confluences in Alexander's time; but, long afterward, in the days of the early Arab writers, all the rivers met at a place called Dosh-i-ab, or "the Meeting of the Waters," in territory now belonging to the Bahawalpur State. Our complete uncertainty as to the courses of the rivers, which have ranged, as the old channels indicate, over a space a hundred and ten miles wide in the region of the final confluence, deprives the remainder of Alexander's river voyage of much of its interest. His course in Upper Sind cannot be indicated even approximately, and it is impossible to fix accurately the position of either the towns or the nations mentioned by the historians.

The confluence of the combined Panjab rivers with the "Indus," wherever it may have been situated, was appointed to be the southern boundary of the satrapy of Philippos, to whom all the Thracians were made over together with an adequate force of infantry to form the garrison of his province. At about the same time the Bactrian nobleman, Oxyartes, father of Alexander's wife, Roxana, was deputed to the Paropanisadai, or the Kabul province, as satrap in succession to Tyriaspes, whose administration had been unsatisfactory. A city was founded at the confluence of the rivers with the "Indus," which Alexander hoped would become prosperous and famous. Dockyards also were constructed. Certain independent tribes, whom Arrian calls Abastanoi, Xathroi or Oxathroi, and Ossadioi, submitted or were subjugated, and it is noted that galleys of thirty oars and transport vessels were built and supplied by the Xathroi. Although it is impossible to determine accurately either the correct names or the true positions of the tribes in Northern Sind mentioned by the various ancient authorities, the region occupied by the tribes referred to seems to be that lying to the north and south of N. lat. 28° and between E. long. 69° and 70° 30′. During this stage of the campaign, Krateros, who hitherto, from the beginning, had always marched on the right, or western, bank of each successive river, was transferred to the left, or eastern, bank, which offered greater facilities for movement and was occupied by tribes less hostile than those on the other bank.

Alexander now hurried on in order to surprise the

powerful monarch called Mousikanos by Arrian, who had proudly abstained from sending envoys or presents to the invader. The capital of this stiff-necked king may be probably, although not certainly, identified with Alor, or Aror, the ancient capital of Sind, now included in the Shikarpur District, and situated in N. lat. 27° 39′, E. long. 68° 59′. The peculiarities of the people of this kingdom excited the surprise and admiration of the Macedonians. The inhabitants were believed to attain the age of a hundred and thirty years, their longevity being the result of good health secured by temperance in diet. Although their country possessed mines of both gold and silver, they refused to make use of either metal. Unlike the other Indians, they kept no slaves, employing in their stead "young men in the flower of their age, as the Cretans employ the Aphamiotai, and the Lacedæmonians the Helots." They also resembled the Lacedæmonians in observing the custom of a public meal, at which the food served was the produce of the chase. They declined to study any science save that of medicine, and were reputed to have no system of civil law, the jurisdiction of the courts being confined to cases of murder and other violent crime.

King Mousikanos, like the Malloi, being completely surprised by the rapidity of the movements of Alexander, who had reached the frontier before his departure from his last camp had been reported, hastened to meet the conqueror, bringing with him all his elephants and the choicest presents which India could offer. Alexander, with his habitual readiness to accept submission, received the king courteously, expressed much admiration of his capital and realm, and confirmed him in his sovereignty. But Mousikanos, acting under the advice of Brahman counsellors, quickly repented of his ready submission, and revolted. Peithon, the son of Agenor, who had been appointed satrap of the country to the south of the territory entrusted to Philippos, was sent in pursuit of the rebel, while Alexander in person operated against the towns, some of which were destroyed, while others were occupied by garrisons. Mousikanos, having been captured by Peithon, was crucified along with the Brahmans who had instigated his defection.

Alexander next marched with a flying column against a chief named Oxykanos, who was taken prisoner. His two principal cities were sacked, and the other towns in the neighbourhood surrendered without attempting resistance; "so much were the minds of all the Indians paralyzed with abject terror by Alexander and the success of his arms." Another chieftain, named Sambos, whose capital was Sindimana, and who had fled in terror, surrendered, and more Brahmans, who had instigated the revolt of an unnamed town, were executed. It is said that during this campaign on the Lower Indus eighty thousand of the natives were killed, and multitudes were sold as slaves.

After the execution of Mousikanos, the ruler of the Delta, which was known to the Greeks as Patalene, from its capital Patala, arrived in camp and proffered the submission of his kingdom, which was accepted. He was sent back to his country to prepare for the reception of the expedition.

About the same time Krateros, one of Alexander's most trusted lieutenants, was detached with orders to conduct a large portion of the army into Karmania by the route leading through the territories of Arachosia (Kandahar) and Drangiana (Sistan). The troops entrusted to Krateros comprised the brigades (τάξις) of Attalos, Meleager, and Antigenes, besides some of the archers, the "companions" or guards, and other Macedonians unfit for further active service. The elephants also accompanied this force.

Alexander in person retained the command of the troops serving as marines, while Hephaistion was given supreme command of the rest of the army, which advanced on the right bank of the river. Krateros, who had been transferred to the left bank in Upper Sind, had, of course, been obliged to recross the stream in order to begin his homeward march. His place on the left bank was now taken by Peithon, son of Agenor, who was given a mounted force of lancers and Agrianians, with instructions to place colonists in certain fortified towns, suppress attempts at insurrection, maintain order, and ultimately to rejoin Alexander at Patala. The prince and people of that city fled in terror, but were mostly reassured and induced to return to their homes.

Alexander, considering Patala to be a position of high strategical importance, caused Hephaistion to construct a citadel there and to dig wells in the adjoining region. He proposed to make a great naval station at the point where the river divided, and remained sufficiently long on the spot to see some progress made in the construction of a roadstead and dockyard. He then resolved to explore personally both arms of the river down to the sea, and first sailed down the western, or right, branch, which probably debouched near or below Debal, the ancient port of Sind, distant about fifteen miles from Thathah (Tatta). His sailors, accustomed to the tideless waters of the Mediterranean, were thrown into a state of great alarm and confusion by the ebb and flow of the tide, but ultimately Alexander succeeded in pushing on with some of the fastest vessels and reaching the open sea. He sailed out a few miles into the deep, sacrificed bulls to Poseidon, and followed up the sacrifice by a libation, casting the golden vessels used in the ceremony into the ocean as a thank-offering.

He then returned to Patala, where he found the works of the new naval station well advanced, and proceeded to explore the eastern, or left, branch of the river. Near its mouth he passed through a large lake, apparently that now known as the Samarah lake to the west of Amarkot, and again reached the seashore in about latitude 25°. Having spent three days in reconnoitring the coast and arranging for the construction of wells, he returned to Patala. Harbours and docks were built on the shores of the lake, and furnished with garrisons. Provisions to supply the forces for four months were collected, and all other necessary preparations were made for the two bold enterprises which he had planned: the voyage of the fleet along the coast to the Persian Gulf, and his own march with the army through Gedrosia in a direction, so far as might be practicable, parallel to the course of the fleet.

His plans were conceived upon a comprehensive scale. Nearchos, the admiral who had successfully commanded the flotilla during the ten months' voyage from Jihlam to the sea, was instructed to bring the fleet round the coast into the Persian Gulf as far as the mouth of the Euphrates, and to record careful observations of the strange lands and seas which he should visit. Alexander himself proposed to conduct the army back to Persia through the wilds of the country then called Gedrosia, and now known as Mukran, hitherto untrodden save by the legendary hosts of Semiramis and Cyrus. The king, who was independent of the winds, started on his march about the beginning of October, 325 B.C. Nearchos, being obliged to watch for the change of the monsoon, did not leave his anchorage in the river until two or three weeks later.

Although Gedrosia has usually remained outside the Indian political system, the province, or part of it, has been included from time to time within the dominions of the sovereigns of Hind, and its history cannot be regarded as altogether foreign to the history of India. But the satrapy of Gedrosia undoubtedly lay beyond the limits of India proper, and a summary narrative of the adventures met with by Nearchos on its coasts and his sovereign in its deserts will be sufficient to complete the story of Alexander's Indian campaign.

Nearchos was detained for several days in the river, and, after much difficulty in making a passage for the ships round a bar, which obstructed the mouth of the western branch, ultimately got out to sea. Contrary winds detained him for twenty-four days in a secure harbour, to which he gave the name of Alexander's Haven. The coast-line has been changed so much by both accretion and denudation, that attempts at detailed identifications of places near the mouth of the river are a waste of time, but it is safe to affirm that the haven where Nearchos found shelter was not very far from the modern Karachi (Kurrachee). The admiral then crept cautiously along the inhospitable coast, his crews often suffering severely from lack of provisions and fresh water. After travelling a hundred miles or so (850 *stadia*), the fleet reached the mouth of the river Arabis (the Purali), which formed the boundary between the Arabioi, the last a people of Indian descent settled in this region, and the Oreitai, who occupied an extensive territory to the west of the river.

Having traversed an estimated distance of eight hundred *stadia* more, the fleet reached a place called Kokala, where the wearied crews were allowed to disembark and enjoy much-needed rest. While the sailors were reposing here in a fortified camp, Nearchos came into touch with Leonnatos, whom Alexander had detached with a field force to subdue the Oreitai. News arrived that a great battle had been fought, in which Leonnatos had defeated the natives with terrible slaughter. The Oreitai are said to have lost six thousand men and all their leaders out of a total force of eight thousand foot and three hundred horse. The Macedonian loss, although numerically small, was noteworthy because it included the colleague of Leonnatos, Apollophanes, who had recently been appointed satrap of the country. Communications between Leonnatos and Nearchos having been established, the fleet was repaired and victualled, and sailors who had proved inefficient at sea were drafted into the army, their places being taken by men selected from the troops under the command of Leonnatos.

Continuing their voyage westward, the ships passed along the coast near the mouth of the river Tomeros, which was inhabited by a race of savages, ignorant of the use of iron, and armed only with wooden spears charred at the point to harden them. These wild men were covered with shaggy hair all over the body, and had clawlike nails strong enough to rip up fish and to split the softer kinds of wood. Their clothing was made of the skins of wild beasts or those of the larger fishes. After a skirmish with the savages, the fleet delayed for five days to effect repairs, and on the sixth day reached the rocky headland named Malana (now Ras Malin), the eastern boundary of the Oreitai, a people who were not savages, but were dressed and armed like the inhabitants of India, although differing from them in language and customs.

When the Malana cape had been passed, the inland

people were known as Gedrosioi, and no longer as Oreitai. The inhabitants of the coast continued to astonish the voyagers by their strange manners and customs. "These poor wretches," we are told, "had nothing but fish to live on," and so they were dubbed Ichthyophagoi, or "Fish-eaters," by the Greeks – what the real name of the race may have been is not known. Whales, which were numerous along this coast, although very alarming to the sailors of the fleet, were extremely useful to the natives on shore, and supplied the materials for the better houses, which were built of whales' bones, the huge jaws serving as doorways.

The seamen on board the ships of Nearchos, being superstitious, like the sailors of all ages and countries, were much frightened at the weird tales told about an uninhabited island, which Arrian calls Nosala, and is now known as Astola or Astalu. It lies nearly midway between Urmera and Pasni headlands, and is to this day as much an object of dread to the Med fisherman as it was long ago to the Greek sailors.

Thus threading their way through all dangers, real or imaginary, the explorers made their way to a port called Badis, near Cape Jask at the entrance to the Straits of Ormuz, and so came into touch with the more civilized province of Karmania. Proceeding through the straits, the delighted mariners found themselves at Harmozeia (Ormuz), a charming place, producing everything that they wanted, except olives. Here the men came ashore and were gratefully enjoying their rest, when some of the more adventurous spirits strolled inland, and were astounded to meet a stranger wearing Greek clothes and speaking Greek. Tears came to their eyes as they heard the familiar sounds of home in that strange and distant land. Explanations having been exchanged, the stranger proved to be a straggler from Alexander's army, and gave the welcome information that the king was only five days' march distant.

Nearchos and Archias at once arranged to go inland to meet their sovereign, and, after many difficulties, made their way to his presence, but so ragged and unkempt were they, that Alexander at first could not recognize them. When at last he was convinced of his friends' identity, he assumed hastily that they must be the sole miserable survivors from his lost fleet, and was in despair at the imagined disaster. But he was soon reassured by Nearchos, who told him that the ships were safe and sound, hauled up at the mouth of the Anamis River for repairs.

The admiral, after volunteering to conduct the fleet up the gulf to Susa, returned to the coast, to which he was obliged to fight his way, and thence sailed on, with little adventure, to the mouth of the Euphrates. He then heard of Alexander's approach to Susa, and, turning back, entered the Tigris to meet him, and "it was thus that the expedition which had started from the mouths of the Indus was brought in safety to Alexander."

The difficulties encountered by the army under the command of Alexander were even greater than those met and overcome by the fleet under Nearchos. The king seems to have been ignorant of the existence of the Hala range of mountains, which terminates in Cape Malin. This great obstacle, which he was obliged to turn, deranged his plans, and compelled him to penetrate far into the interior, and for a time to lose touch with the fleet. The army suffered agonies from thirst, and the unfortunate followers perished by thousands. "The blazing heat and want of water," Arrian tells us, "destroyed a great part of the army, and especially the beasts of burden, which perished from the great depth of the sand, and the heat which scorched like fire, while a great many died of thirst." Ultimately, the remnant of the force worked its way back to the coast, emerging near the harbour of Pasni, almost on the line where the telegraph-wire now runs, and its sufferings were at an end. But the soldiers had been obliged "to burn the rich spoils taken from their enemies, for the sake of which they had marched to the utmost extremities of the East." The success of the general was the ruin of the private.

While the army was still in Karmania, a report was received that Philippos, satrap of the Indian provinces north of the confluence of the Akesines with the Indus, had been treacherously murdered by his mercenary troops. Although this disquieting communication was accompanied by the information that the murderers had been slain by the satrap's Macedonian body-guard, Alexander was not then in a position to make permanent arrangements, and was obliged to content himself with sending a despatch to India, directing Ambhi, King of Taxila, and Eudamos, commandant of a Thracian contingent on the Upper Indus, to assume the administration of the province until a satrap could be appointed in due course. The death of Alexander at Babylon in the following year (June, 323 B.C.) effectually prevented any attempt being made to retain control over the conquered countries east of the Indus.

When the second partition of the empire was effected at Triparadeisos in 321 B.C., Antipater practically recognized the independence of India by appointing the native kings Poros and Ambhi, as a matter of form, to the charge of the Indus valley and Panjab. Peithon, whom Alexander had appointed Satrap of the Indus Delta, was transferred to the provinces "which bordered on the Paropanisadai," *i.e.* to Arachosia, etc., west of the Indus, and India was abandoned by the Macedonian government in reality, though not in name. Eudamos, alone of the Macedonian officers, retained some authority in the Indus valley until 317.

The Indian expedition of Alexander may be said to have lasted for three years, from May, 327 B.C., when he crossed the Hindu Kush, to May, 324 B.C., when he entered Susa. Out of this period, about nineteen months were spent in India east of the Indus, from March, 326 B.C., when he crossed the bridge at Ohind, until September or October in the following year, when he entered the territory of the Arabioi.

Looked at merely from the soldier's point of view, the achievements wrought in that brief space of time are marvellous and incomparable. The strategy, tactics, and organization of the operations give the reader of the story the impression that in all these matters perfection was attained. The professional military critic may justly blame Alexander, as his own officers blamed him, for excessive display of personal heroism, and needless exposure to danger of the precious life upon which the safety of the whole army depended, but criticism is silenced by admiration, and by the reflection that the example set by the king's reckless daring was of incalculable value as a stimulus and encouragement to troops often ready to despair of success.

The descent of the rivers to the ocean through the territories of civilized and well-armed nations, admittedly the best soldiers in the East, and the voyage of Nearchos from the Indus to the Tigris, may fairly be described as unqualified successes. The third great enterprise, the retirement of the army led by Alexander in person through Gedrosia, would have been equally prosperous but for the occurrence of physical difficulties, which could not be foreseen, owing to the imperfection of the information at the king's command. But even this operation was not a failure. Notwithstanding the terrible privations endured and the heavy losses suffered, the army emerged from the deserts as an organized and disciplined force, and its commander's purpose was attained.

On the whole, Alexander's Indian campaign was a success. It was not really marred by the mutiny at the Hyphasis. If his soldiers had permitted him to plunge more deeply into the interior, he would probably have been unable to maintain the communication with his European base, on which his safety depended, and his small, isolated force might have been overwhelmed by the mere numbers of his adversaries. Koinos and his fellow remonstrants may be credited with having prevented the annihilation of the Macedonian army.

The triumphant progress of Alexander from the Himalaya to the sea demonstrated the inherent weakness of the greatest Asiatic armies when confronted with European skill and discipline. The dreaded elephants lost their terrors, and proved to be a poor defence against the Macedonian cavalry. The unopposed march of Krateros from Sind to Persia through Sistan opened up an alternative land route and solved the problem of easy overland communication with Europe. The circumnavigation of the coast by Nearchos gave Alexander a third line of communication by sea, and, if he had lived, there is no reason to suppose that he would have experienced serious difficulty in retaining his hold upon the Panjab and Sind.

All his proceedings prove conclusively that he intended the permanent annexation of those provinces to his empire, and the measures which he took for the purpose were apparently adequate to ensure success. But Alexander's premature death destroyed the fruits of his well-planned and successful enterprise. Within three years of his departure, his officers had been ousted, his garrisons destroyed, and all trace of his rule had disappeared. The colonies which he founded in India, unlike those established in the other Asiatic provinces, took no root. The campaign, although carefully designed to secure a permanent conquest, was in actual effect no more than a brilliantly successful raid on a gigantic scale, which left upon India no mark save the horrid scars of bloody war.

India remained unchanged. The wounds of battle were quickly healed; the ravaged fields smiled again as the patient oxen and no less patient husbandmen resumed their interrupted labours; and the places of the slain myriads were filled by the teeming swarms of a population which knows no limits save those imposed by the cruelty of man or the still more pitiless operations of nature. India was not Hellenized. She continued to live her life of "splendid isolation," and soon forgot the passing of the Macedonian storm.

"The East bowed low before the blast
In patient, deep disdain;
She let the legions thunder past,
And plunged in thought again."

FRIEZE FROM A BUDDHIST STUPA.

CHAPTER V

CHANDRAGUPTA MAURYA AND BINDUSARA

321 B. C. TO 272 B. C.

WHEN Alexander quitted the Panjab, he posted no Macedonian garrisons in that province, making over the care of his interests to King Poros, who must have been independent in practice. Ambhi, King of Taxila, was also entrusted with authority as a colleague of Poros. After the assassination of Philippos, Alexander had sent orders from Karmania to Eudamos, commandant of a Thracian garrison on the Indus, to act as resident pending the appointment of a satrap, and to supervise the native princes. But this officer had no adequate force at his command to enforce his authority, which must have been purely nominal. He managed, however, to remain in India, probably somewhere in the basin of the Indus, until about 317 B. C., when he departed to help Eumenes against Antigonos, taking with him a hundred and twenty elephants, and a small force of infantry and cavalry. He had obtained the elephants by treacherously slaying a native prince, perhaps Poros, with whom he had been associated as a colleague.

The province of Sind, on the Lower Indus, below the great confluence of the rivers, which had been entrusted by Alexander to Peithon, son of Agenor, remained under Greek influence for a still shorter period. At the time of the second partition of the Macedonian empire in 321 B. C. at Triparadeisos, Antipater was avowedly unable to exercise any effective control over the Indian rajas, and Peithon had been obliged already to retire to the west of the Indus. The Indian provinces to the east of the river were consequently ignored in the partition, and Peithon was content to accept the government of the regions bordering on the Paropanisadai, or Kabul country. That country probably continued to be administered by Roxana's father Oxyartes, whom Alexander had appointed satrap. Sibyrtios was confirmed in the government of Arachosia and Gedrosia; Stasandros, the Cyprian, was given Aria and Drangiana; and his countryman Stasanor was appointed governor of Bactria and Sogdiana. These arrangements clearly prove that in 321 B. C., within two years of Alexander's death, the Greek power to the east of the Indus had been extinguished, with the slight exception of the small territory, wherever it may have been, which Eudamos managed to hold for some four years longer.

The insecurity of the Macedonian authority in the newly annexed Indian provinces had been proved by the assassination of Philippos, the report of which was received while Alexander was in Karmania, and might be expected to return some day to the scene of his victories. His death in June, 323 B. C., dispelled all fears of his return, and the native princes undoubtedly took the earliest possible opportunity to assert their independence and exterminate the weak foreign garrisons. The news of Alexander's decease was known in India probably as early as August, but no serious fighting would have been undertaken by ordinary commanders until the beginning of the cold season in October; for Alexander's indifference to climatic conditions was not shared by Indian chiefs, who were accustomed to regulate their military movements strictly in accordance with precedent. We may feel assured that as soon as the news of the conqueror's death had been confirmed beyond doubt, and the season permitted the execution of military operations with facility, a general rising took place, and that Macedonian authority in India was at an end early in 322 B.C., except for the small remnant to which Eudamos continued to cling.

The leader of the revolt against the foreigners was an able adventurer, Chandragupta by name, at that time a young man, probably not more than twenty-five years of age. Although he was on his father's side a scion of the royal house of Magadha,—the principal State in Northern India,—his mother was of lowly origin, and, in accordance with Hindu law, he belonged to her caste and had to bear the reproach of inferior social rank. The family name Maurya, assumed by the members of the dynasty founded by Chandragupta, is said to be a derivative from Mura, his mother's name. In some way or other, young Chandragupta incurred the displeasure of his kinsman, Mahapadma Nanda, the reigning King of Magadha, and was obliged to go into exile. During his banishment he had the good fortune to see Alexander, and is said to have expressed the opinion that the Macedonian king, if he had advanced, would have made an easy conquest of the great kingdom on the Ganges, by reason of the extreme unpopularity of the reigning monarch. Mahapadma Nanda was reputed to be the son of a barber, who had secured the affections of the late queen. The guilty pair had then murdered the king, whose throne was seized by the barber-paramour. His son, the now reigning monarch, was avaricious and profligate, and naturally possessed few friends.

Chandragupta, having collected, during his exile, a formidable force of the warlike and predatory clans on the northwestern frontier, attacked the Macedonian garrisons immediately after Alexander's death, and conquered the Panjab. He then turned his victorious arms against his enemy, the King of Magadha, and, taking advantage of that monarch's unpopularity, dethroned and slew him, utterly exterminating every member of his family. His adviser in this revolution was a subtle Brahman named Chanakya, by whose aid he succeeded in seizing the vacant throne. But the people did not gain much by the change of masters, because Chandragupta, "after his victory, forfeited by his tyranny all title to the name of liberator, oppressing with servitude the very people whom he had emancipated from foreign thraldom." He inherited from his Nanda predecessor a huge army, which he increased until it numbered thirty thousand cavalry, nine thousand elephants, six hundred thousand infantry, and a multitude of chariots. With this irresistible force, all the northern States, probably as far as the Narmada, or even farther, were overrun and subjugated; so that the dominions of Chandragupta, the first paramount sovereign or emperor in India, extended from the Bay of Bengal to the Arabian Sea.

While Chandragupta was engaged in the consolidation of his empire, a rival was laying the foundations of his power in Western and Central Asia, and preparing to attempt the recovery of Alexander's Indian conquests. In the course of the internecine struggle between the generals of Alexander, two had emerged as competitors for supreme power in Asia—Antigonos and Seleukos, who afterward became known as Nikator, or the Conqueror. Fortune at first favoured Antigonos and drove his antagonist into exile; but in 312 B.C. Seleukos recovered possession of Babylon, and six years later felt himself justified in assuming the regal style and title. He is conventionally described as King of Syria, but was in reality the lord of Western and Central Asia. The eastern provinces of his realm extended to the borders of India; and he naturally desired to recover the Macedonian conquests in that country, which had been practically abandoned, although never formally relinquished. In pursuit of this object, Seleukos crossed the Indus in 305 B.C., and attempted to imitate the victorious march of Alexander. The details of the campaign are not known, and it is impossible to determine how far the invading army penetrated into the Ganges valley, if at all, but the result of the war is certain.

When the shock of battle came, the hosts of Chandragupta were too strong for the invader, and Seleukos was obliged to retire and conclude a humiliating peace. Not only was he compelled to abandon all thought of conquest in India, but he was constrained to surrender a large part of Ariana to the west of the Indus. In exchange for the comparatively trifling equivalent of five hundred elephants, Chandragupta received the satrapies of the Paropanisadai, Aria, and Arachosia, the capitals of which were respectively the cities now known as Kabul, Herat, and Kandahar. The satrapy of Gedrosia, or at least the eastern portion of it, seems also to have been included in the cession, and the high contracting powers ratified the peace by "a matrimonial alliance," which phrase probably means that Seleukos gave a daughter to his Indian rival. This treaty may be dated in 303 B. C. As soon as it was concluded, Seleukos started on his long march westward to confront Antigonos, whom he defeated and slew at Ipsos in Phrygia in 301 B. C. As Ipsos was at least 2500 miles distant from the Indus, the march to it must have occupied a year or more.

The range of the Hindu Kush Mountains, known to the Greeks as the Paropanisos or Indian Caucasus, in this way became the frontier between Chandragupta's provinces of Herat and Kabul on the south, and the Seleukidan province of Bactria on the north. The first Indian emperor, more than two thousand years ago, thus entered into possession of that "scientific frontier" sighed for in vain by his English successors, and never held in its entirety even by the Mogul monarchs of the sixteenth and seventeenth centuries.

In the course of some eighteen years Chandragupta had expelled the Macedonian garrisons from the Panjab and Sind, repulsed and humbled Seleukos the Conqueror, and established himself as undisputed supreme lord of at least all Northern India and a large part of Ariana. These achievements fairly entitle him to rank among the greatest and most successful kings known to history. A realm so vast and various as that of Chandragupta was not to be governed by weakness. The strong hand which won the empire was needed to keep it, and the government was administered with stern severity. About six years after the withdrawal of Seleukos, Chandragupta died (297 B. C.), and handed on the imperial succession to his son Bindusara.

Soon after the conclusion of peace in 303 B. C., Seleukos had sent as his envoy to the court of Chandragupta an officer named Megasthenes, who had been employed under Sibyrtios, Satrap of Arachosia. The envoy resided for a considerable time at Pataliputra (now Patna), the capital of the Indian empire, and employed his leisure in compiling an excellent account of the geography, products, and institutions of India, which continued to be the principal authority on the subject until modern times. Although often misled by erroneous information received from others, Megasthenes is a veracious and trustworthy witness concerning matters which came under his personal observation, and his vivid account of Chandragupta's civil and military administration may be accepted without hesitation as true and accurate. That account, although preserved in a fragmentary form, is so full and detailed that the modern reader is more minutely informed in many respects concerning the institutions of Chandragupta than he is about those of any Indian sovereign until the days of Akbar, the contemporary of Queen Elizabeth.

Pataliputra, the imperial capital, which had been founded in the fifth century B. C., stood in the tongue of land formed by the confluence of the Son with the Ganges, on the northern bank of the former, and a few miles distant from the latter. The site is now occupied by the large native city of Patna and the English civil station of Bankipur, but the rivers changed their courses many centuries ago, and the confluence is at present near the cantonment of Dinapur, about twelve miles above Patna. The ancient city, which lies buried below its modern successor, was, like it, a long, narrow parallelogram, measuring about nine miles in length and a mile and a half in breadth. It was defended by a massive timber palisade, pierced by sixty-four gates, crowned by five hundred and seventy towers, and protected externally by a broad and deep moat, filled from the waters of the Son.

The royal palace, although chiefly constructed of timber, was considered to excel in splendour and magnificence the palaces of Susa and Ekbatana, its gilded pillars being adorned with golden vines and silver birds. The buildings stood in an extensive park, studded with fish-ponds and furnished with a great variety of ornamental trees and shrubs.

Here the imperial court was maintained with barbaric and luxurious ostentation. Basins and goblets of gold, some measuring six feet in width, richly carved tables and chairs of state, vessels of Indian copper set with precious stones, and gorgeous embroidered robes were to be seen in profusion, and contributed to the brilliancy of the public ceremonies. When the king condescended to show himself in public on state occasions, he was carried in a golden palanquin, adorned with tassels of pearls, and was clothed in fine muslin embroidered with purple and gold. When making short journeys, he rode on horseback, but when travelling longer distances he was mounted like a modern raja, on an elephant with golden trappings. Combats of animals were a favourite diversion, as they still are at the courts of native princes, and the king took delight in witnessing the fights of bulls, rams, elephants, rhinoceroses, and other animals. Gladiatorial contests between men were also exhibited. A curious entertainment, which seems not to be known in the present age, was afforded by ox-races, which were made the subject of keen betting, and were watched by the king with the closest interest. The course was one of thirty *stadia*, or six thousand yards, and the race was run with cars, each of which was drawn by a mixed team of horses and oxen, the horses being in the centre, with an ox on each side. Trotting oxen are still largely used for drawing travelling-carriages in many parts of India, but the breed of racers seems to be extinct.

The principal royal amusement was the chase, which was conducted with great ceremony, the game in an enclosed preserve being driven up to a platform occupied by the king, who shot the animals with arrows; but, if the hunt took place in the open country, he used to ride an elephant. When hunting, he was closely attended by armed female guards, who were obtained by purchase from foreign countries, and formed an indispensable element in the courts of the ancient Indian monarchs. The road for the sovereign's procession was marked off with ropes, which it was death for any one, even a woman, to pass. The institution of the royal hunt was abolished by Chandragupta's grandson, Asoka, in 259 B. C.

As a rule, the king remained within the precincts of the inner palace, under the protection of his Amazonian body-guard, and appeared in public only to hear cases, offer sacrifice, and to go on military or hunting expeditions. Probably he was expected to show himself to his subjects at least once a day, and then to receive petitions and decide disputes in person. Like the modern Indians, Chandragupta took pleasure in massage or friction of the limbs, and custom required that he should indulge in this luxury while giving public audience; four attendants used to massage him with ebony rollers during the time that he was engaged in disposing of cases. In accordance with Persian custom, which had much influence upon the Indian court and administration, the king ceremonially washed his hair on his birthday, which was celebrated by a splendid festival, at which the nobles were expected to make rich presents to their sovereign.

In the midst of all the gold and glitter, and in spite of the most elaborate precautions, uneasy lay the head that wore the crown. The king's life was so constantly threatened by plots that he dared not incur the risk either of sleeping in the daytime, or of occupying the same bedroom two nights in succession. The dramatist brings vividly before us the astuteness of the Brahman counsellor who detected the plots both of the poisoners and of —

> "The brave men who were concealed
> In the subterrene avenue that led
> To Chandragupta's sleeping chamber — thence
> To steal by night, and kill him as he slept."

The army, to which Chandragupta owed his throne and empire, was maintained at enormous numerical strength, and so organized, equipped, and administered as to attain a high degree of efficiency, as measured by an Oriental standard. It was not a militia, but a standing army, drawing liberal and regular pay, and supplied by the government with horses, arms, equipment, and stores. The force at the command of Mahapadma Nanda is said to have numbered eighty thousand horse, two hundred thousand foot, eight thousand chariots, and six thousand fighting elephants. This huge force was greatly augmented by Chandragupta, who raised the numbers of the infantry to six hundred thousand, and also had thirty thousand horse, and nine thousand elephants, besides chariots, all permanently enrolled in a regularly paid establishment.

Each horseman carried two lances, resembling the kind called *saunia* by the Greeks, and a buckler. All the infantry carried the broadsword as their principal weapon, and as additional arms, either javelins, or bow and arrows. The arrow was discharged with the aid of pressure from the left foot on the extremity of the bow resting upon the ground, and with such force that neither shield nor breastplate could withstand it.

Each chariot, which might be drawn by either four or two horses, accommodated two fighting-men besides the driver; and an elephant, in addition to the mahout, or driver, carried three archers. The nine thousand elephants therefore implied a force of thirty-six thousand men, and the eight thousand chariots, supposing them to be no more numerous than those kept by Mahapadma Nanda, required twenty-four thousand men to work them. The total number of soldiers in the army would thus have been six hundred thousand infantry, thirty thousand horsemen, thirty-six thousand men with the elephants, and twenty-four thousand with the chariots, or 690,000 in all, excluding followers and attendants.

These high figures may seem incredible at first sight, but are justified by our knowledge of the unwieldy hosts used in war by Indian kings in later ages. For instance, Nuñez, the Portuguese chronicler, who was contemporary with Krishna Deva, the Raja of Vijayanagar, in the sixteenth century (1509-30), affirms that that prince led against Raichur an army consisting of 703,000 foot, 32,600 horse, and 551 elephants, besides camp-followers.

The formidable force at the disposal of Chandragupta, by far the largest in India, was controlled and administered under the direction of a War Office organized on an elaborate system. A commission of thirty members was divided into six boards, each with five members, to which departments were severally assigned as follows: Board No. 1, in co-operation with the admiral—Admiralty; Board No. 2—Transport, Commissariat, and Army Service, including the provision of drummers, grooms, mechanics, and grass-cutters; Board No. 3—Infantry; Board No. 4—Cavalry; Board No. 5—War-chariots; Board No. 6—Elephants.

INDIAN FOOT-SOLDIERS.
From an Ajanta Cave Painting. (After Griffiths.)

All Indian armies had been regarded from time immemorial as normally comprising the four arms, cavalry, infantry, elephants, and chariots; and each of these arms would naturally fall under the control of a distinct authority; but the addition of co-ordinate supply and admiralty departments appears to be an innovation due to the genius of Chandragupta. His organization must have been as efficient in practice as it was systematic on paper, for it enabled him not only, in the words of Plutarch, to "overrun and subdue all India," but also to expel the Macedonian garrisons, and to repel the invasion of Seleukos.

The details recorded concerning the civil administration of Chandragupta's empire, if not so copious as we might desire, are yet sufficient to enable us to realize the system of government, which, although of course based upon the personal autocracy of the sovereign, was something better than a merely arbitrary tyranny.

The administration of the capital city, Pataliputra, was regarded as a matter of the highest importance, and was provided for by the formation of a Municipal Commission, consisting of thirty members, divided, like the War Office Commission of equal numbers, into six boards or committees of five members each. These boards may be regarded as an official development of the ordinary non-official *panchayat*, or committee of five members, by which every caste and trade in India has been accustomed to regulate its internal affairs from time immemorial.

The first Municipal Board, which was entrusted with the superintendence of everything relating to the industrial arts, was doubtless responsible for fixing the rates of wages, and must have been prepared to enforce the use of pure and sound materials, as well as the performance of a fair day's work for fair wages, as determined by the authorities. Artisans were regarded as being in a special manner devoted to the royal service, and capital punishment was inflicted on any person who impaired the efficiency of a craftsman by causing the loss of a hand or an eye.

The second Board devoted its energies to the case of foreign residents and visitors, and performed duties which in modern Europe are entrusted to the consuls representing foreign powers. All foreigners were closely watched by officials, who provided suitable lodgings, escorts, and, in case of need, medical attendance. Deceased strangers were decently buried, and their estates were administered by the commissioners, who forwarded the assets to the persons entitled. The existence of these elaborate regulations is conclusive proof that the Maurya empire in the third century B.C. was in constant intercourse with foreign states, and that large numbers of strangers visited the capital on business.

The third Board was responsible for the systematic registration of births and deaths, and we are expressly informed that the system of registration was enforced for the information of the government, as well as for facility in levying the taxes. The taxation referred to was probably a poll-tax, at the rate of so much a head annually. Nothing in the legislation of Chandragupta is more astonishing to the observer familiar with the lax methods of ordinary Oriental governments than this registration of births and deaths. The spontaneous adoption of such a measure by an Indian native state in modern times is unheard-of, and it is impossible to imagine an old-fashioned raja feeling anxious "that births and deaths among both high and low might not be concealed." Even the Anglo-Indian administration, with its complex organization and European notions of the value of statistical information, did not attempt the collection of vital statistics until very recent times, and has always experienced great difficulty in securing reasonable accuracy in the figures.

The important domain of trade and commerce was the province of the fourth Board, which regulated sales, and enforced the use of duly stamped weights and measures. Merchants paid a license tax, and the trader who dealt in more than one class of commodity paid double.

The fifth Board was responsible for the supervision of manufactures on similar lines. A curious and not easily intelligible regulation prescribed the separation of new from old goods, and imposed a fine for violation of the rule.

The collection of a tithe of the value of the goods sold was the business of the sixth and last Board, and evasion of this tax was punishable with death. Similar taxation on sales has always been common in India, but rarely, if ever, has its collection been enforced by a penalty so formidable as that exacted by Chandragupta.

Our detailed information relates only to the municipal administration of Pataliputra, the capital, but it is reasonable to infer that Taxila, Ujjain, and the other great cities of the empire were governed on the same principles and by similar methods. The "Provincials' Edict" of Asoka is addressed to the officers in charge of the city of Tosali in Kalinga.

In addition to the special departmental duties above detailed the Municipal Commissioners in their collective capacity were required to control all the affairs of the city, and to keep in order the markets, temples, harbours, and, generally speaking, all public works.

The administration of the distant provinces was entrusted to viceroys, probably, as a rule, members of the royal family. Chandragupta's brother-in-law was, as we have seen, governor of remote Kathiawar on the western coast. The information concerning the viceroyalties being more complete for Asoka's reign than for that of Chandragupta, the subject will be referred to again when Asoka's system of administration is discussed.

In accordance with the usual practice of Oriental monarchies, the court kept watch over the more remote functionaries by means of special agents, or "news-writers," the *akhbar navis* of modern times, who are called "overseers" and "inspectors" by the Greek authors, and are mentioned in the Asoka Edicts as the king's "men" or "reporters." The duty of these officers was to superintend or oversee all that occurred in town or country, and to make private reports to the government. Arrian notes that similar officers were employed by the authorities of the independent nations as well as by the monarchical governments of India. They did not disdain to utilize as coadjutors the courtesans of the camp and city, and these must have transmitted at times to their masters strange packets of scandalous gossip. Arrian's informants assured him that the reports sent in were always true, and that no Indian could be accused of lying; but it is permissible to doubt the strict accuracy of this statement, although it is certainly the fact that the people of ancient India enjoyed a wide-spread and enviable reputation for straightforwardness and honesty.

The general honesty of the people and the efficient administration of the criminal law are both attested by the observation recorded by Megasthenes, that while he resided in Chandragupta's camp, containing four hundred thousand persons, the total of the thefts reported in any one day did not exceed two hundred *drachmai*, or about eight pounds sterling. When crime did occur, it was repressed with terrible severity. Ordinary wounding by mutilation was punished by the corresponding mutilation of the offender, in addition to the amputation of his hand. If the injured person happened to be an artisan devoted to the royal service, the penalty was death. The crime of giving false evidence was visited with mutilation of the extremities, and in certain unspecified cases serious offences were punished by the shaving of the offender's hair, a penalty regarded as specially infamous. Injury to a sacred tree, evasion of the municipal tithe on goods sold, and intrusion on the royal procession going to the hunt were all alike capitally punishable. These recorded instances of severity are sufficient to prove that the code of criminal law, as a whole, must have been characterized by uncompromising sternness and slight regard for human life.

The native law of India has always recognized agricultural land as being Crown property, and has admitted the undoubted right of the ruling power to levy a Crown rent, or "land revenue," amounting to a considerable portion, either of the gross produce or of its cash value. Even the English laws, which, contrary to ancient custom, recognize private property in culturable land, insist that the land revenue is the first charge on the soil, and permit the enforcement of the charge by sale of the land free of all incumbrances, in the event of default. The land revenue is still the mainstay of Indian finance. So it must have been in the days of Chandragupta. The details of his system of "settlement," or valuation and assessment of the land, have not been preserved, and it is not known whether a fresh valuation was made annually, or at longer intervals. The normal share of the gross produce taken by the Crown is said to have been one-fourth; but in practice, no doubt, the proportion taken varied largely, as it does to this day, and all provinces could not be treated alike. Certain other unspecified dues were also levied. Since the army was a professional force, recruited from the fighting castes, the agricultural population was exempt from military service, and Megasthenes noted with surprise and admiration that the husbandmen could pursue their calling in peace, while the professional soldiers of hostile kings engaged in battle.

The proper regulation of irrigation is a matter of prime importance in India, and it is much to the credit of Chandragupta that he maintained a special Irrigation Department, charged with the duty of measuring the lands and of so regulating the sluices that every one should receive his fair share of the life-giving water.

The allusion to the measurement of lands as part of the duty of the Irrigation Department seems to indicate that a water-rate was levied, and the reference to sluices implies a regular system of canals.

The inscription of the Satrap Rudradaman, engraved about the year 150 A. D. on the famous rock at Girnar in Kathiawar, on which Asoka, four centuries earlier, had recorded a version of his immortal edicts, bears direct testimony to the care bestowed by the central government upon the question of irrigation, even in the most remote provinces. Although Girnar is situated close to the Arabian Sea, at a distance of at least a thousand miles from the Maurya capital, the needs of the local farmers did not escape the imperial notice. Chandragupta's brother-in-law Pushyagupta, who was viceroy of the western provinces, saw that by damming up a small stream a reservoir of great value for irrigation could be provided. He accordingly formed a lake called Sudarsana, "the Beautiful," between the citadel on the east side of the hill and the "inscription rock" farther to the east, but failed to complete the necessary supplemental channels. These were constructed in the reign of Chandragupta's grandson Asoka, under the superintendence of his representative Tushaspa, the Persian, who was then governor. These beneficent works constructed under the patronage of the Maurya emperors endured for four hundred years, but in the year 150 A. D. a storm of exceptional violence destroyed the embankment, and with it the lake.

The embankment was rebuilt "three times stronger"

than before by order of the local Saka Satrap Rudradaman, who has recorded the history of the work in an inscription which is the only known epigraphic record containing the names of Chandragupta and Asoka Maurya. Notwithstanding the triple strength of Rudradaman's masonry, it, too, failed to withstand the fury of the elements, and the dam again burst at some time unknown. The lake thus finally disappeared, and its site, buried in deep jungle, was so utterly forgotten that modern local inquirers have experienced difficulty in ascertaining its exact position.

The fact that so much pains and expense were lavished upon this irrigation work in a remote dependency of the empire is conclusive evidence that the provision of water for the fields was recognized as an imperative duty by the great Maurya emperors, and is a striking illustration of the accuracy of Megasthenes' remark that imperial officers were wont to "measure the land, as in Egypt, and inspect the sluices by which water is distributed into the branch canals, so that every one may enjoy his fair share of the benefit."

The central government, by means of local officers, exercised strict control and maintained close supervision over all classes and castes of the population. Even the Brahman astrologers, soothsayers, and sacrificial priests, whom Megasthenes erroneously described as forming a separate caste of "philosophers" or "sophists," received their share of official attention, and were rewarded or punished according as their predictions and observations proved correct or mistaken.

Among the artisans, ship-builders and armour-makers were salaried public servants, and were not permitted, it is said, to work for any private person. The wood-cutters, carpenters, blacksmiths, and miners were subject to special supervision, of which the nature is not defined.

According to Strabo, no private person was permitted to keep either a horse or an elephant, the possession of either animal being a royal privilege. But this assertion is undoubtedly inaccurate, and is contradicted by the reasonable and detailed observations of Arrian. That author tells us that the mounts used commonly were horses, camels, and asses, elephants being used only by the wealthy, and considered specially appropriate for the service of royalty. Except as regards asses, which are now looked upon with contempt and restricted to the humblest services as beasts of burden for potters and washermen, the statement of Arrian applies accurately to modern India. To ride an elephant or camel, or to travel in a four-horse chariot, was, he says, a mark of distinction, but anybody might ride or drive a single horse.

The roads were maintained in order by the officers of the proper department, and pillars, serving as mile-stones and sign-posts, were set up at intervals of ten *stadia*, equivalent to half a *kos*, according to the Indian reckoning, or 2022½ English yards. The provision of these useful marks was made more liberally than it was afterward by the Mogul emperors, who were content with one pillar to each *kos*. A royal road, or grand

An Indian Charger Fully Caparisoned.
From a Photograph.

highway, ten thousand *stadia* in length, connected the northwestern frontier with the capital.

The foregoing review of the civil and military system of government during the reign of Chandragupta proves clearly that Northern India in the time of Alexander the Great had attained to a high degree of civilization, which must have been the product of evolution continued through many centuries. Unfortunately, no monuments have been discovered which can be referred with certainty to the period of Chandragupta and his son, and the archæologist is unable to bring the tangible evidence afforded by excavation to support the statements of the Greek observers.

The earliest known examples of Indian art and architecture, with very slight exceptions, still date from the reign of Asoka. No trace of stone architecture prior to the age of Asoka has been detected. Writing was certainly in common use long before the days of Chandragupta, when, according to the Greek authors, the bark of trees and cotton cloth served as writing material, and it is surprising that no inscriptions of his time have yet been found. But some records, either on stone or metal, probably exist, and may be expected to come to light whenever the really ancient sites shall be examined.

Chandragupta ascended the throne at an early age, and, inasmuch as he reigned only twenty-four years, must have died before he was fifty years of age. In this brief space of life he did much. The expulsion of the Macedonian garrisons, the decisive repulse of Seleukos the Conqueror, the subjugation of all Northern India from sea to sea, the formation of a gigantic army, and the thorough organization of the civil government of a vast empire were no mean achievements. The power of Chandragupta was so firmly established that it passed peaceably into the hands of his son and grandson, and his alliance was courted by the potentates of the Hellenistic world. The Greek princes made no attempt to renew the aggressions of Alexander and Seleukos upon secluded India, and were content to maintain friendly diplomatic and commercial relations with her rulers for three generations.

The Maurya empire was not, as some recent writers fancy that it was, in any way the result of Alexander's splendid but transitory raid. The nineteen months which he spent in India were consumed in devastating warfare, and his death rendered fruitless all his grand constructive plans. Chandragupta did not need Alexander's example to teach him what empire meant. He and his countrymen had had before their eyes for ages the stately fabric of the Persian monarchy, and it was that empire which impressed their imagination and served as the model for their institutions, in so far as they were not indigenous. The little touches of foreign manners in the court and institutions of Chandragupta, which chance to have been noted by our fragmentary authorities, are Persian, not Greek; and the Persian title of satrap continued to be used by Indian provincial governors for centuries, down to the close of the fourth century A. D.

The military organization of Chandragupta shows no trace of Hellenic influence. It is based upon the ancient Indian model, and his vast host was merely a development of the considerable army maintained by the kingdom of Magadha. The Indian kings relied upon their elephants, chariots, and huge masses of infantry, the cavalry being few in comparison, and inefficient. Alexander, on the contrary, made no use of elephants or chariots, and put his trust in small bodies of highly trained cavalry, handled with consummate skill and calculated audacity. In the art of war he had no successor. The Seleukid kings were content to follow the Oriental system and put their trust in elephants.

When Chandragupta died, in the year 297 B. C., he was succeeded by his son Bindusara. The Greek writers, however, do not know this name, and call the successor of Chandragupta by appellations which seem to be attempts to transcribe the Sanskrit epithet Amitraghata, "Slayer of foes." The friendly relations between India and the Hellenistic powers, which had been initiated by Chandragupta and Seleukos, continued unbroken throughout the reign of Bindusara, at whose court Megasthenes was replaced by Deïmachos, as ambassador. The new envoy followed his predecessor's example by recording notes on the country to which he was accredited, but, unfortunately, very few of his observations have been preserved. When the aged founder of the Seleukid monarchy was assassinated in 280 B. C., his place was taken by his son and colleague,

Antiochos Soter, who continued to follow his father's policy in regard to India.

The anecdote concerning the correspondence between Antiochos and Bindusara, although trivial in itself, is worth quoting as a tangible proof of the familiar intercourse between the sovereign of India and his ally in Western Asia. Nothing, we are told, being sweeter than figs, Bindusara begged Antiochos to send him some figs and raisin wine, and added that he would like him also to buy and send a professor. Antiochos replied that he had much pleasure in forwarding the figs and raisin wine, but regretted that he could not oblige his correspondent with the last-named article, because it was not lawful for Greeks to sell a professor.

Nothing is recorded concerning the internal policy of Bindusara, whose reign lasted for twenty-five years, nor is any monument or inscription of his time known. But it is probable that he continued his father's career of annexation and conquest within the borders of India. The limits of the empire ruled by Asoka, son and successor of Bindusara, are known with sufficient accuracy, and it is certain that his dominions extended as far south as Madras. The country south of the Narmada was not conquered by Asoka, whose only annexation was that of the kingdom of Kalinga, on the coast of the Bay of Bengal.

The Deccan, or peninsular India, down to approximately the latitude of Madras, must have been subjugated by either Chandragupta or Bindusara, because it was inherited from the latter by Asoka; and it is more probable that the conquest of the south was the work of Bindusara than that it was effected by his busy father. But the ascertained outline of the career of Chandragupta is so wonderful and implies his possession of such exceptional ability, that it is possible that the conquest of the south must be added to the list of his achievements. With this brief glance the shadowy figure of Bindusara passes from our view, and the next two chapters will be devoted to the history of Asoka, who rightfully claims a place in the front rank of the great monarchs, not only of India, but of the world.

CHAPTER VI

ASOKA MAURYA

ACCORDING to credible tradition, Asoka-vardhana, or Asoka, as he is generally called, served his apprenticeship to the art of government during the lifetime of his father, Bindusara, as viceroy successively of the northwestern frontier province and of Western India. He was one of several sons, and was no doubt selected by his father, in accordance with the usual practice, as *Yuvaraja*, or crown prince, on account of his ability and fitness for the imperial succession.

Taxila, the capital of the northwestern viceroyalty, which probably included Kashmir, the Panjab, and the provinces to the west of the Indus, was in those days one of the greatest and most splendid of the cities of the East, and enjoyed a special reputation as the headquarters of Hindu learning. The sons of people of all the upper classes, chiefs, Brahmans, and merchants, flocked to Taxila, as to a university town, in order to study the circle of Indian arts and sciences. The territory surrounding the capital was rich and populous, and, two generations earlier, had formed a small independent state, weak enough to be in terror of its neighbours, and yet strong enough to render Alexander valuable assistance.

The Greeks, who considered the little state to be well governed, noted with interest, and without disapprobation, the local customs, which included polygamy, the exposure of the dead to be devoured by vultures, and the sale in open market of maidens who had failed to secure husbands in the ordinary course.

OLD ASTRONOMICAL OBSERVATORY AT UJJAIN.
From a photograph.

The position of the city on the highroad from Central Asia to the interior of India fitted it to be the capital of the northwestern viceroy, and its strategical advantages are still recognized. Hasan Abdal, close to its ruins, is a favourite ground for the manœuvres of the Indian army, and at Rawalpindi, a few miles to the southeast, a huge cantonment guards the road to India against possible Alexanders advancing from the northwest.

Ujjain, the capital of Western India, was equally famous, and equally suitable as the seat of a viceregal government. Reckoned to be one of the seven sacred cities, and standing on the road leading from the busy ports of the western coast to the markets of the interior, it combined the advantages of a favourite place of pilgrimage with those of a great commercial depot. The city was recognized as the headquarters of Indian astronomy, and latitudes were computed from its meridian.

The Ceylonese tradition that Asoka was residing at Ujjain when he was summoned to the capital by the news of his father's mortal illness may well be believed, but no credence can be given to the tales which relate that Asoka had a hundred brothers, ninety-nine of whom he slew, and so forth. These idle stories seem to have been invented chiefly in order to place a dark background of early wickedness behind the bright picture of his mature piety. Asoka certainly had brothers and sisters alive in the seventeenth year of his reign, whose households were objects of his anxious care; and there is nothing to indicate that he regarded his relatives with jealousy. His grandfather, Chandragupta, "a man of blood and iron," who had fought his way from poverty and exile to the imperial throne, naturally was beset by jealousies and hatreds, and constrained to live a life of distrustful suspicion. But Asoka, who was born in the purple and inherited an empire firmly established by half a century of masterful rule, presumably was free from the "black care" which haunted his ancestor. His edicts display no sense of insecurity or weakness from first to last, and the probability is that he succeeded peaceably in accordance with his predecessor's nomination.

Inasmuch as the reign of Asoka lasted for fully forty years, he must have been a young man when, in the year 272 B. C., he undertook the government of the vast empire which had been won and kept by his grandfather and father. Nothing is recorded concerning the first eleven years of his rule, which were spent presumably in the current work of administration. His solemn coronation did not take place until the year 269 B. C., about three years after his accession, and this fact is the only circumstance which supports the notion that his succession was disputed. The anniversary of his coronation was always celebrated with ceremony and specially marked by the pardon and release of prisoners.

In the twelfth year of his reign, or the ninth, as reckoned from the coronation, Asoka embarked upon the one aggressive war of his life, and rounded off his dominions by the conquest of the kingdom of Kalinga, the strip of territory extending along the coast of the Bay of Bengal from the Mahanadi to the Godavari. The campaign was wholly successful, and Kalinga became an integral part of the Maurya dominions. Two special edicts published a few years later show that the administration of the newly acquired territory caused much anxiety to the emperor, who, like all sovereigns, sometimes was not well served by his officers. The royal instructions, which enjoined just and paternal government, and specially insisted on sympathetic, tactful treatment of the wilder tribes, were disregarded at times by officials, who had to be warned that disobedience of orders was not the way to win the favour either of heaven or their master.

The kingdom of Kalinga had maintained a considerable military force, which was estimated by Megasthenes as numbering sixty thousand infantry, one thousand cavalry, and seven hundred war elephants. The opposition offered to the invaders was so stubborn that the conquest involved immeasurable suffering. The victor records with sorrow that 150,000 persons were carried into captivity, one hundred thousand were slain, and that many times that number perished from famine, pestilence, and the other calamities which follow in the train of armies.

The sight of all this misery and the knowledge that he alone had caused it smote the conscience of Asoka, and awakened in his breast feelings of "remorse, profound sorrow, and regret." These feelings crystallized into a steadfast resolve that never again would ambition lead him to inflict such grievous wrongs upon his fellow creatures, and four years after the conquest he was able to declare that "the loss of even the hundredth or the thousandth part of the persons who were then slain, carried away captive, or done to death in Kalinga would now be a matter of deep regret to his Majesty."

The king acted up to the principles which he professed, and abstained from aggressive war for the rest of his life. About this time he came under the influence of Buddhist teaching, his devotion to which increased more and more as the years rolled on. The "chiefest conquest," he declares, is that won by the Law of Piety, and he begs his descendants to rid themselves of the popular notion that conquest by arms is the duty of kings; and, even if they should find themselves engaged in warfare, he reminds them that they might still find pleasure in patience and gentleness, and should regard as the only true conquest that which is effected through the Law of Piety.

Asoka from this time forth made it the business of his life to employ his unlimited autocratic power over a vast empire in the teaching, propagation, and enforcement of the ethical system which he called the Law of Piety (*dhamma*) and had learned chiefly from his Buddhist instructors.

In the sixteenth and seventeenth years of his reign, he definitely decided upon his line of action, and proclaimed the principles of his government to his people in a series of fourteen edicts engraved upon the rocks, and laid down the general rules which must guide the conduct of the lieges. These extraordinary documents were followed by others specially concerning the conquered province of Kalinga, the purport of which has been referred to above.

In the year 249 B. C., when he had occupied the throne for twenty-three years, Asoka made a solemn pilgrimage to the most sacred spots in the Buddhist Holy Land. Starting from Pataliputra, the capital, he advanced northwards along the royal road, the course of which is marked by five great monolithic pillars, through the districts now known as Muzaffarpur and Champaran, until he approached the base of the outer Himalayan range.

Probably he then turned westwards, without crossing the hills, and first visited the famous Lumbini Garden, —the Bethlehem of Buddhism,—where, according to the legend, the pains of travail came upon Maya, and she gave birth to Buddha as she stood under a tree. At this spot his guide and preceptor, Upagupta, addressed Asoka and said: "Here, great king! was the Venerable One born." A pillar inscribed with these words, still as legible as when they were incised, was set up by Asoka to preserve the memory of his visit, and stands to this day.

In due course Saint Upagupta led his royal disciple to Kapilavastu, the home of Buddha's childhood; to Sarnath, near Benares, the scene of the Master's first success as a preacher; to Sravasti, where he lived for many years; to the Bodhi tree of Gaya, where he overcame the powers of darkness; and to Kusinagara, where he died. At all these holy places the king granted liberal endowments, and set up memorials, some of which have come to light in these latter days, after long ages of oblivion.

In the year 242 B.C., when his reign had lasted for thirty years, Asoka undertook a formal retrospect of all the measures adopted by him in furtherance of the ethical reforms which he had at heart, and took the opportunity of laying down a concise code of regulations concerning the slaughter and mutilation of animals, practices which he regarded with abhorrence.

Birthplace of Buddha.
Pillar Erected by King Asoka in Lumbini Garden.

TOPE AT SARNATH, NEAR BENARES.

About two years later, Asoka, recognizing fully the validity of the Buddhist doctrine that no layman could attain *nirvana*, determined to ensure his final deliverance from rebirth so far as possible by entering the order of monks, and actually assuming the yellow robe. He does not appear to have abdicated at the same time, for edicts issued six years later were still published by his authority and with his sanction; it is probable, however, that he withdrew from active participation in secular affairs, and left the administration in the hands of his ministers and the heir apparent or crown prince. But this supposition is not necessary to explain his conduct. His submission to the Ten Precepts, or ascetic rules, binding upon ordained monks, did not inevitably involve his withdrawal from the duties of royalty, and he would have found no difficulty in formally complying with the obligations of mendicancy by a begging tour within the spacious palace precincts.

The case of Asoka is not unique. A perfect parallel is furnished by Chinese history, which records that Hsiao Yen, the first emperor of the Liang dynasty, who was a devout Buddhist, actually adopted the monastic garb on two occasions, in 527 and 529 A. D. A less completely parallel case is supplied by the story of a Jain king of Western India in the twelfth century, who assumed the title of "Lord of the Order," and at various periods of his reign bound himself by vows of continence and abstinence.

Whatever may have been the exact procedure adopted, there is no doubt that Asoka was formally ordained as a monk, and the fact was so notorious that a thousand years later his statues were still to be seen, vested in monastic garb. The latter years of his reign were undoubtedly devoted in a special degree to works of piety, but there is no sufficient reason for believing the legends which depict the emperor in his old age as a dotard devotee incapable of administering the affairs of the empire.

The latest edicts, dated 256 years after the death of Buddha, that is to say, in the year 232 or 231 B.C., must have been published very shortly before the emperor's death, which is supposed to have occurred at a holy hill near Rajagriha, the ancient capital of Magadha.

A large body of tradition affirms that a Buddhist church council was held at the capital by the command and under the patronage of Asoka in order to settle the canon of scripture and reform abuses in monastic discipline. Although the legendary details of the constitution and proceedings of the council are clearly unhistorical, the fact of the assembly may be accepted without hesitation. If it had met before the thirty-first year of the reign in which the emperor published the Pillar Edicts, recording his retrospect of the measures taken for the promotion of piety, the council would assuredly have been mentioned in those documents. But they are silent on the subject, and the fair inference is that the council was held

Pillar of Asoka at Allahabad.

at a date subsequent to their publication, and after the emperor had assumed the monastic robe.

The one document in the whole series of the Asoka inscriptions which is avowedly Buddhist in explicit terms—the Bhabra Edict—evidently belongs to the same period as the council, and is to be interpreted as the address of the emperor-monk to his brethren of the order.

The extent of the enormous empire governed by Asoka can be ascertained with approximate accuracy. On the northwest, it extended to the Hindu Kush mountains, and included most of the territory now under the rule of the Ameer of Afghanistan, as well as the whole, or a large part, of Baluchistan, and all of Sind. The secluded valleys of Suwat and Bajaur were probably more or less thoroughly controlled by the imperial officers, and the valleys of Kashmir and Nepal were certainly integral parts of the empire. Asoka built a new capital in the vale of Kashmir, named Srinagar, at a short distance from the city which now bears that name.

In the Nepal valley, he replaced the older capital, Manju Patan, by a city named Patan, Lalita Patan, or Lalitpur, which still exists, two and a half miles to the southeast of Kathmandu, the modern capital. Lalita Patan subsequently became the seat of a separate principality, and it retains the special Buddhist stamp impressed upon it by Asoka. His foundation of this city was undertaken as a memorial of the visit which he paid to Nepal in 250 or 249 B. C., when he undertook the tour of the holy places. He was accompanied by his daughter Charumati, who adopted a religious life, and remained in Nepal, when her imperial father returned to the plains. She founded a town called Devapatana, in memory of her husband, Devapala Kshatriya, and settled down to the life of a nun at a convent built by her to the north of Pasupatinath, which bears her name to this day. Asoka treated Lalita Patan as a place of great sanctity, erecting in it five great *stupas*, one in the centre of the town, and four others outside the walls at the cardinal points. All these monuments still exist, and differ conspicuously from more recent edifices. Some minor buildings are also attributed to Asoka or his daughter.

Eastwards, the empire comprised the whole of Bengal as far as the mouths of the Ganges, where Tamralipti (generally identified with the modern Tamluk) was the principal port. The strip of coast to the north of the Godavari River, known as Kalinga, was annexed in 261 B.C. Farther south, the Andhra kingdom, between the Godavari and the Krishna (Kistna), appears to have been treated as a protected state, administered by its own rajas.

On the southeast, the Palar River, the northern frontier of the Tamil race, may be regarded as the limit of the imperial jurisdiction. The Tamil states extending to the extremity of the peninsula, and known as the Chola and Pandya kingdoms, were certainly independent, as were the Keralaputra and Satiyaputra states on the southwestern, or Malabar, coast. The southern frontier of the empire must nearly have coincided with the thirteenth degree of north latitude, or it may be described approximately as a line drawn from the mouth of the Palar River near Sadras on the eastern coast (N. lat. 12° 13′ 15″) through Bangalore (N. lat. 12° 58′) to the river Chandragiri on the western coast (N. lat. 13° 15′).

The wilder tribes on the northwestern frontier and in the jungle tracts of the Vindhya Mountains separating Northern from Southern India seem to have enjoyed a limited autonomy under the suzerainty of the paramount power. The empire comprised, therefore, in modern terminology, Afghanistan south of the Hindu Kush, Baluchistan, Sind, the valley of Kashmir, Nepal, the lower Himalaya, and the whole of India proper, except the southern extremity.

The central regions seem to have been governed directly from Pataliputra under the king's personal supervision. The outlying provinces were administered by members of the royal family, holding the rank of viceroys, of whom, apparently, there were four. The ruler of the northwest was stationed at Taxila, and his jurisdiction may be assumed to have included the Panjab, Sind, the countries beyond the Indus, and Kashmir. The eastern territories, including the conquered kingdom of Kalinga, were governed by a viceroy stationed at Tosali, the exact position of which has not been ascertained. The western provinces of Malwa, Guzerat, and Kathiawar were under the government of a prince, whose headquarters were at the ancient city of Ujjain, and the southern provinces, beyond the Narmada, were ruled by the fourth viceroy.

Asoka was a great builder, and so deep was the impression made on the popular imagination by the extent and magnificence of his architectural works that legend credited him with the erection of eighty-four thousand *stupas*, or sacred cupolas, within the space of

BHARAHAT SCULPTURE OF A BUDDHIST STUPA.
(After Cunningham.)

three years. When Fa-hien, the first Chinese pilgrim, visited Pataliputra, the capital, at the beginning of the fifth century A.D., in the reign of Chandragupta Vikramaditya, the palace of Asoka was still standing, and was deemed to have been wrought by supernatural agency.

"The royal palace and halls in the midst of the city, which exist now as of old, were all made by the spirits which he employed, and which piled up the stones, reared the walls and gates, and executed the elegant carving and inlaid sculpture work in a way which no human hands of this world could accomplish."

These stately buildings have all vanished, and their remains lie buried for the most part beyond hope of recovery deep below the silt of the Ganges and Son Rivers, overlaid by the East Indian railway, the city of Patna, and the civil station of Bankipur. Slight and desultory excavations have revealed enough to attest the substantial truth of the pilgrim's enthusiastic description, and I have myself seen two huge and finely carved sandstone capitals—one with the acanthus-leaf ornament—dug up near Bankipur.

The numerous and magnificent monasteries founded by Asoka have shared the fate of his palaces, and are ruined beyond recognition. The only buildings of the Asokan period which have escaped destruction and remain in a state of tolerable preservation are those forming the celebrated group of *stupas*, or cupolas, at and near Sanchi, in Central India, not very far from Ujjain, where Asoka held court as viceroy of the west before his accession to the throne. The elaborately carved gateways of the railing round the principal monument, which have been so often described and figured, may have been constructed to the order of the great Maurya, and are certainly not much later than his time.

The massive monolithic sandstone pillars, inscribed and uninscribed, which Asoka erected in large numbers throughout the home provinces of the empire, some of which are fifty feet in height and about fifty tons in weight, are not only worthy monuments of his magnificence, but also of the highest interest as the earliest known examples of the Indian stone-cutter's art in architectural forms. The style is Persian rather than Greek, and the mechanical execution is perfect.

Bas-relief on Left-hand Pillar, Northern Gateway of the Rail at Sanchi.

The caves, with highly polished walls, excavated in the intensely hard quartzose gneiss of the Barabar hills near Gaya by order of Asoka, for the use of the Ajivika ascetics, a penitential order closely connected with the Jains, recall Egyptian work by the mastery displayed over intractable material.

The most interesting monuments of Asoka are his famous inscriptions, more than thirty in number, incised upon rocks, boulders, cave walls, and pillars, which supply the only safe foundation for the history of his reign, and must be briefly described before I can enter upon the discussion of his doctrine and policy. The more important documents, which expound fully both his principles of government and his system of practical ethics, supply many interesting autobiographical details. The shorter documents include dedications, brief commemorative records, and other matter; but all, even the most concise, have interest and value.

The area covered by the inscriptions comprises nearly the whole of India, and extends from the Himalaya to Mysore, and from the Bay of Bengal to the Arabian Sea.

The documents are all written in various forms of Prakrit, that is to say, vernacular dialects closely allied both to literary Sanskrit and to the Pali of the Ceylonese Buddhist books, but not identical with either. They were, therefore, obviously intended to be read and understood by the public generally, and their existence presupposes a fairly general knowledge of the art of writing. The inscriptions designed for public instruction were placed either in suitable positions on high-roads or at frequented places of pilgrimage where their contents were ensured the greatest possible publicity.

Two recensions of the Fourteen Rock Edicts, inscribed on rocks at places near the northwestern frontier of India, were executed in the script locally current, now generally known to scholars as the Kharoshthi, which is a modified form of an ancient Aramaic alphabet, written from right to left, introduced into the Panjab during the period of Persian domination in the fifth and fourth centuries B. C. All the other inscriptions are incised in one or other variety of the early Brahmi alphabet, from which the Devanagari and other forms of the modern script in Northern and Western India have been evolved, and which is read from left to right.

The inscriptions readily fall into eight classes, which

may be arranged in approximate chronological order as follows:—

1. The Fourteen Rock Edicts, in seven recensions, dating from the thirteenth and fourteenth regnal years, as reckoned from the coronation, corresponding to 257 and 256 B. C.

2. The two Kalinga Edicts, issued probably in 256 B. C., and concerned only with the newly conquered province.

3. The three dedicatory Cave Inscriptions at Barabar near Gaya, 257 and 250 B. C.

4. The two Tarai Pillar Inscriptions, 249 B. C.

5. The Seven Pillar Edicts, in six recensions, 243 and 242 B. C.

6. The Supplementary Pillar Edicts, about 240 B. C.

7. The Minor Rock Edicts, dated in the year 256 after the death of Buddha, 232 or 231 B. C.

8. The Bhabra Edict, of about the same date as the Minor Rock Edicts.

The Fourteen Rock Edicts contain an exposition of Asoka's principles of government and ethical system, each edict being devoted to a special subject. The different recensions vary considerably, and some do not include all the fourteen edicts. The whole series, in all its varieties, is confined to remote frontier provinces, which were under the government of viceroys. The emperor evidently was of opinion that in the home provinces, under his immediate control, it was not necessary to engrave his instructions on the rocks, as other and more convenient methods of publication were available. But many years later he perpetuated his revised code in the home provinces also by incising it upon several of the monolithic monumental pillars which it was his pleasure to erect in numerous localities.

The two Kalinga Edicts are special supplements to

the series of the Fourteen Rock Edicts, intended to fix the principles on which the administration of the newly conquered province and the wild tribes dwelling on its borders should be conducted. They were substituted for certain edicts (Nos. 11, 12, 13) of the regular series, which were omitted from the Kalinga recension, as being unsuitable for local promulgation.

The three Cave Inscriptions at Barabar in the Gaya District are merely brief dedications of costly cave-dwellings for the use of a monastic sect known as Ajivika, the members of which went about naked and were noted for ascetic practices of the most rigorous kind. These records are chiefly of interest as a decisive proof that Asoka was sincere in his solemn declaration that he honoured all sects, for the Ajivikas had little or nothing in common with the Buddhists and were intimately connected with the Jains.

The two Tarai Pillar Inscriptions, although extremely brief, are of much interest for many reasons, one of which is that they prove beyond question the truth of the literary tradition that Asoka performed a solemn pilgrimage to the sacred spots of the Buddhist Holy Land. The Rummindei, or Padaria, inscription, which is in absolutely perfect preservation, has the great merit of determining, beyond the possibility of doubt, the exact position of the famous Lumbini Garden, where, according to the legend, Gautama Buddha first saw the light. This determination either solves, or supplies the key to, a multitude of problems. The companion record at Nigliva, which is less perfectly preserved, gives the unexpected and interesting information that Asoka's devotion was not confined to Gautama Buddha, but included in its catholic embrace his predecessors, the "former Buddhas."

The Seven Pillar Edicts, issued in their complete form in the year 242 B.C., when Asoka had reigned for thirty years and was nearing the close of his career of activity in worldly affairs, must be read along with the Fourteen Rock Edicts, to which they refer, and of which they may be considered an appendix. The principles enunciated in the earlier instructions are re-iterated and emphasized in the later; the regulations enforcing the sanctity of animal life are amplified and codified; and the series closes with the most valuable of all the documents, Pillar Edict No. 7, preserved on one monument only, which recounts in orderly fashion the measures adopted by the emperor in the course of his long reign to promote "the growth of piety."

The Supplementary Pillar Edicts are brief dedicatory records, more curious than important.

The Minor Rock Edicts, on the other hand, although of small bulk, are in some respects the most interesting of the inscriptions, and until recently presented a puzzling enigma, or series of enigmas. It now seems to be fairly well established that these Minor Rock Edicts were published thirty-eight complete years after Asoka's coronation, or about forty-one years after his accession, and that they must therefore be referred either to the year 232 or 231 B.C., the last year of the aged emperor's life. They are dated expressly 256 years after the death of Buddha, and thus fix that event as having occurred in or about the year 487 B. C., according to the belief current at the court of Pataliputra, only two centuries and a half after its occurrence. When thus interpreted, these brief documents gain intense interest as the valedictory address of the dying emperor-monk to the people whom he loved to regard as his children.

The extremely curious Bhabra Edict, which forms a class by itself, should be referred apparently to the same period as the Minor Rock Edicts, that is to say, to the closing years of Asoka's life, when, although still retaining his imperial dignity, he had assumed the monastic robe and rule, and had abandoned the active direction of worldly affairs to others. This document, recorded, close to a recension of one of the Minor Rock Edicts, at a lonely monastery in the Rajputana hills, is an address by Asoka, as King of Magadha, to the Buddhist monastic order generally, directing the attention of monks and nuns, as well as of the laity, male and female, to seven passages of scripture deemed by the royal judgment to be specially edifying. But, while earnestly recommending devout meditation upon and profound study of these particular texts, the princely preacher is careful to add the explanation that "all that has been said by the Venerable Buddha has been well said," whereas the selection of texts is merely the work of the king's individual judgment. The importance of this edict in the history of Buddhism cannot be easily overrated.

The rank growth of legend which has clustered round the name of Asoka bears eloquent testimony to the commanding influence of his personality. In the Buddhist world his fame is as great as that of Charlemagne in mediæval Europe, and the tangle of mythological legend which obscures the genuine history of Asoka may be compared in mass with that which drapes the figures of Alexander, Arthur, and Charlemagne. The Asoka legend is not all either fiction or myth, and includes some genuine historical traditions, but it is no better suited to serve as the foundation of sober history than the stories of the Morte d'Arthur or Pseudo-Kallisthenes are adapted to form the bases of chronicles of the doings of the British champion or the Macedonian conqueror. This obvious canon of criticism has been forgotten by most writers upon the Maurya period, who have begun at the wrong end with the late legends, instead of at the right end with the contemporary testimony found in the various edicts of the great king himself.

The legends have reached us in two main streams, the Ceylonese and the North Indian. The accident that the Ceylonese varieties of the stories happen to be recorded in books which assume the form of chronicles with a detailed chronology, and have been known to European readers for seventy years, has given to the southern tales an illusory air of authenticity. The earliest of the Ceylonese chronicles, the Dipavamsa, which was probably compiled late in the fourth century A. D., is some six centuries posterior to the death of Asoka, and has little claim to be regarded as a first-rate authority.

The North Indian legends are at least as old, but, being recorded in fragments scattered through many books, Indian, Nepalese, Chinese, and Tibetan, have received scant consideration. All legendary material must of course be used with extreme caution, and only as a supplement to authentic data, but a moment's consideration will show that legends preserved in Northern India, the seat of Asoka's imperial power, are more likely to transmit genuine tradition than those which reached the distant island of Ceylon in translations brought nobody knows how, when, or whence, and subsequently largely modified by local influences. This presumption is verified when the two groups of legends are compared, and it then clearly appears that, in certain matters of importance in which they differ, the Northern version is distinctly the more credible.

ASSYRIAN HONEYSUCKLE ORNAMENT FROM CAPITAL OF LAT, AT ALLAHABAD.

CHAPTER VII

ASOKA MAURYA AND HIS SUCCESSORS

THE edicts are devoted mainly to the exposition, inculcation, and enforcement of a scheme of practical ethics, or rule of conduct, which Asoka called *Dhamma.* No English word or phrase is exactly equivalent to the Prakrit *dhamma* (Sanskrit *dharma*), but the expression Law of Piety, or simply Piety, comes tolerably close to the meaning of the Indian term. The validity of this Law of Piety is assumed in the edicts, and no attempt is made to found it upon any theological or metaphysical basis. Theological ideas are simply ignored by Asoka, as they were by his master Gautama, and the current Hindu philosophy of rebirth, inaccurately called metempsychosis, is taken for granted, and forms the background of the ethical teaching.

The leading tenet of Asoka's Buddhism, as of the cognate Jain system, and some varieties of Brahmanical Hinduism, was a passionate, uncompromising belief in the sanctity of animal life. The doctrine of the absolute, unconditional right of the meanest animal to retain the breath of life until the latest moment permitted by nature, is that of the edicts, and was based upon the belief that all living creatures, including men, animals, gods, and demons, form links in an endless chain of existence, or rather of "becoming."

The being that is now a god in heaven may be reborn in the course of æons as an insect, and the insect,

BUDDHIST WHEEL OF THE LAW OF PIETY, DHARMA-CHAKRA.
From the Bharahat Sculpture. (After Cunningham.)

in its turn, may work up to the rank of a god. This belief, associated with the faith that the mode of rebirth is conditioned by the *karma*, the net ethical result, or balance of good or evil of the life of each creature at the moment of its termination, lies deep down at the roots of Indian thought, and is inseparably bound up with almost every form of Indian religion. Sometimes it is combined with theories which recognize the existence of a personal soul, but it is also firmly held by persons who utterly deny all forms of the soul theory.

It is easy to understand that believers in ideas of this kind may be led logically to regard the life of an insect as entitled to no less respect than that of a man. In practice, indeed, the sanctity of animal was placed above that of human life, and the absurd spectacle was sometimes witnessed of a man being put to death for killing an animal, or even for eating meat. The most pious Buddhist and Jain kings had no hesitation about inflicting capital punishment upon their subjects, and Asoka himself continued to sanction the death penalty throughout his reign. He was content to satisfy his humanitarian feelings by a slight mitigation of the sanguinary penal code inherited from his stern grandfather in conceding to condemned prisoners three days' grace to prepare for death.

In early life Asoka is believed to have been a Brahmanical Hindu, specially devoted to Siva, a god who delights in bloody sacrifices, and he had consequently no scruple about the shedding of blood. Thousands of living creatures used to be slain on the occasion of a banquet (*samaja*) to supply the kitchens of the overgrown royal household with curries for a single day. As he became gradually imbued with the spirit of Buddhist teaching, this wholesale daily slaughter became abominable in his eyes and was stopped, only three living creatures at the most, namely, two peacocks and one deer, being killed each day, and in 257 B.C. even this limited butchery was prohibited.

Two years earlier, in 259 B.C., Asoka had abolished the royal hunt, which formed such an important element in the amusements of his grandfather's court. "In times past," he observes, "their Majesties were wont to go out on pleasure tours, during which hunting and other similar amusements used to be practised." But his Sacred and Gracious Majesty no longer cared for such frivolous outings, and had substituted for them solemn progresses devoted to inspection of the country and people, visits and largess to holy men, and preaching and discussion of the Law of Piety.

As time went on, Asoka's passionate devotion to the doctrine of the sanctity of animal life grew in intensity and, in 243 B.C., resulted in the production of a stringent code of regulations applicable to all classes of the population throughout the empire, without distinction of creed. Many kinds of animals were absolutely protected from slaughter in any circumstances, and the slaying of animals commonly used for food by the flesh-eating population, although not totally prohibited, was hedged round by severe restrictions. On fifty-six specified days in the year, killing under any pretext was categorically forbidden, and in many ways the liberty of the subject was very seriously contracted. While Asoka lived, these regulations were, no doubt, strictly enforced by the special officers appointed for the purpose, and it is not unlikely that deliberate breach of the more important regulations was visited with the capital penalty.

The second cardinal doctrine inculcated and insisted

on by Asoka was that of the obligation of reverence to parents, elders, and preceptors. Conversely, superiors, while receiving their due of reverence, were required to treat their inferiors, including servants, slaves, and all living creatures, with kindness and consideration. As a corollary to these obligations, men were taught that the spirit which inspires reverence on the one side, and kindness on the other, should further induce them to behave with courteous decorum to relatives, ascetics, and Brahmans, and likewise to practise liberality to the same classes, as well as to friends and acquaintances.

The third primary duty laid upon men was that of truthfulness. These three guiding principles are most concisely formulated in the Second Minor Rock Edict, which may be quoted in full:—

"Thus saith his Majesty:

"'Father and mother must be obeyed; similarly, respect for living creatures must be enforced; truth must be spoken. These are the virtues of the Law of Piety which must be practised. Similarly, the teacher must be reverenced by the pupil, and proper courtesy must be shown to relatives.

"'This is the ancient standard of piety; this leads to length of days, and according to this men must act.'"

Among secondary duties, a high place was given to that of showing toleration for and sympathy with the beliefs and practices of others, and a special edict, No. 12 of the Rock series, was devoted to the exposition of this topic. The subjects of the imperial moralist were solemnly warned to abstain from speaking evil of their neighbours' faith, remembering that all forms of religion alike aim at the attainment of self-control and purity of mind, and are thus in agreement about essentials, however much they may differ in externals. In connection with these instructions, men were admonished that all "extravagance and violence of language" should be carefully avoided.

Asoka openly avowed his readiness to act upon these latitudinarian principles by doing reverence to men of all sects, whether ascetics or householders, by means of donations and in other ways. The Cave Inscriptions, which record costly gifts bestowed upon the Ajivikas, a sect of self-mortifying ascetics, more nearly allied to the Jains than the Buddhists, testify that Asoka, like many other ancient Kings of India, really adopted the policy of universal toleration and concurrent endowment.

But his toleration, although perfectly genuine, must be understood with two limitations. In the first place, all Indian religions, with which alone Asoka was concerned, had much in common, and were all alike merely variant expressions of Hindu modes of thought and feeling. There was no such gap dividing them as that which yawns between Islam and Puranic Brahmanism. In the second place, the royal toleration, although perfect as regarding beliefs, did not necessarily extend to all overt practices. Sacrifices involving the death of a victim, which are absolutely indispensable for the correct worship of some of the gods, were categorically

Cave at Ajanta

The Cave Temples of India are of the highest importance because of their antiquity and historic significance. The most famous are in Western India at Ajanta, Ellora. Karli, Kanhari, and Elephanta. These stupendous monuments, hewn out of the solid rock, impress the beholder by their grandeur and by the beauty of the decorations on pillar and wall. The marvellous frescoes painted on the walls of the Ajanta caves date back to the Buddhist ages; the paintings are of great value for the history of art and as illustrations of the life of the Hindus during the centuries to which they belong.

prohibited, at least at the capital, from an early period in the reign, and were further restricted, in all parts of the empire, by the code promulgated later in the Pillar Edicts. The conscientious objector was not permitted to allege his conscience as a justification for acts disapproved on principle by the government. Men might believe what they liked, but must do as they were told.

While almsgiving was commended, the higher doctrine was taught that "there is no such charity as the charitable gift of the Law of Piety, no such distribution as the distribution of piety." The sentiment recurs in curiously similar language in Cromwell's earliest extant letter. He wrote from St. Ives: "Building of hospitals provides for men's bodies, to build material temples is judged a work of piety; but they that procure spiritual food, they that build up spiritual temples, they are the men truly charitable, truly pious."

Asoka cared little for ritual, and was inclined to look with some scorn upon ordinary ceremonies, which are, as he observes, "of doubtful efficacy." Just as true charity consists in a man's efforts to diffuse a knowledge of the Law of Piety among his fellow creatures, so true ceremonial consists in the fulfilment of that law, which "bears great fruit," and includes kind treatment of slaves and servants, honour to teachers, respect for life, and liberality to ascetics and Brahmans. These things, with others of the same kind, are called "the ceremonial of piety."

The preacher looked to men's hearts rather than to

their outward acts, and besought his congregation, the inhabitants of a vast empire, to cultivate the virtues of "compassion, liberality, truth, purity, gentleness, and saintliness." He hoped that the growth of piety would be promoted by the imperial regulations devised for that purpose; but, while enforcing those regulations with all the power of an autocrat, he relied more upon the meditations of individuals, stimulated by his teaching. "Of these two means," he says, "pious regulations are of small account, whereas meditation is of greater value."

Notwithstanding his avowal of the comparative powerlessness of regulations, the emperor did not neglect to provide official machinery for the promulgation of his doctrine and the enforcement of his orders. All the officers of state, whom, in modern phraseology, we may call lieutenant-governors, commissioners, and district magistrates, were commanded to make use of opportunities during their periodical tours for convoking assemblies of the lieges and instructing them in the whole duty of man. Certain days in the year were particularly set apart for this duty, and the officials were directed to perform it in addition to their ordinary work.

A special agency of censors was also organized for the purpose of enforcing the regulations concerning the sanctity of animal life and the observance of filial piety, in the most extended sense. These officers were expressly enjoined to concern themselves with all sects, and with every class of society, not excluding the royal family, while separate officials were charged with the delicate duty of supervising female morals. In practice, this system must have led to much espionage and tyranny, and, if we may judge from the proceedings of kings in later ages, who undertook a similar task, the punishments inflicted for breach of the imperial regulations must have been terribly severe.

It is recorded by contemporary testimony that in

INTERIOR VIEW OF AJANTA CAVE.

the seventh century King Harsha, who obviously aimed at copying closely the institutions of Asoka, did not shrink from inflicting capital punishment, without hope of pardon, on any person who dared to infringe his commands by slaying any living thing or using flesh as food in any part of his dominions.

In the twelfth century, Kumarapala, King of Gujarat in Western India, after his conversion to Jainism in 1159 A.D., took up the doctrine of the sanctity of animal life with the most inordinate zeal, and imposed savage penalties upon violators of his rules. An unlucky merchant, who had committed the atrocious crime of cracking a louse, was brought before the special court at Anhilwara, and punished by the confiscation of his whole property, the proceeds of which were devoted to the building of a temple. Another wretch, who had outraged the sanctity of the capital by bringing in a dish of raw meat, was put to death. The special court constituted by Kumarapala had functions similar to those of Asoka's censors, and the working of the later institution sheds much light upon the unrecorded proceedings of the earlier one.

More modern parallels to Asoka's censors are not lacking. In 1876, when a pious Maharaja was in power in Kashmir, breaches of the commandments of the Hindu scriptures were treated by the state as offences, and investigated by a special court composed of five eminent pandits, belonging to families in which the office was hereditary, who determined appropriate penalties.

Up to the middle of the nineteenth century, and possibly until a later date, similar hereditary Brahman officers exercised jurisdiction over offenders charged with breaches of caste rules in Khandesh, the Deccan, and some parts of the Konkan, and imposed suitable expiation in the shape of fine, penance, or excommunication.

These cases, ancient and modern, are sufficient to prove that when Asoka made an innovation by appointing censors, officers who "had never been appointed in all the long ages past," the new departure was in accordance with Hindu notions, and was consequently readily imitated in later times by rulers of various religions.

The practical piety of Asoka was exhibited in many works of benevolence, on which he dwells with evident pleasure and satisfaction. His theory of true charity did not hinder him from bestowing liberal alms. The distribution of the charitable grants made by the sovereign and members of the royal family was carefully supervised both by the censors and other officials, who seem to have been organized in a royal almoner's department.

Special attention was devoted to the needs of travellers, which have at all times evoked the sympathy of pious Indians. The provision made for wayfarers, including the dumb animals, who were never forgotten by Asoka, is best described in the monarch's own words: "On the roads," he says, "I have had banyan-trees planted to give shade to man and beast; I have had groves of mango-trees planted, and at every half *kos* I have had wells dug; rest-houses have been erected, and numerous watering-places have been prepared here and there for the enjoyment of man and beast." Distances were carefully marked by pillars erected at convenient intervals, ever since Chandragupta's time.

The lively sympathy of Asoka with his suffering fellow creatures, human and animal, also found expression in the extensive provision of relief for the sick. Arrangements for the healing of man and beast were provided, not only throughout all provinces of the empire, but also in the friendly independent kingdoms of Southern India and Hellenistic Asia, medicinal herbs and drugs, wherever lacking, being planted, imported, and supplied as needed.

The animal hospitals which existed recently, and may still exist, at Bombay and Surat, may be regarded as either survivals or copies of the institutions founded by the Maurya monarch. The following account of the Surat hospital, as it was maintained late in the eighteenth century, would probably have been applicable with little change to the prototype at Pataliputra.

"The most remarkable institution in Surat is the Banyan Hospital, of which we have no description more recent than 1780. It then consisted of a large piece of ground enclosed by high walls and subdivided into several courts or wards for the accommodation of animals. In sickness they were attended with the greatest care, and here found a peaceful asylum for the infirmities of old age.

"When an animal broke a limb, or was otherwise disabled, his owner brought him to the hospital, where he was received without regard to the caste or nation of his master. In 1772, this hospital contained horses, mules, oxen, sheep, goats, monkeys, poultry, pigeons, and a variety of birds; also an aged tortoise, which was known to have been there seventy-five years. The most extraordinary ward was that appropriated for rats, mice, bugs, and other noxious vermin, for whom suitable food was provided."

The active official propaganda carried on by various agencies throughout the empire and protected states did not satisfy the zeal of Asoka, who burned with a desire to diffuse the blessings of both his ethical system

ANIMAL HOSPITAL.

and distinctive Buddhist teaching in all the independent kingdoms with which he was in touch. For this purpose he organized an efficient system of foreign missions under his personal supervision, the results of which are visible to this day. His conception of the idea of foreign missions on a grand scale was absolutely original, and produced a well-considered and successful scheme, carried out with method and thoroughness in conjunction and harmony with his measures of domestic propaganda.

Before the year 256 B. C., when the Rock Edicts were published collectively, the royal missionaries had been despatched to all the protected states and tribes on the frontiers of the empire, to the independent kingdoms of Southern India, to Ceylon, and to the Hellenistic monarchies of Syria, Egypt, Cyrene, Macedonia, and Epirus, then governed respectively by Antiochos Theos, Ptolemy Philadelphos, Magas, Antigonos Gonatas, and Alexander. The missionary organization thus embraced three continents, Asia, Africa, and Europe.

The protected states and tribes brought in this way within the circle of Buddhist influence included the Kambojas of Tibet, with other Himalayan nations; the Gandharas and Yavanas of the Kabul valley and regions still farther west; the Bhojas, Pulindas, and Pitenikas dwelling among the hills of the Vindhya range and Western Ghats; and the Andhra kingdom between the Krishna and Godavari Rivers.

The Dravidian peoples of the extreme south, below the thirteenth degree of latitude, being protected by their remoteness, had escaped annexation to the northern empire. In Asoka's time their territories formed four independent kingdoms, the Chola, Pandya, Keralaputra, and Satiyaputra. The capital of the Chola kingdom was probably Uraiyur, or Old Trichinopoly, and that of the Pandya realm was doubtless Korkai in the Tinnevelli District. The Keralaputra State comprised the Malabar coast south of the Chandragiri River, and the Satiyaputra country may be identified with the region where the Tulu language is spoken, of which Mangalore is the centre. With all these kingdoms Asoka was on such friendly terms that he was at liberty to send his missionaries to preach to the people, and even to found monasteries in several places. One such institution was established by his younger brother Mahendra in the Tanjore District, where its ruins were still visible nine hundred years later.

An ancient Chinese writer assures us that "according to the laws of India, when a king dies, he is succeeded by his eldest son (*Kumararaja*); the other sons leave the family and enter a religious life, and they are no longer allowed to reside in their native kingdom." This compulsory withdrawal from secular affairs did not necessarily imply the disappearance of the younger brother into obscurity. The Church in India, especially in Buddhist India, as in Roman Catholic Europe, offered a career to younger sons, and the able ecclesiastic sometimes attained higher fame than his royal relative. Mahendra's assumption of the yellow robe, in accordance with the rule above stated, was, in the first instance, probably due to political necessity rather than to free choice; but, whatever motive may have led him to adopt the monastic life, he became a devout and zealous monk and a most successful missionary.

When Asoka determined to extend his propaganda to Ceylon, he selected as head of the mission his monk brother, who probably was already settled at his monastery in Southern India and then crossed over to Ceylon with his four colleagues. The teaching of the preachers, backed as it was by the influence of a monarch so powerful as Asoka, was speedily accepted by King Tissa of Ceylon and the members of his court, and the new religion soon gained a hold on the affections of the people at large. Mahendra spent the rest of his life in Ceylon, and devoted himself to the establishment and organization of the Buddhist Church in the island, where he is revered as a saint. His ashes rest under a great cupola or *stupa* at Mihintale, one of the most remarkable among the many notable Buddhist monuments which are the glory of Ceylon.

The Mahavamsa chronicle, which gives a list of Asoka's missionaries and the countries to which they were deputed, makes no mention of the missions to the Tamil kingdoms of Southern India. This reticence is probably to be explained by the fierce hostility between the Sinhalese and the Tamils of the mainland, which lasted for centuries. If I am right in believing that Mahendra migrated from his monastery near Tanjore to the island, this fact would have been most distasteful to the monks of the Great Vihara, who could not bear to think that they were indebted to a resident among the hated Tamils for instruction in the rudiments of the faith, and much preferred that people should believe their religion to have come direct from the Holy Land of Buddhism. Some motive of this kind seems to have originated the Sinhalese legend of Mahendra, who is represented as an illegitimate son of Asoka, and is said to have been followed by a sister named Sanghamitra (" Friend of the Order "), who did for the nuns of Ceylon all that her brother did for the monks.

This legend, which is overlaid by many marvellous inventions, is fiction. The true version, representing Mahendra as the younger brother of Asoka, was well remembered at the imperial capital, Pataliputra, where Fa-hien, at the beginning of the fifth century, was shown the hermitage of Asoka's saintly brother; and it was still the only version known to Hiuen Tsang in the seventh century. Even when the latter pilgrim took down the Sinhalese legends from the lips of the island monks whom he met at Kanchi, he applied the stories to the brother, not to the son of Asoka.

The Mahavamsa seems also to err in attributing to Asoka the despatch of missionaries to Pegu (*Sovanabhumi*). No such mission is mentioned in the inscriptions, and it is very improbable that Asoka had any dealings with the countries to the east of the Bay of Bengal. His face was turned westwards toward the Hellenistic kingdoms. The Ceylon form of Buddhism appears to have been introduced into Burma and Pegu at a very much later date, and there is reason to believe that the earliest Burmese Buddhism was of the Tantric Mahayana type, imported direct from Northern India many centuries after Asoka's time.

Unfortunately, no definite record has been preserved of the fortunes of the Buddhist missions in the Hellenistic kingdoms of Asia, Africa, and Europe, nor are the names of the missionaries known. The influence of Buddhist doctrine on the heretical Gnostic sects appears to be undoubted, and many writers have suspected that the more orthodox forms of Christian teaching owe some debt to the lessons of Gautama; but the subject is too obscure for discussion in these pages.

It is, however, certain that Asoka, by his comprehensive and well-planned measures of evangelization, succeeded in transforming the doctrine of a local Indian sect into one of the great religions of the world. The personal ministry of Gautama Buddha was confined to a comparatively small area, comprising about four degrees of latitude and as many of longitude, between Gaya, Allahabad, and the Himalaya. Within these limits he was born, lived, and died. When he died, about 487 B.C., Buddhism was merely a sect of Hinduism, unknown beyond very restricted limits, and with no better apparent chance of survival than that enjoyed by many other contemporary sects now long forgotten.

The effective organization of the monastic system by the Buddhists was probably the means of keeping their system alive and in possession of considerable influence in the Ganges valley for the two centuries and a quarter which elapsed between the death of Gautama and the conversion of Asoka. His imperial patronage, gradually increasing as his faith grew in intensity, made the fortune of Buddhism, and raised it to the position which enables it still to dispute with Christianity the first place among the religions of the world, so far as the number of believers is concerned.

Asoka did not attempt to destroy either Brahmanical Hinduism or Jainism, but his prohibition of bloody sacrifices, the preference which he openly avowed for Buddhism, and his active propaganda undoubtedly brought his favourite doctrine to the front, and established it as the dominant religion both in India and Ceylon. It still retains that position in the southern island, but has vanished from the land of its birth, and has failed to retain its grasp upon many of its distant conquests.

Still, notwithstanding many failures, fluctuations, developments, and corruptions, Buddhism now commands, and will command for countless centuries to come, the devotion of hundreds of millions of men. This great result is the work of Asoka alone, and entitles him to rank for all time with that small body of men who may be said to have changed the faith of the world.

The obvious comparison of Asoka with Constantine has become a commonplace, but, like most historical parallels, it is far from exact. Christianity, when the emperor adopted it as the state creed, was already a power throughout the Roman Empire, and Constantine's adherence was rather an act of submission to an irresistible force than one of patronage to an obscure sect. Buddhism, on the contrary, when Asoka accorded to it his invaluable support, was but one of many sects struggling for existence and survival, and without any pretension to dictate imperial policy. His personal action, probably prompted and directed by his teacher, Upagupta, was the direct cause of the spread of the doctrine beyond the limits of India; and, if a Christian parallel must be sought, his work is comparable with that of Saint Paul, rather than with that of Constantine.

Upagupta, to whom the conversion of Asoka is ascribed, is said to have been the son of Gupta, a perfumer, and to have been born either at Benares or Mathura. Probably he was a native of the latter city, where the monastery built by him still existed in the seventh century. Tradition also associated his name with Sind, in which country he is said to have made frequent missionary journeys.

The vigorous and effective action taken by Asoka to propagate his creed and system of morals is conclusive proof of his absolute honesty of purpose, and justifies the modern reader in giving full credence to the devout professions made by him in the edicts. "Work I must," he observed, "for the public benefit;" and work he did. The world still enjoys the fruit of his labours, and his words, long lost, but now restored to utterance, ring with the sound of sincerity and truth.

Asoka was a hard-working king, as unwearied in business as Philip II of Spain, ready to receive reports "at any hour and any place," and yet dissatisfied with the outcome of his industry. "I am never," he laments, "fully satisfied with my exertions and despatch of business." Probably he worked too hard, and would have effected still more if he had done less. But his ideal of duty was high, and, like the Stoic philosopher,

ENTRANCE TO KARLI CAVE.

he felt bound to obey the law of his nature, and to toil on, be the result success or failure.

The character of Asoka must be deduced from his

words. The edicts are written in a style far too peculiar and distinctive to be the work of a secretary of state, and are alive with personal feeling. No secretary would have dared to put into his master's mouth the passionate expressions of remorse for the misery caused by the Kalinga war, leading up to the resolve to eschew aggressive warfare for the rest of his life, and the declaration that "although a man do him an injury, his Majesty holds that it must be patiently borne, as far as it possibly can be borne."

The edicts reveal Asoka as a man who sought to combine the piety of the monk with the wisdom of the king, and to make India the kingdom of righteousness as he conceived it, a theocracy without a God, in which the government should act the part of Providence, and guide the people in the right way. Every man, he maintained, must work out his own salvation, and eat the fruit of his deeds. "The fruit of exertion is not to be obtained by the great man only, because even the small man by exertion can win for himself much heavenly bliss; and for this purpose was given the precept—'Let small and great exert themselves.'" There could be no progress without individual effort; the government could point out the road, but each man must travel it for himself.

Reverence, compassion, truthfulness, and sympathy were the virtues which he inculcated; irreverence, cruelty, falsehood, and intolerance were the vices which he condemned. The preacher was no mere sermon-writer. He was a man of affairs, versed in the arts of peace and war, the capable ruler of an immense empire, a great man, and a great king.

Asoka, like all Oriental monarchs, was a polygamist, and had at least two consorts, who ranked as queens. The name of the second of these ladies, Karuvaki, is preserved in a brief edict signifying the royal pleasure that her charitable donations should be regarded by all officials concerned as her act and deed, redounding to her accumulation of merit. She is described as the mother of Tivara, who may be considered as a favourite child of the aged emperor at the time the edict was issued, late in his reign.

Tradition avers that his faithful chief queen for many years was named Asandhimitra, and that when she died, and Asoka was old, he married a dissolute young woman named Tishyarakshita, concerning whom and her stepson Kunala, the old folk-lore tale, known to the Greeks as that of Phædra and Hippolytus, is related with much imaginative embellishment. But folk-lore is not history, and the pathetic story of the blinded Kunala must not be read or criticized as matter-of-fact narrative. The legend appears in diverse forms with various names.

Another son of Asoka, named Jalauka, who plays a large part in Kashmir tradition, although rather a shadowy personage, has more appearance of reality than Kunala. He was reputed to have been an active and vigorous King of Kashmir, who expelled certain intrusive foreigners, and conquered the plains as far as Kanauj. He was hostile to Buddhism and devoted to the worship of Siva and the Divine Mothers, in whose honour he and his queen, Isanadevi, erected many temples at places which can be identified. But the story of Jalauka, notwithstanding the topographical details, is essentially legendary, and no independent corroboration of the Kashmir tradition has been discovered.

Tivara, the son mentioned in the Queen's Edict, is not heard of again, and may have died before his father. Dasaratha, the grandson of Asoka, who is described in the *Vishnu Purana* as the son of Suyasas, or Suparsva, was certainly a reality, being known from brief dedicatory inscriptions on the walls of cave-dwellings at the Nagarjuni hills, which he bestowed upon the Ajivikas, as his grandfather had done in the neighbouring Barabar hills. The script, language, and style of Dasaratha's records prove that his date was very close to that of Asoka, whom probably he directly succeeded. Assuming this to be the fact, the accession of Dasaratha may be dated in 231 B. C. His reign appears to have been short, and is allotted (under other names) eight years in two of the Puranas.

The whole duration of the Maurya dynasty according to Puranic authority was 137 years, and if this period be accepted and reckoned from the accession of Chandragupta in 321 B. C., the dynasty must have come to an end in 184 B. C., which date is certainly approximately correct. Four princes who succeeded Dasaratha, each of whom reigned for a few years, are mere names. The empire seems to have broken up very soon after Asoka's death, his descendants, whose names are recorded in the Puranic lists, retaining only Magadha and the neighbouring home provinces. The Andhra protected state between the Krishna and Godavari Rivers was among the earliest defections, and rapidly grew into a powerful kingdom, stretching right across India, as will be narrated in the next chapter. The last king of the imperial Maurya line, a weak prince named Brihadratha, was treacherously assassinated by his commander-in-chief, Pushyamitra.

But descendants of the great Asoka continued as local rajas in Magadha for many centuries, the last of them being Purna-varman, who was nearly contemporary with the Chinese pilgrim, Hiuen Tsang, in the seventh century. Petty Maurya dynasties, probably connected in some way with the imperial line, ruled in the Konkan, between the Western Ghats and the sea, and some other parts of Western India, during the sixth, seventh, and eighth centuries, and are frequently mentioned in inscriptions.

BUDDHIST SCULPTURE.

CHAPTER VIII

THE SUNGA, KANVA, AND ANDHRA DYNASTIES

184 B.C. TO 236 A.D.

THE SUNGA DYNASTY

PUSHYAMITRA, the commander-in-chief, having slain his master, Brihadratha Maurya, and imprisoned the minister, usurped the vacant throne, and established himself as sovereign of the now contracted Maurya dominions, thus founding a dynasty known to history as that of the Sungas.

The capital continued to be, as of old, Pataliputra, and probably all the central or home provinces of the empire recognized the usurper's authority, which extended to the south as far as the Narmada River, and presumably embraced the territories in the Ganges basin, corresponding with the modern Bihar, Tirhut, and the United Provinces of Agra and Oudh. It is unlikely that either the later Mauryas or the Sungas exercised any jurisdiction in the Panjab.

During the latter years of his reign, the usurper

was threatened by serious dangers menacing from both east and west. Menander, a relative of the Bactrian

TOWER OF VICTORY, CHITOR.

monarch Eukratides, the King of Kabul and the Panjab, formed the design of emulating the exploits of Alexander, and advanced with a formidable force into the interior of India. He annexed the Indus delta, the peninsula of Surashtra (Kathiawar), and some other territories on the western coast, occupied Mathura on the Jumna, besieged Madhyamika (now Nagari near Chitor) in Rajputana, invested Saketam in southern Oudh, and threatened Pataliputra, the capital.

About the same time, or a little earlier, Kharavela, King of Kalinga on the coast of the Bay of Bengal, invaded Magadha. He claims to have won some successes, and to have humbled his adversary, but whatever advantage he gained would seem to have been temporary or to have affected only the eastern frontier of the Magadhan kingdom.

The more formidable invasion of Menander was certainly repelled after a severe struggle, and the Greek king was obliged to retire to his own country, but probably retained his conquests in Western India for a few years longer.

Thus ended the last attempt by a European general to conquer India by land. All subsequent invaders from the western continent have come in ships, trusting to their command of the sea, and using it as their base. From the repulse of Menander in 153 B. C. until the bombardment of Calicut by Vasco da Gama in 1502 A. D., India enjoyed immunity from European attack.

During the progress of these wars the outlying southern provinces extending to the Narmada River were administered by the crown prince, Agnimitra, as viceroy, who had his capital at Vidisa, the modern

Bhilsa on the Betwa in Sindhia's territory. Agnimitra's youthful son, Vasumitra, was employed on active service under the orders of the king, his grandfather. Pushyamitra, who at this time must have been advanced in years, resolved to crown his military successes by proclaiming and substantiating a formal claim to the rank of Lord Paramount of Northern India. His pretensions received confirmation by the success of Agnimitra in a local war with his southern neighbour, the Raja of Vidarbha (Berar), which resulted in the complete defeat of the raja, who was obliged to cede half of his dominions to a rival cousin, the river Varada (Warda) being constituted the dividing line.

HORSE-SACRIFICE.

Pushyamitra determined to revive and celebrate with appropriate magnificence the ancient rite of the horse-sacrifice (*asvamedha*), which, according to immemorial tradition, could only be performed by a paramount sovereign, and involved as a preliminary a formal and successful challenge to all rival claimants to supreme power, delivered after this fashion:—

"A horse of a particular colour was consecrated by the performance of certain ceremonies, and was then turned loose to wander for a year. The king, or his representative, followed the horse with an army, and when the animal entered a foreign country, the ruler of that country was bound either to fight or to submit. If the liberator of the horse succeeded in obtaining or enforcing the submission of all the countries over which it passed, he returned in triumph with all the vanquished rajas in his train; but if he failed, he was disgraced and his pretensions ridiculed. After his successful return, a great festival was held, at which the horse was sacrificed."[1]

The command, at least nominally, of the guard attendant on the consecrated steed liberated by Pushyamitra was entrusted to his young grandson, Vasumitra, who is said to have encountered and routed a band of certain Yavanas, or western foreigners, who took up the challenge on the banks of the river Sindhu, which now forms the boundary between Bundelkhand and the Rajputana States. These disputants may have been part of the division of Menander's army which had undertaken the siege of Madhyamika in Rajputana.

The Yavanas and all other rivals having been disposed of in due course, Pushyamitra was justified in his claim to rank as the paramount power of Northern

[1] Dowson, *Classical Dict.*, s. v. Asvamedha.

India, and straightway proceeded to announce his success by a magnificent celebration of the sacrifice at his capital. The dramatist Kalidasa, who has so well preserved the traditions of the time in his play on King Agnimitra, professes to record the very words of the invitation addressed by the victorious king to his son, the crown prince, as follows:—

"May it be well with thee! From the sacrificial enclosure the commander-in-chief Pushyamitra sends this message to his son Agnimitra, who is in the territory of Vidisa, affectionately embracing him. Be it known unto thee that I, having been consecrated for the *Rajasuya* [i. e. *asvamedha*] sacrifice, let loose free from all check or curb a horse which was to be brought back after a year, appointing Vasumitra as its defender, girt with a guard of a hundred Rajputs. This very horse wandering on the right [or 'south'] bank of the Sindhu was claimed by a cavalry squadron of the Yavanas. Then there was a fierce struggle between the two forces. Then Vasumitra, the mighty bowman, having overcome his foes, rescued by force my excellent horse, which they were endeavouring to carry off. Accordingly I will now sacrifice, having had my horse brought back to me by my grandson, even as Ansumat brought back the horse to Sagara. Therefore you must dismiss anger from your mind, and without delay come with my daughters-in-law to behold the sacrifice."

The exaggerated regard for the sanctity of animal life, which was one of the most cherished features of Buddhism, and the motive of Asoka's most characteristic legislation, had nécessarily involved the prohibition of bloody sacrifices, which are essential to certain forms of Brahmanical worship and were believed by the orthodox to possess the highest saving efficacy. The memorable horse-sacrifice of Pushyamitra marked the beginning of the Brahmanical reaction, which was fully developed five centuries later in the time of Samudragupta and his successors.

But the revival of the practice of ṣacrifice by an orthodox Hindu ruler did not necessarily involve persecution of Jains and Buddhists who abhorred the rite. There is no evidence that any member of those sects was ever compelled to sacrifice against his will, as, under Buddhist and Jain domination, the orthodox were forced to abstain from ceremonies regarded by them as essential to salvation. Pushyamitra has been accused of persecution, but the evidence is merely that of a legend of no authority.

But, although the alleged proscription of Buddhism by Pushyamitra is not supported by evidence, and it is true that the gradual extinction of that religion in India was due in the main to causes other than persecution, it is also true that from time to time fanatic kings indulged in savage outbursts of cruelty, and committed genuine acts of persecution directed against Jains or Buddhists as such. Well-established instances of such proceedings will be met with in the course of this history, and others, which do not come within its limits, are on record. That such outbreaks of wrath should have occurred is not wonderful, if we consider the extreme oppressiveness of the Jain and Buddhist prohibitions when ruthlessly enforced, as they certainly were by some rajas, and probably by Asoka. The wonder rather is that persecutions were so rare, and that as a rule the various sects managed to live together in harmony, and in the enjoyment of fairly impartial official favour.

When Pushyamitra, some five years subsequent to the retreat of Menander, died, after a long and eventful reign, he was succeeded by his son, the crown prince Agnimitra, who had governed the southern provinces during his father's lifetime. He reigned but a few years, and was succeeded by Sujyeshtha, probably a brother, who was followed seven years later by Vasumitra, a son of Agnimitra, who as a youth had guarded the sacrificial horse on behalf of his aged grandfather. The next four reigns are said to have been abnormally short, amounting together to only seventeen years.

The inference that the extreme brevity of these reigns indicates a period of confusion, during which palace revolutions were frequent, is strongly confirmed by the one incident of the time which has survived in tradition. Sumitra, another son of Agnimitra, who was, we are told, inordinately devoted to the stage, was surprised when in the midst of his favourite actors by one Mitradeva, who "severed his head with a scimitar, as a lotus is shorn from its stalk." The ninth king, Bhagavata, is credited with a long reign of twenty-six years, but we know nothing about him. The tenth king, Devabhuti, or Devabhumi, was, we are assured, a man of licentious habits, and lost his life while engaged in a discreditable intrigue. The dynasty thus came to an unhonoured end after having occupied the throne for a hundred and twelve years.

THE KANVA OR KANVAYANA DYNASTY

The plot which cost the royal debauchee Devabhuti his throne and life was contrived by his Brahman minister Vasudeva, who seems to have controlled the state even during the lifetime of his nominal master. Mitradeva, the slayer of Prince Sumitra, probably belonged to the same powerful family, which is known to history as that of the Kanvas, or Kanvayanas. There is reason to believe that the later Sunga kings enjoyed little real power, and were puppets in the hands of their Brahman ministers, like the Mahratta rajas in the hands of the Peshwas. But the distinct testimony of both the Puranas and Bana that Devabhuti, the tenth and last Sunga, was the person slain by Vasudeva, the first Kanva, forbids the acceptance of Professor Bhandarkar's theory that the Kanva dynasty should be regarded as contemporary with the Sunga.

Vasudeva seized the throne rendered vacant by his crime, and was succeeded by three of his descendants. The whole dynasty, comprising four reigns, covers a period of only forty-five years. The figures indicate, as in the case of the Sungas, that the times were disturbed, and that succession to the throne was often effected by violent means. Nothing whatever is known about the reigns of any of the Kanva kings. The last of them was slain in 27 B.C. by a king of the Andhra, or Satavahana, dynasty, which at that time possessed wide dominions stretching across the table-land of the Deccan from sea to sea.

The Puranas treat the whole Andhra dynasty as following the Kanva, and consequently identify the slayer of the last Kanva prince with Simuka, or Sipraka, the first of the Andhra line. But, as a matter of fact, the independent Andhra dynasty had begun about 220 B.C., long before the suppression of the Kanvas in 27 B.C., and the Andhra king who slew Susarman cannot possibly have been Simuka. It is impossible to affirm with certainty who he was, because the dates of accession of the various Andhra princes are not known with accuracy.

ANDHRA DYNASTY

Before proceeding to narrate the history of the Andhra kings after the extinction of the Kanva dynasty, we must cast back a glance to the more distant past, and trace the steps by which the Andhra kingdom became one of the greatest powers in India.

In the days of Chandragupta Maurya and Megasthenes the Andhra nation, probably a Dravidian people, now represented by the large population speaking the Telugu language, occupied the deltas of the Godavari and Krishna (Kistna) Rivers on the eastern side of India, and was reputed to possess a military force second only to that at the command of the King of the Prasii, Chandragupta Maurya. The Andhra territory included thirty walled towns, besides numerous villages, and the army consisted of one hundred thousand infantry, two thousand cavalry, and one thousand elephants. The capital of the state was then Sri Kakulam, on the lower course of the Krishna.

The nation thus described was evidently independent, and it is not known at what time, in the reign either of Chandragupta or Bindusara, the Andhras were compelled to submit to the irresistible forces at the command of the Maurya kings and recognize the suzerainty of Magadha.

When next heard of in Asoka's edicts (256 B.C.), they were enrolled among the tribes resident in the outer circle of the empire, subject to the imperial commands, but doubtless enjoying a considerable degree of autonomy under their own raja. The withdrawal of the strong arm of Asoka was the signal for the disruption of his vast empire. While the home provinces continued to obey his feeble successors upon the throne of Pataliputra, the distant governments shook off the imperial yoke and re-asserted their independence.

The Andhras were not slow to take advantage of the opportunity given by the death of the great emperor, and, very soon after the close of his reign, set up as an independent power under the government of a king named Simuka. The new dynasty extended its sway with such extraordinary rapidity that, in the reign of the second king, Krishna (Kanha), the town of Nasik, near the source of the Godavari in the Western Ghats, was included in the Andhra dominions, which thus stretched across India.

A little later, either the third or fourth king, who is described as Lord of the West, was able to send a force of all arms to the aid of his ally, Kharavela, King of Kalinga in the east, which kingdom had also recovered its independence after the death of Asoka.

Nothing more is heard of the Andhra kings until one of them, as above related, in 27 B. C., slew the last of the Kanvas, and no doubt annexed the territory, whatever it was, which still recognized the authority of that dynasty. The Andhra kings all claimed to belong to the Satavahana family, and most of them assumed the title of Satakarni. They are consequently often referred to by one or other of these designations, without mention of the personal name of the monarch, and it is thus sometimes impossible to ascertain which king is alluded to. As already observed, the real name of the slayer of Susarman Kanva is not known.

The name of Hala, the seventeenth king, by virtue of its association with literary tradition, possesses special interest as marking a stage in the development of Indian literature. In his time, the learned dialect elaborated by scholars, in which the works of Kalidasa and other famous poets are composed, had not come into general use as the language of polite literature, and even the most courtly authors did not disdain to seek royal patronage for compositions in the vernacular dialects. On such literature the favour of King Hala was bestowed, and he himself is credited with the composition of the anthology of erotic verses, called the "Seven Centuries," written in the ancient Maharashtri tongue. A collection of tales, entitled the "Great Story-book," written in the Paisachi dialect, and a Sanskrit grammar, arranged with special reference to the needs of students more familiar with the vernacular speech than with the so-called "classical" language, are attributed to his ministers.

The next kings concerning whom anything is known are those numbered twenty-one to twenty-three in the dynastic list, who form a group distinguished by peculiar personal names and a distinctive coinage, and are commemorated by a considerable number of inscriptions and coins. Vilivayakura I, the first of the group, whose accession would seem to indicate a break in the continuity of the dynasty, perhaps due to the ambition of a junior branch, obtained power in 84 A.D., and, according to the Puranas, enjoyed it only for half a year. Some rare coins struck in his western dominions are his sole memorial.

He was succeeded by Sivalakura, presumably his son, who, after a reign of twenty-eight years, transmitted the sceptre to Vilivayakura II, who bore his grandfather's name, in accordance with Hindu custom. His reign of about twenty-five years was distinguished by successful warfare against his western neighbours, the Sakas, Pahlavas, and Yavanas of Malwa, Gujarat, and Kathiawar. The names of these foreign tribes demand some explanation.

The Sakas, the Se (Sek) of Chinese historians, were

a horde of pastoral nomads, like the modern Turkomans, occupying territory to the west of the Wu-sun horde, apparently situated between the Chu and Jaxartes Rivers, to the north of the Alexander Mountains. About 160 B. C., they were expelled from their pasture grounds by another similar horde, the Yueh-chi, and compelled to migrate southwards. They ultimately reached India, but the road by which they travelled is not known with certainty.

Princes of Saka race established themselves at Taxila in the Panjab and Mathura on the Jumna, where they displaced the native rajas, and ruled principalities for several generations, assuming the ancient Persian title of satrap. Probably they recognized Mithradates I (174-136 B. C.) and his successors, the early kings of the Parthian, or Arsakidan, dynasty of Persia, as their overlords.

Another branch of the horde advanced farther to the south, presumably across Sind, which was then a well-watered country, and carved out for themselves a dominion in the peninsula of Surashtra, or Kathiawar, and some of the neighbouring districts on the mainland.

The Pahlavas seem to have been Persians, in the sense of being Parthians of Persia, as distinguished from the Parsikas, or Persians proper. The name is believed to be a corruption of Parthiva, "Parthian," and is almost certainly identical with Pallava, the designation of a famous southern dynasty, which is frequently mentioned in inscriptions during the early centuries of the Christian era, and had its capital at

Kanchi, or Conjevaram, in the Chingleput District, Madras.

The word Yavana is etymologically the same as "Ionian," and originally meant "Asiatic Greek," but has been used with varying connotation at different periods. In the third century B. C. Asoka gave the word its original meaning, describing Antiochos Theos and the other contemporary Hellenistic kings as Yavanas. In the second century A. D. the term had a vaguer signification, and was employed as a generic term to denote foreigners coming from the old Indo-Greek kingdoms on the northwestern frontier.

These three foreign tribes, Sakas, Pahlavas, and Yavanas, at that time settled in Western India as the lords of a conquered native population, were the objects of the hostility of Vilivayakura II. The first foreign chieftain in the west whose name has been preserved is Bhumaka the Kshaharata, who attained power at about the beginning of the second century A. D., and was followed by Nahapana, who aggrandized his dominions at the expense of his Andhra neighbours. The Kshaharata clan seems to have been a branch of the Sakas.

In the year 126 A. D. the Andhra king Vilivayakura II recovered the losses which his kingdom had suffered at the hands of the intruding foreigners, and utterly destroyed the power of Nahapana. The hostility of the Andhra monarch was stimulated by the disgust felt by all Hindus, and especially by the followers of the orthodox Brahmanical system, at the outlandish practices of foreign barbarians, who ignored caste rules, and treated with contempt the precepts of the holy *sastras*. This disgust is vividly expressed in the long inscription recorded in 144 A. D. by the queen-mother Balasri, of the Gautama family, in which she glorifies herself as the mother of the hero who "destroyed the Sakas, Yavanas, and Pahlavas . . . properly expended the taxes which he levied in accordance with the sacred law . . . and prevented the mixing of the four castes."

RIVER SIPRA AT UJJAIN.
From a photograph.

After the destruction of Nahapana, the local government of the west was entrusted to one Chashtana, who seems to have been a Saka, and to have acted as viceroy under the Andhra conqueror. Chashtana, whose capital was at Ujjain in Malwa, is mentioned by his contemporary, Ptolemy the geographer, under the slight disguise of Tiastanes. From him sprang a long line of satraps, who retained the government of Western India with varying fortune, until the last of them was overthrown at the close of the fourth century by Chandragupta Vikramaditya.

In the year 138 A. D. Vilivayakura II was succeeded on the Andhra throne by his son Pulumayi II, the Siro Polemaios of Ptolemy, and about the same time the satrap Rudradaman, grandson of Chashtana, assumed the government of the western provinces. His daughter, Dakshamitra, was married to Pulumayi, but this relationship did not deter Rudradaman, who was an ambitious and energetic prince, from levying war upon his son-in-law. The satrap was victorious, and when the conflict was renewed, success still attended on his arms (145 A. D.). Moved by natural affection for his daughter, the victor did not pursue his advantage to the uttermost, and was content with the retrocession of territory, while abstaining from inflicting utter ruin upon his opponent.

The peninsula of Kathiawar, or Surashtra, the whole of Malwa, Kachchh (Cutch), Sind, and the Konkan, or territory between the Western Ghats and the sea, besides some adjoining districts, thus passed under the sway of the satraps, and were definitely detached from the Andhra dominions.

Although Pulumayi II was a son of Vilivayakura II, his accession seems to mark a dynastic epoch, emphasized by a transfer of the capital and the abandonment of the peculiar type of coinage known to numismatists as the "bow and arrow," favoured by the Vilivayakura group. The western capital, which in the time of Vilivayakura II (Baleokouros) had been at a town called Hippokoura by Ptolemy, probably the modern Kolhapur, was removed by Pulumayi II to Paithan, or Paithana, on the upper waters of the Godavari, two hundred miles farther north. Pulumayi II enjoyed a long reign over the territories diminished by the victories of his father-in-law, and survived until 170 A. D.

The next two kings, Siva Sri and Siva Skanda, who are said to have reigned each for seven years, seem to have been brothers of Pulumayi II. Nothing is known about them, except that the former struck some rude leaden coins in his eastern provinces.

The most important and powerful of the last seven kings of the dynasty evidently was Yajna Sri, who reigned from 184 to 213 A. D. for twenty-nine years. His rare silver coins, imitating the satrap coinage, certainly prove a renewal of relations with the western satraps, and probably point to unrecorded conquests. It would seem that Yajna Sri must have renewed the struggle in which Pulumayi II had been worsted, and recovered some of the provinces lost by that prince. The silver coins would then have been struck for circulation in the conquered districts, just as similar coins were minted by Chandragupta Vikramaditya when he finally shattered the power of the Saka satraps. The numerous and varied, although rude, bronze and leaden coins of Yajna Sri, which formed the currency of the eastern provinces, confirm the testimony of inscriptions by which the prolonged duration of his reign is attested. Some pieces bearing the figure of a ship probably should be referred to this reign, and suggest the inference that Yajna Sri's power was not confined to the land.

His successors, Vijaya, Vada Sri, and Pulumayi III, with whom the long series of Andhra kings came to an end about 236 A. D., are mere names; but the real existence of Vada Sri is attested by the discovery of a few leaden coins bearing his name. Research will probably detect coins struck by both his next predecessor and immediate successor.

The testimony of the Puranas that the dynasty endured for 456½ years, or, in round numbers, four centuries and a half, appears to be accurate. The number of the kings also appears to be correctly stated as having been either thirty or thirty-one.

At present nothing is known concerning the causes which brought about the downfall of this dynasty, which had succeeded in retaining power for a period so unusually prolonged. The fall of the Andhras happens to coincide very closely with the death of Vasudeva, the last of the great Kushan kings of Northern India, as well as with the rise of the Sasanian dynasty of Persia (226 A. D.), and it is possible that the coincidence may not be merely fortuitous. But the third century A. D. is one of the dark spaces in the spectrum of Indian history, and almost every event of that time is concealed from view by an impenetrable veil of oblivion. Vague speculation, unchecked by the salutary limitations of verified fact, is, at the best, unprofitable, and so we must be content to let the Andhras pass away in the darkness.

CHAPTER IX

THE INDO-GREEK AND INDO-PARTHIAN DYNASTIES

250 B.C. TO 50 A.D.

THE story of the native dynasties in the interior must now be interrupted to admit a brief review of the fortunes of the various foreign rulers who established themselves in the Indian territories once conquered by Alexander, after the sun of the Maurya empire had set, and the northwestern frontier was left exposed to foreign attack. The daring and destructive raid of the great Macedonian, as we have seen, had effected none of the permanent results intended. The Indian provinces which he had subjugated, and which Seleukos had failed to recover, passed into the iron grip of Chandragupta, who transmitted them to the keeping of his son and grandson. I see no reason to doubt that the territories west of the Indus ceded by Seleukos to his Indian opponent continued in possession of the successors of the latter, and that consequently the Hindu Kush range was the frontier of the Maurya empire up to the close of Asoka's reign.

But it is certain that the unity of the empire did

not survive Asoka, and that when the influence of his dominating personality ceased to act, the outlying provinces shook off their allegiance and set up as independent states. The history of some of these has been told in the preceding chapter. The regions of the northwestern frontier, when no longer protected by the arm of a strong paramount native power in the interior, offered a tempting field to the ambition of the Hellenistic princes of Bactria and Parthia, as well as to the cupidity of the warlike races on the border. This chapter will be devoted, so far as the very imperfect materials available permit, to a sketch of the leading events in the annals of the Panjab and trans-Indus provinces from the close of Asoka's reign to the establishment of the Indo-Scythian, or Kushan, power.

The spacious Asiatic dominion consolidated by the genius of Seleukos Nikator passed in the year 262 or 261 B. C. into the hands of his grandson Antiochos, a drunken sensualist, miscalled even in his lifetime Theos, or "the god," and, strange to say, worshipped as such. This worthless prince occupied the throne for fifteen or sixteen years, but toward the close of his reign his empire suffered two grievous losses by the revolt of the Bactrians, under the leadership of Diodotos, and of the Parthians, under that of Arsakes.

The loss of Bactria was especially grievous. This province, the rich plain watered by the Oxus (Amu Darya) after its issue from the mountains, had been occupied by civilized men from time immemorial, and its capital, Zariaspa, or Balkh, had been from ancient days one of the most famous cities of the East. The country, which was said to contain a thousand towns, had been always regarded, during the time of the Achæmenian kings, as the premier satrapy, and reserved as an appanage for a prince of the blood. When Alexander shattered the Persian power and seated himself upon the throne of the Great King, he continued to bestow his royal favour upon the Bactrians, who in return readily assimilated the elements of Hellenic civilization. Two years after his death, at the final partition of the empire in 321 B.C., Bactria fell to the share of Seleukos Nikator, and continued to be one of the most valuable possessions of his son and grandson.

The Parthians, a race of rude and hardy horsemen, with habits similar to those of the modern Turkomans, dwelt beyond the Persian deserts in the comparatively infertile regions to the southeast of the Caspian Sea. Their country, along with the territories of the Chorasmioi, Sogdioi, and Arioi (Khwarizm, Samarkand, and Herat), had been included in the sixteenth satrapy of Darius, and all the tribes named, armed like the Bactrians, with cane bows and short spears, supplied contingents to the host of Xerxes. In the time of Alexander and the early Seleukids, Parthia proper and Hyrkania, adjoining the Caspian, were combined to form a satrapy. The Parthians, unlike the Bactrians, never adopted Greek culture, and, although submissive to their Persian and Macedonian masters, retained unchanged the habits of a horde of mounted shepherds, equally skilled in the management of their steeds and the use of the bow.

These two nations, so widely different in history and manners,—the Bactrians, with a thousand cities, and the Parthians, with myriads of moss-troopers,—were moved at almost the same moment, about the middle of the third century B. C., to throw off their allegiance to their Seleukidan lord, and assert their independence. The exact dates of these rebellions cannot be determined, but the Bactrian revolt seems to have been the earlier, and there is reason to believe that the Parthian struggle continued for several years, and was not ended until after the death of Antiochos Theos in 246 B. C., although the declaration of Parthian autonomy seems to have been made in 248 B. C.

The Bactrian revolt was a rebellion of the ordinary Oriental type, headed by Diodotos, the governor of the province, who seized an opportunity to shake off the authority of his sovereign and assume the royal state. The Parthian movement was rather a national rising, led by a chief named Arsakes, who is described as being a man of uncertain origin but undoubted bravery, and inured to a life of rapine. Arsakes slew Andragoras, the Seleukidan viceroy, declared his independence, and so founded the famous Arsakidan dynasty of Persia, which endured for nearly five centuries (248 B. C. to 226 A. D.). The success of both the Bactrian and Parthian rebels was facilitated by the war of succession which disturbed the Seleukidan monarchy after the death of Antiochos Theos.

The line of Bactrian kings initiated by Diodotos was destined to a briefer and stormier existence than that enjoyed by the dynasty of the Arsakids. Diodotos himself wore his newly won crown for a brief space only, and after a few years was succeeded (*cir.* 245 B. C.) by his son of the same name, who entered into an alliance with the Parthian king.

Diodotos II was followed (*cir.* 230 B. C.) by Euthydemos, a native of Magnesia, who seems to have belonged to a different family, and to have gained the crown by successful rebellion. This monarch became involved in a long-contested war with Antiochos the Great of Syria (223 - 187 B. C.), which was terminated (*cir.* 208 B. C.) by a treaty recognizing the independence of the Bactrian kingdom. Shortly afterward Antiochos crossed the Hindu Kush, and compelled an Indian king named Subhagasena, who probably ruled in the Kabul valley, to surrender a considerable number of elephants and large treasure. Leaving Androsthenes of Cyzicus to collect this war indemnity, Antiochos in person led his main force homeward by the Kandahar route through Arachosia and Drangiana to Karmania.

Demetrios, son of Euthydemos and son-in-law of Antiochos, who had given him a daughter in marriage when the independence of Bactria was recognized, repeated his father-in-law's exploits with still greater success, and conquered a considerable portion of Northern India, presumably including Kabul, the Panjab, and Sind (*cir.* 190 B. C.).

The distant Indian wars of Demetrios necessarily

weakened his hold upon Bactria, and afforded the opportunity for successful rebellion to one Eukratides, who made himself master of Bactria about 175 B.C., and became involved in many wars with the surrounding states and tribes, which he carried on with varying fortune and unvarying spirit. Demetrios, although he had lost Bactria, long retained his hold upon his eastern conquests, and was known as "King of the Indians," but after a severe struggle the victory rested with Eukratides, who was an opponent not easily beaten. It is related that on one occasion, when shut up for five months in a fort with a garrison of only three hundred men, he succeeded in repelling the attack of a host of sixty thousand under the command of Demetrios.

But the hard-won triumph was short-lived. While Eukratides was on his homeward march from India, attended by his son Apollodotos, whom he had made his colleague in power, he was barbarously murdered by the unnatural youth, who is said to have gloried in his monstrous crime, driving his chariot wheels through the blood of his father, to whose corpse he refused even the poor honour of burial.

The murder of Eukratides shattered to fragments the kingdom for which he had fought so valiantly. Another son, named Heliokles, who assumed the title of "the Just," perhaps as the avenger of his father's cruel death, enjoyed for a brief space a precarious tenure of power in Bactria. Strato, who also seems to have belonged to the family of Eukratides, held a principality in the Panjab for a few years, and was perhaps the immediate successor of Apollodotos. Agathokles and Pantaleon, whose coins are specially Indian in character, were earlier in date, and contemporary with Euthydemos and Demetrios.

It is evident from the great variety of the royal names in the coin-legends, which are nearly forty in number, that both before and after the death of Eukratides, the Indian borderland was parcelled out among a crowd of Greek princelings, for the most part related either to the family of Euthydemos and Demetrios or to that of their rival, Eukratides. Some of these princelings, among whom was Antialkidas, were subdued by Eukratides, who, if he had lived, might have consolidated a great border kingdom. But his death in the hour of victory increased the existing confusion, and it is quite impossible to make a satisfactory territorial and chronological arrangement of the Indo-Greek frontier kings contemporary with and posterior to Eukratides. Their names, with two exceptions, are known from coins only.

One name, that of Menander, stands out conspicuously amid the crowd of obscure princes. He seems to have belonged to the family of Eukratides, and to have had his capital at Kabul, whence he issued in 155 B.C. to make the bold invasion of India described in the last chapter. Two years later he was obliged to retire and devote his energies to the encounter with dangers which menaced him at home, due to the never-ending quarrels with his neighbours on the frontier.

Menander was celebrated as a just ruler, and when he died was honoured with magnificent obsequies. He is supposed to have been a convert to Buddhism, and has been immortalized under the name of Milinda in a celebrated dialogue entitled "The Questions of Milinda," which is one of the most notable books in Buddhist literature.

Heliokles, the son of Eukratides, who had obtained Bactria as his share of his father's extensive dominion, was the last king of Greek race to rule the territories to the north of the Hindu Kush. While the Greek princes and princelings were struggling one with the other in obscure wars which history has not condescended to record, a deluge was preparing in the steppes of Mongolia, which was destined to sweep them all away into nothingness.

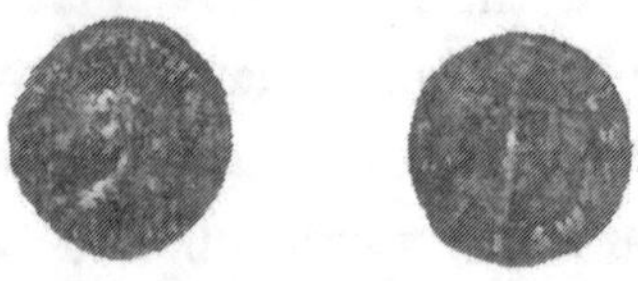

COIN OF THE INDO-GREEK KING MENANDER.
Second Century B.C.

A horde of nomads, named the Yueh-chi, whose movements will be more particularly described in the next chapter, were driven out of northwestern China in the year 165 B.C., and compelled to migrate westwards by the route to the north of the deserts. Some years later, about 160 B.C., they encountered another horde, the Sakas or Se, who seem to have occupied the territories lying to the north (or, possibly, to the south) of the Alexander Mountains, between the Chu and Jaxartes (Syr Darya) Rivers, as already mentioned.

The Sakas, accompanied by cognate tribes, were forced to move in a southerly direction, and in course of time entered India, possibly by more roads than one. This flood of barbarian invasion burst upon Bactria in the period between 140 and 130 B.C., finally extinguishing the Hellenistic monarchy, which must have been weakened already by the growth of the Parthian or Persian power. The last Græco-Bactrian king was Heliokles, with whom Greek rule to the north of the Hindu Kush disappeared for ever.

The Saka flood, still pouring on, surged into the valley of the Helmund (Erymandrus) River, and so filled that region, the modern Sistan, that it became known as Sakastene, or the Saka country.

Other branches of the barbarian stream which penetrated the Indian passes deposited settlements at Taxila in the Panjab and at Mathura on the Jumna, where Saka princes, with the title of satrap, ruled for more than a century, seemingly in subordination to the Parthian power. Another section of the horde, at a later date, pushed on southwards and occupied the peninsula of Surashtra, or Kathiawar, founding a Saka dynasty which lasted for centuries.

Strato I, a Greek King of Kabul and the Panjab, who was to some extent contemporary with Heliokles, seems to have been succeeded by Strato II, probably his grandson, who, in turn, was apparently displaced at Taxila by the Saka satraps. The satraps of Mathura were closely connected with those of Taxila, and belong to the same period, a little before and after 100 B.C.

The movements of the Sakas and allied nomad tribes were closely connected with the development of the

Parthian or Persian power under the Arsakidan kings. Mithradates I, a very able monarch (174 to 136 B.C.), who was for many years the contemporary of Eukratides, King of Bactria, succeeded in extending his dominion so widely that his power was felt as far as the Indus, and possibly even to the east of that river. The Saka chiefs of Taxila and Mathura would not have assumed the purely Persian title of satrap, if they had not regarded themselves as subordinates of the Persian or Parthian sovereign, and the close relations between the Parthian monarchy and the Indian borderland at this period are demonstrated by the appearance of a long line of princes of Parthian origin, who now enter on the scene.

The earliest of these Indo-Parthian kings apparently was Maues, or Mauas, who attained power in the Kabul valley and Panjab about 120 B.C., and adopted the title of "Great King of Kings" (βασιλέως βασιλέων μεγάλου), which had been used for the first time by Mithradates I. His coins are closely related to those of that monarch, as well as to those of the unmistakably Parthian border chief, who called himself Arsakes Theos. The King Moga, to whom the Taxila satrap was immediately subordinate, was almost certainly the personage whose name appears on the coins as *Mauou* in the genitive case.

Vonones, or Onones, whose name is unquestionably Parthian, was probably the immediate successor of Maues on the throne of Kabul. He was succeeded by his brother Spalyris, who was followed in order by

Azes (Azas) I, Azilises, Azes II, and Gondophares. The princes prior to the last named are known from their coins only. Gondophares, whose accession may be dated with practical certainty in 21 A. D., and whose coins are Parthian in style, enjoyed a long reign of some thirty years, and is a more interesting personage. He reigned, like his predecessors, in the Kabul valley and the Panjab.

The special interest attaching to Gondophares is due to the fact that his name is associated with that of St. Thomas, the apostle of the Parthians, in very ancient Christian tradition. The belief that the Parthians were allotted as the special sphere of the missionary labours of St. Thomas goes back to the time of Origen, who died in the middle of the third century, and is also mentioned in the *Clementine Recognitions*, a work of the same period, and possibly somewhat earlier in date.

The nearly contemporary *Acts of St. Thomas*, as well as later tradition, generally associate the Indians, rather than the Parthians, with the name of the apostle, but the terms "India" and "Indians" had such vague signification in ancient times that the discrepancy is not great. The earliest form of the tradition clearly deserves the greater credit, and there is no apparent reason for discrediting the statement handed down by Origen that Thomas received Parthia as his allotted region. According to the *Clementine Recognitions*, the apostolic preaching brought about very desirable reforms in the morals and manners of the Medes and

Persians, who were induced to abandon scandalous practices, forbidden by religion, although sanctioned by immemorial usage.

The legend connecting St. Thomas with King Gondophares appears for the first time in the Syrian text of the *Acts of St. Thomas*, which was composed at about the same date as the writings of Origen. The substance of the long story may be set forth briefly as follows:—

"When the twelve apostles divided the countries of the world among themselves by lot, India fell to the share of Judas, surnamed Thomas, or the Twin, who showed unwillingness to start on his mission. At that time an Indian merchant named Habban arrived in the country of the south, charged by his master, Gundaphar, King of India, to bring back with him a cunning artificer able to build a palace meet for the king. In order to overcome the apostle's reluctance to start for the East, our Lord appeared to the merchant in a vision, sold the apostle to him for twenty pieces of silver, and commanded St. Thomas to serve King Gundaphar and build the palace for him.

"In obedience to his Lord's commands, the apostle sailed next day with Habban the merchant, and during the voyage assured his companion concerning his skill in architecture and all manner of work in wood and stone. Wafted by favouring winds, their ship quickly reached the harbour of Sandaruk. Landing there, the voyagers shared in the marriage-feast of the king's daughter, and used their time so well that bride and bridegroom were converted to the true faith. Thence the saint and the merchant proceeded on their voyage, and came to the court of Gundaphar, King of India. St. Thomas promised to build him the palace within the space of six months, but expended the moneys given to him for that purpose in alms-giving, and, when called to account, explained that he was building for the king a palace in heaven, not made with hands. He preached with such zeal and grace that the king, his brother Gad, and multitudes of the people embraced the faith. Many signs and wonders were wrought by the holy apostle.

"After a time, Sifur, the general of King Mazdai, arrived, and besought the apostle to come with him and heal his wife and daughter. St. Thomas hearkened to his prayer, and went with Sifur to the city of King Mazdai, riding in a chariot. He left his converts in the country of King Gundaphar, under the care of Deacon Xanthippos. King Mazdai waxed wroth when his queen Tertia and a noble lady named Mygdonia were converted by St. Thomas, who was accordingly sentenced to death and executed by four soldiers, who pierced him with spears on a mountain without the city. The apostle was buried in the sepulchre of the ancient kings; but the disciples secretly removed his bones, and carried them away to the West."

Writers of later date, subsequent to the seventh century, profess to know the name of the city where the apostle suffered martyrdom, and call it variously Kalamina, Kalamita, Kalamena, or Karamena, and much ingenuity has been expended in futile attempts to identify this city. But the scene of the martyrdom is anonymous in the earlier versions of the tale, and Kalamina should be regarded as a place in fairyland, which it is vain to try to locate on a map. The same observation applies to the attempts at the identification of the port variously called Sandaruk, Andrapolis, and so forth.

The whole story is pure mythology, and the geography is as mythical as the tale itself. Its interest in the eyes of the historian of India is confined to the fact that it proves that the real Indian king, Gondophares, was remembered two centuries after his death, and was associated in popular belief with the apostolic mission to the Parthians. Inasmuch as Gondophares was certainly a Parthian prince, it is reasonable to believe that a Christian mission actually visited the Indo-Parthians of the northwestern frontier during his reign, whether or not that mission was conducted by St. Thomas in person. The traditional association of the name of the apostle with that of King Gondophares is in no way at variance with the chronology of the reign of the latter.

The alleged connection of the apostle with Southern India and with the shrine near Madras dubbed San Thomé by the Portuguese stands on a different footing. The story of the southern mission of St. Thomas first makes its appearance in Marco Polo's work in the thirteenth century, and has no support in either probability or ancient tradition. It may be dismissed without hesitation as a late invention of the local Nestorian Christians, concocted as a proof of their orthodox descent.

The coins of Abdagases, the son of Gondophares' brother, are found in the Panjab only, while those of Orthagnes occur in Kandahar, Sistan, and Sindh. It would seem that the Indo-Parthian princes were gradually driven southward by the advancing Yueh-chi, who had expelled the last of them from the Panjab by the end of the first century A. D.[1]

For a period of some two centuries after the beginning of the Saka and Parthian invasions, the northern portions of the Indian borderland, comprising probably the valley of the Kabul River, the Suwat valley, and some neighbouring districts to the north and northwest of Peshawar, remained under the government of local Greek princes, who, whether independent or subject to the suzerainty of a Parthian overlord, certainly exercised the perogative of coining silver and bronze money.

The last of these Indo-Greek rulers was Hermaios, who succumbed to the Yueh-chi chief, Kadphises I, about 50 A. D., when that enterprising monarch added Kabul to the growing Yueh-chi empire. The Yueh-chi chief at first struck coins jointly in the name of himself and the Greek prince, retaining on the obverse the portrait of Hermaios with his titles in Greek letters. After a time, while still preserving the familiar portrait, he substituted his own name and style in the legend. The next step taken was to replace the bust of Hermaios by the effigy of Augustus, as in his later years, and so to do homage to the expanding fame of that

[1] The successors of Gondophares seem to have followed in this order: Abdagases, Orthagnes, Arsakes, Pakores, Sanabares.

emperor, who, without striking a blow, and by the mere terror of the Roman name, had compelled the Parthians to restore the standards of Crassus (20 B. C.), which had been captured thirty-three years earlier.

Still later probably are those coins of Kadphises I which dispense altogether with the royal effigy, and present on the obverse an Indian bull, and on the reverse a Bactrian camel, devices fitly symbolizing the conquest of India by a horde of nomads.

Thus the numismatic record offers a distinctly legible abstract of the political history of the times, and tells in outline the story of the gradual supersession of the last outposts of Greek authority by the irresistible advance of the hosts from the steppes of Central Asia.

When the European historian, with his mind steeped in the conviction of the immeasurable debt owed to Hellas by modern civilization, stands by the side of the grave of Greek rule in India, it is inevitable that he should ask what was the result of the contact between Greece and India. Was Alexander to Indian eyes nothing more than the irresistible cavalry leader before whose onset the greatest armies were scattered like chaff, or was he recognized, consciously or unconsciously, as the pioneer of Western civilization and the parent of model institutions? Did the long-continued government of Greek rulers in the Panjab vanish before the assault of rude barbarians without leaving a trace of its existence save coins, or did it impress a Hellenic stamp upon the ancient fabric of Indian polity?

Questions such as these have received widely divergent answers, but undoubtedly the general tendency of European scholars has been to exaggerate the Hellenizing effects of Alexander's invasion and of the Indo-Greek rule on the northwestern frontier. The most extreme "Hellenist" view is that expressed by Herr Niese, who is convinced that all the later development of India depends upon the institutions of Alexander, and that Chandragupta Maurya recognized the suzerainty of Seleukos Nikator. Such extravagant notions are so plainly opposed to the evidence that they might be supposed to need no refutation, but they have been accepted to a certain extent by English writers of repute, who are, as already observed, inclined naturally to believe that India, like Europe and a large part of Asia, must have yielded to the subtle action of Hellenic ideas.

It is therefore worth while to consider impartially and without prejudice the extent of the Hellenic influence upon India from the invasion of Alexander to the Kushan or Indo-Scythian conquest at the end of the first century of the Christian era, a period of four centuries in round numbers.

The author's opinion that India was not Hellenized by the operations of Alexander has been expressed in the chapter of this work dealing with his retreat from India, but it is advisable to remind the reader of the leading facts in connection with the more general question of Hellenic influence upon Indian civilization during four hundred years. In order to form a correct judgment in the matter, it is essential to bear dates in mind. Alexander stayed only nineteen months in India, and however far-reaching his plans may have been, it is manifestly impossible that during those few months of incessant conflict he should have founded Hellenic institutions on a permanent basis or materially affected the structure of Hindu polity and society. As a matter of fact he did nothing of the sort, and within two years of his death, with the exception of some small garrisons under Eudamos in the Indus valley, the whole apparatus of Macedonian rule had been swept away. After the year 316 B.C. not a trace of it remained. The only mark of Alexander's direct influence on India is the existence of a few coins modelled in imitation of Greek types which were struck by Saubhuti (Sophytes), the chief of the Salt Range, whom he subdued at the beginning of the voyage down the rivers.

Twenty years after Alexander's death, Seleukos Nikator attempted to recover the Macedonian conquests east of the Indus, but failed, and more than failed, being obliged not only to forego all claims on the provinces temporarily occupied by Alexander, but to surrender a large part of Ariana, west of the Indus, to Chandragupta Maurya. The Indian administration and society so well described by Megasthenes, the ambassador of Seleukos, were Hindu in character, with some features borrowed from Persia, but none from Greece. The assertion that the development of India depended on the institutions of Alexander is a grotesque travesty of the truth.

For eighty or ninety years after the death of Alexander the strong arm of the Maurya emperors held India for the Indians against all comers, and those monarchs treated with their Hellenistic neighbours on equal terms. Asoka was much more anxious to communicate the blessings of Buddhist teaching to Antiochos and Ptolemy than to borrow Greek notions from them. Although it appears to be certainly true that Indian plastic and pictorial art, such as it was, drew its inspiration from Hellenistic Alexandrian models during the Maurya period, the Greek influence merely touched the fringe of Hindu civilization, and was powerless to modify the structure of Indian institutions in any essential respect.

For almost a hundred years after the failure of Seleukos Nikator no Greek sovereign presumed to attack India. Then Antiochos the Great (*cir.* 206 B.C.) marched through the hills of the country now called Afghanistan, and went home by Kandahar and Sistan, levying a war indemnity of treasure and elephants upon a local chief. This brief campaign can have had no appreciable effect on the institutions of India, and its occurrence was probably unknown to many of the courts east of the Indus.

The subsequent invasions of Demetrios, Eukratides, and Menander, which extended with intervals over a period of about half a century (190 - 153 B.C.), penetrated more deeply into the interior of the country; but they, too, were transient raids, and cannot possibly have affected seriously the ancient and deeply rooted civilization of India. It is noticeable that the Hindu astronomer refers to Menander's Greeks as the "viciously valiant Yavanas." The Indians were impressed by both Alexander and Menander as mighty captains, not as missionaries of culture, and no doubt regarded both those sovereigns as impure barbarians, to be feared, but not imitated.

The East has seldom shown much readiness to learn from the West, and when Indians have condescended, as in the cases of relief sculpture and the drama, to borrow ideas from European teachers, the thing borrowed has been so cleverly disguised in native trappings that the originality of the Indian imitators is stoutly maintained even by acute and learned critics.

The Panjab, or a considerable part of it, with some of the adjoining regions, remained more or less under Greek rule for nearly two centuries and a half, from the time of Demetrios (190 B. C.) to the overthrow of Hermaios by the Kushans (*cir.* 50 A. D.), and we might reasonably expect to find clear signs of Hellenization in those countries. But the traces of Hellenic influence even there are surprisingly slight and trivial. Except the coins, which retain Greek legends on the obverse, and are throughout mainly Greek in type, although they begin to be bilingual from the time of Demetrios and Eukratides, scarcely any indication of the prolonged foreign rule can be specified. The coinage undoubtedly goes far to prove that the Greek language was that used in the courts of the frontier princes, but the introduction of native legends on the reverses demonstrates that it was not understood by the people at large. No inscriptions in that tongue have yet been discovered, and the single Greek name, Theodore, met with in a native record, comes from the Suwat valley, and is of late date, probably 56 A. D.

There is no evidence that Greek architecture was ever introduced into India. A temple with Ionic pillars, dating from the time of Azes (either Azes I, 50 B. C., or Azes II, some fifty years later), has been discovered at Taxila; but the plan of the building is not Greek, and the pillars of foreign pattern are merely borrowed ornaments. The earliest known example of Indo-Greek sculpture belongs to the same period, the reign of Azes, and not a single specimen can be referred to the times of Demetrios, Eukratides, and Menander, not to speak of Alexander. The well-known sculptures of Gandhara, the region around Peshawar, are much later in date, and are the offspring of cosmopolitan Græco-Roman art.

The conclusion of the matter is that the invasions of Alexander, Antiochos the Great, Demetrios, Eukratides, and Menander were in fact, whatever their authors may have intended, merely military incursions, which left no appreciable mark upon the institutions of India. The prolonged occupation of the Panjab and neighbouring regions by Greek rulers had extremely little effect in Hellenizing the country. Greek political institutions and architecture were rejected, although to a small extent Hellenic example was accepted in the decorative arts, and the Greek language must have been familiar to the officials at the kings' courts. The literature of Greece was probably known more or less to some of the native officers, who were obliged to learn their masters' language for business purposes, but that language was not widely diffused, and the impression made by Greek authors upon Indian literature and science is not traceable until after the close of the period under discussion.

CHAPTER X

THE KUSHAN OR INDO-SCYTHIAN DYNASTY

FROM 56 TO 225 A. D.

THE migrations of the nomad nations of the Mongolian steppes, briefly noticed in the preceding chapter, produced on the political fortunes of India effects so momentous that they deserve and demand fuller treatment.

A tribe of Turki nomads, known to Chinese authors as the Hiung-nu, succeeded in inflicting upon a neighbouring and rival horde of the same stock a decisive defeat about the middle of the second century B. C. The date of this event is fixed as 165 B. C. by most scholars, but M. Chavannes puts it some twenty or twenty-five years later. The Yueh-chi were compelled to quit the lands which they occupied in the province of Kan-suh in Northwestern China, and to migrate westwards in search of fresh pasture-grounds. The moving horde mustered a force of bowmen, estimated to number from one hundred to two hundred thousand, and the whole multitude must have comprised at least from half a million to a million persons of all ages and both sexes.

In the course of their westward migration in search of grazing-grounds adequate for the sustenance of their vast numbers of horses, cattle, and sheep, the Yueh-chi, moving along the route past Kucha (N. lat. 41° 38′, E. long. 83° 25′), to the north of the desert of Gobi, came into conflict with a smaller horde, named Wu-sun, which occupied the basin of the Ili River and its southern tributaries, the Tékès and Kongès. The Wu-sun, although numbering a force of only ten thousand bowmen, could not submit patiently to the devastation of their lands, and sought to defend them. But the superior numbers of the Yueh-chi assured the success of the invaders, who slew the Wu-sun chieftain, and then passed on westwards, beyond Lake Issyk-kul, the Lake Tsing of Hiuen Tsang, in search of more spacious pastures. A small section of the immigrants, diverging to the south, settled on the Tibetan border, and became known as the Little Yueh-chi, while the main body, which continued the westward march, was designated the Great Yueh-chi.

The next foes encountered by the Yueh-chi were the Sakas, or Se, who probably included more than one horde, for, as Herodotus observes, the Persians were accustomed to use the term Sakai to denote all Scythian nomads. The Sakas, who dwelt to the west of the Wu-sun, probably in the territory between the Jaxartes (Syr Darya) and Chu Rivers, also attempted to defend their lands, but met with even worse success than the Wu-sun, being compelled to vacate their pasture-grounds in favour of the victorious Yueh-chi, who occupied them. The Sakas were forced to migrate in search of new quarters, and, ultimately, as stated in the last preceding chapter, made their way into India and Sistan.

For some fifteen or twenty years the Yueh-chi remained undisturbed in their usurped territory. But meantime their ancient enemies, the Hiung-nu, had protected the infant son of the slain Wu-sun chieftain, who had grown to manhood under their care. This youth, with Hiung-nu help, attacked the Yueh-chi, and avenged his father's death by driving them from the lands which they had wrested from the Sakas. Being thus forced to resume their march, the Yueh-chi moved into the valley of the Oxus, and reduced to subjection its peaceful inhabitants, known to the Chinese as Ta-hia. The political domination of the Yueh-chi was probably extended at once over Bactria, to the south of the Oxus, but the headquarters of the horde continued for many years to be on the north side of the river, and the pastures on that side sufficed for the wants of the newcomers.

In the course of time, which may be estimated at two or three generations, the Yueh-chi lost their nomad habits, became a settled, territorial nation, in actual occupation of the Bactrian lands south of the river, as well as of Sogdiana to the north, and were divided into five principalities. As a rough approximation to the truth, this political and social development, with its accompanying growth of population, may be assumed to have been completed about 70 B.C.

For the next century nothing is known about Yueh-chi history; but more than a hundred years after the division of the nation into five territorial principalities situated to the north of the Hindu Kush, the chief of the Kushan section of the horde, who is conventionally known to European writers as Kadphises I, succeeded in imposing his authority on his colleagues and establishing himself as sole monarch of the Yueh-chi nation. His accession as such may be dated in the year 45 A. D., which cannot be very far wrong.

The pressure of population upon the means of subsistence, which had impelled the Yueh-chi horde to undertake the long and arduous march from the borders of China to the Hindu Kush, now drove it across that barrier, and stimulated Kadphises I to engage in the formidable task of subjugating the provinces to the south of the mountains.

He made himself master of Ki-pin (Kashmir?) as well as of the Kabul territory, and, in the course of a long reign, consolidated his power in Bactria, and found time to attack the Parthians. His empire thus extended from the frontiers of Persia to the Indus, and included Sogdiana, now the Khanate of Bukhara, with probably all the territories comprised in the existing kingdom of Afghanistan. The complete subjugation of the hardy mountaineers of the Afghan highlands, who have withstood so many invaders with success, must have occupied many years, and cannot be assigned to any particular year, but 60 A. D. may be taken as a mean date for the conquest of Kabul.

The Yueh-chi advance necessarily involved the suppression of the Indo-Greek and Indo-Parthian chiefs of principalities to the west of the Indus, and in the preceding chapter proof has been given of the manner in which the coinage legibly records the outline of the story of the gradual supersession of Hermaios, the last Greek prince of Kabul, by the barbarian invaders. The final extinction of the Indo-Parthian power in the Panjab and the Indus valley was reserved, however, for the reign of the successor of Kadphises I, who is most conveniently designated as Kadphises II.

At the age of eighty Kadphises I closed his victorious reign, and was succeeded, in or about 85 A. D., by his son Kadphises II. This prince, no less ambitious and enterprising than his father, devoted himself to the further extension of the Yueh-chi dominion, and even ventured to measure swords with the Chinese emperor.

The embassy of Chang-kien in 125 - 115 B. C. to the Yueh-chi, while they still resided in Sogdiana to the north of the Oxus, had brought the western barbarians into touch with the Middle Kingdom, and for a century and a quarter the Emperors of China kept up intercourse with the Scythian powers. In the year 8 A. D. official relations ceased, and when the first Han dynasty came to an end in 23 or 24 A. D., Chinese influence in the western countries had been reduced to nothing. Fifty years later Chinese ambition re-asserted itself, and for a period of thirty years, from 73 to 102 A. D., General Pan-chao led an army from victory to victory as far as the confines of the Roman empire. The King of Khotan, who had first made his submission in 73 A. D., was followed by several other princes, including the King of Kashgar, and the route to the west along the southern edge of the desert was thus opened to the arms and commerce of China. The reduction of Kuché and Kharachar in 94 A. D. similarly threw open the northern road.

The steady advance of the victorious Chinese evidently alarmed Kadphises II, who regarded himself as the equal of the emperor and had no intention of accepting the position of a vassal. Accordingly, in 90 A. D., he boldly asserted his equality by demanding a Chinese princess in marriage. General Pan-chao, who considered the proposal an affront to his master, arrested the envoy and sent him home. Kadphises II, unable to brook this treatment, equipped a formidable force of seventy thousand cavalry under the command of his viceroy Si, which was despatched across the Tsung-ling range, or Taghdumbash Pamir, to attack the Chinese. The army of Si probably advanced by the Tashkurghan pass, some fourteen thousand feet high, and was so shattered by its sufferings during the passage of the mountains, that, when it emerged into the plain below, either that of Kashgar or Yarkand, it fell an easy prey to Pan-chao, and was totally defeated. Kadphises II was compelled to pay tribute to China, and the Chinese annals record the arrival of several missions bearing tribute at this period.

This serious check did not crush the ambition of

the Yueh-chi monarch, who now undertook the easier task of attacking India. Success in this direction compensated for failure against the power of China, and the Yueh-chi dominion was gradually extended (90 to 100 A. D.) all over Northwestern India, with the exception of Southern Sind, probably as far east as Benares. The conquered Indian provinces were administered by military viceroys, to whom apparently should be attributed the large issues of coins known to numismatists as those of the Nameless King. These pieces, mostly copper, but including a few in base silver, are certainly contemporary with Kadphises II, and are extremely common all over Northern India from the Kabul valley to Benares and Ghazipur on the Ganges.

The Yueh-chi conquests opened up the path of commerce between the Roman empire and India. Kadphises I, who struck coins in bronze or copper only, imitated, after his conquest of Kabul, the coinage either of Augustus in his later years, or the similar coinage of Tiberius (14 to 38 A. D.). When the Roman gold of the early emperors began to pour into India in payment for the silks, spices, gems, and dye-stuffs of the East, Kadphises II perceived the advantage of a gold currency, and struck an abundant issue of Orientalized *aurei*, agreeing in weight with their prototypes, and not much inferior in purity. In Southern India, which, during the same period, maintained an active maritime trade with the Roman empire, the local

COPPER COIN OF KADPHISES, KUSHAN DYNASTY.

kings did not attempt to copy the imperial *aurei*, which, however, they imported in large quantities, and used for currency purposes, just as English sovereigns now are in many parts of the world.

The Indian embassy, which offered its congratulations to Trajan after his arrival in Rome in 99 A. D., was probably despatched by Kadphises II to announce his conquest of Northwestern India.

The temporary annexation of Mesopotamia by Trajan in 116 A. D. brought the Roman frontier within six hundred miles of the western limits of the Yueh-chi empire. Although the province beyond the Euphrates was retroceded by Hadrian the year after its annexation, there can be no doubt that at this period the rulers of Northern and Western India were well acquainted with the fame and power of the great Western empire, and were sensibly influenced by its example.

The victorious reign of Kadphises II was undoubtedly prolonged, and may be supposed to have covered a space of thirty-five or forty years, from about 85 to 120 or 125 A. D., when he was succeeded by Kanishka, who alone among the Kushan kings has left a name cherished by tradition, and famous far beyond the limits of India. His name, it is true, is unknown in Europe, save to a few students of unfamiliar lore, but it lives in the legends of Tibet, China, and Mongolia, and is scarcely less significant to the Buddhists of those lands than that of Asoka himself.

Notwithstanding the widespread fame of Kanishka, his authentic history is scanty, and his chronological position strangely open to doubt. Unluckily, no passage in the works of the accurate Chinese historians has yet been discovered which synchronizes him with any definite name or event in the well-ascertained history of the Middle Kingdom. The Chinese books which mention him are all, so far as is yet known, merely works of edification, and not well adapted to serve as mines of historic fact. They are, in truth, translations or echoes of Indian tradition, as are the books of Tibet and Mongolia, and no student needs to be told how baffling are its vagaries.

Kanishka and his proximate successors certainly are mentioned in an exceptionally large number of inscriptions, of which more than a score are dated, and it might be expected that this ample store of epigraphic material would set at rest all doubts and establish beyond dispute the essential outlines of the Kushan chronology. But, unfortunately, the dates are recorded in such a fashion as to be open to most various interpretations, and eminent scholars are still to be found who place the accession of Kanishka in 57 B. C., as well as others who date that event in 278 A. D. Many lines of evidence, which are of great collective force when brought together, lead to the conclusion that Kanishka was the contemporary of Hadrian and Marcus Aurelius, and came to the throne about 120 or 125 A. D., directly succeeding Kadphises II.

Kanishka unquestionably belonged to the Kushan section of the Yueh-chi nation, as did the Kadphises kings, and there does not seem to be sufficient reason for believing that he was not connected with them. The coins both of Kadphises II and Kanishka frequently display in the field the same four-pronged symbol, and agree accurately in weight and fineness, besides exhibiting a very close relationship in the obverse devices. The inevitable inference is that the two kings were very near in time to one another—in fact, that one immediately followed the other. Now Kadphises II (Yen-kao-ching) was beyond doubt not only the successor, but the son of Kadphises I (Kieu-tsieu-k'io), who died at the age of eighty after a long reign. It is quite impossible to bring Kanishka into close association with Kadphises II, except on the generally admitted assumption that Kanishka was his immediate successor. Without further pursuing in detail a tedious archæological argument, it will suffice to say here that ample reason can be shown for holding that the great majority of Indianists are right in placing the Kanishka group directly after that of the Kadphises kings.

Kanishka then may be assumed to have succeeded Kadphises II, to whom he was presumably related, in or about 120 or 125 A. D. Tradition and the monuments and inscriptions of his time prove that his sway, like that of his predecessor, extended all over Northwestern India, probably as far south as the Vindhyas. His coins are found constantly associated with those of Kadphises II from Kabul to Ghazipur on the Ganges, and their vast number and variety indicate a reign of considerable length. His dominions included Upper Sind, and his high reputation as a conqueror suggests the probability that he extended his power to the mouths of the Indus and swept away the petty Parthian princes who still ruled that region at the close of the first century A. D., but are no more heard of afterward.

He probably completed the subjugation and annexation of the secluded vale of Kashmir, and certainly showed a marked preference for that delightful country, in which he erected numerous monuments, and founded a town, which, although now reduced to a petty village, still bears his honoured name.

Tradition affirms that he carried his arms far into the interior, and attacked the king residing at the ancient imperial city of Pataliputra. It is said that he carried off from that city a Buddhist saint named Asvaghosha. But little dependence can be placed upon ecclesiastical traditions which connect the names of famous saints with those of renowned kings, and all such traditions need confirmation.

Kanishka's capital was Purushapura, the modern Peshawar, the city which then guarded, as it now does, the main road from the Afghan hills to the Indian plains. There, in his latter days, when he had become a fervent Buddhist, he erected a great relic tower, which seems to have deserved to rank among the wonders of the world. The superstructure of carved wood rose in thirteen stories to a height of at least four hundred feet, surmounted by a mighty iron pinnacle. When Song-yun, a Chinese pilgrim, visited the spot at the beginning of the sixth century, this structure had been thrice destroyed by fire, and as often rebuilt by pious kings. A monastery of exceptional magnificence stood by its side. Faint traces of the substructures of these buildings may even now be discerned at the "King's Mound" (*Shahji-ki-Dheri*) outside the Lahore gate of Peshawar.

The monastery was still flourishing as a place of Buddhist education as late as the ninth or tenth century, when Prince Vira Deva of Magadha was sent there to

FORT JAMRUD, PESHAWAR.

benefit by the instruction of the resident teachers, who were famous for their piety. The final demolition of this celebrated establishment was undoubtedly due to the Mohammedan invasions of Mahmud of Ghazni and his successors. Moslem zeal against idolatry was always excited to acts of destruction by the spectacle of the innumerable images with which Buddhist holy places were crowded.

The ambition of Kanishka was not confined by the

limits of India. He engaged in successful war with the Parthians, when attacked by the king of that nation, who is described by the tradition as "very stupid and with a violent temper." The prince referred to may be either Chosroes (Khusru) or one of the rival kings who disputed the possession of the Parthian throne between 108 and 130 A.D.

The most striking military exploit of Kanishka was his conquest of Kashgar, Yarkand, and Khotan, extensive provinces lying to the north of Tibet and the east of the Pamirs, and at that time, as now, dependencies of China. Kadphises II, when he attempted the same arduous adventure in 90 A.D., had failed ignominiously, and had been compelled to pay tribute to China. Kanishka, secure in the peaceful possession of India and Kashmir, was better prepared to surmount the appalling difficulties of conveying an effective army across the passes of the Taghdumbash Pamir, which no modern ruler of India would dare to face, and he had no longer General Pan-chao to oppose him. Where his predecessor had failed, Kanishka succeeded, and he not only freed himself from the obligation of paying tribute to China, but compelled the defeated kings to surrender hostages, including a son of the Han Emperor of China, who built a Buddhist shrine at the place of his detention in the province of Kapisa.

These hostages were treated, as beseemed their rank, with the utmost consideration, and were assigned suitable residences at different Buddhist monasteries for each of the three seasons,—the hot, the cold, and the rainy. During the time of the summer heats, when the burning plains are not pleasant to live in, they enjoyed the cool breezes at a monastery in the hills of Kapisa beyond Kabul, which was erected specially for their accommodation. The Chinese prince deposited a store of jewels as an endowment for this establishment before his return home, and was gratefully remembered for centuries. When Hiuen Tsang visited the place in the seventh century, he found the walls adorned with paintings of the prince and his companions attired in the garb of China, while the resident monks still honoured the memory of their benefactor with prayers and offerings. The residence of the hostages during the cold season was at an unidentified place in the Eastern Panjab, to which the name of Chinapati was given in consequence. The situation of their abode during the rains is not mentioned. An incidental result of the stay of the hostages in Kanishka's dominions was the introduction of the pear and peach, both of which had been previously unknown in India.

The biographer of Hiuen Tsang tells a curious story about the treasure deposited by the Chinese prince as an endowment for the Chinapati shrine, which was known to be buried under the feet of the image of Vaisravana, the Great Spirit King, at the south side of the eastern gate of the hall of Buddha. An impious raja who tried to appropriate the hoard was frightened away by portents which seemed to indicate the displeasure of its guardian spirit, and when the monks endeavoured to make use of it for the purpose of repairing the shrine, in accordance with the donor's intention, they too were terrified by similar manifestations.

While Hiuen Tsang was lodging at the shrine during the rainy season, the monks besought him to use his influence with the spirit to obtain permission to expend the treasure on urgently needed repairs of the steeple. The pilgrim complied, burned incense, and duly assured the guardian spirit that no waste or misappropriation would be permitted. The workmen who were set to dig up the spot then suffered no molestation, and at a depth of seven or eight feet found a great copper vessel containing several hundredweights of gold and a quantity of pearls. The balance of the treasure left after the repairs to the steeple has doubtless been appropriated long since by excavators less scrupulous than the pious Master of the Law.

The monks of the Chinapati monastery were followers of the ancient form of Buddhism known as the Hinayana, or Lesser Vehicle, and the narrative implies that the Chinese prince belonged to the same sect. If he was really a Buddhist, it is of interest to speculate whether he brought his creed with him or learned it in India. The stories dating from the seventh century which narrate the arrival of Buddhist missionaries in China in 217 B.C., although favourably regarded by Professor Terrien de Lacouperie, are generally disbelieved and are highly improbable.

The missionaries despatched by Asoka in the middle of the third century B.C. were directed to the south and west, not to the east, and there is little or no evidence of intercourse between India and China before the time of the Yueh-chi invasion. The statement that the Emperor Ming-ti sent for Buddhist teachers in or about 64 A.D., although rejected by Wassiljew, has been accepted by most writers; but even those authors who admit the fact that Buddhist missionaries reached China at that date allow that their influence was very slight and limited. The effective introduction of Buddhism into China appears not to have taken place until the reign of Hwan-ti, about the middle of the second century, when "the people of China generally adopted this new religion, and its followers became numerous." This development of Chinese Buddhism was apparently the direct result of Kanishka's conquest of Khotan, and it is consequently improbable that the Han prince brought his Buddhist creed with him. It may be assumed that he adopted it during his stay in India and that when he returned home he became an agent for its diffusion in his native land. Wassiljew's view that the Buddhist religion did not become widely known in China until the fourth century is not inconsistent with the belief that the Indian system was effectively introduced to a limited extent two centuries earlier.

The stories told about Kanishka's conversion and his subsequent zeal for Buddhism have so much resemblance to the Asoka legends that it is difficult to decide how far they are traditions of actual fact, and how far merely echoes of an older tradition. The Yueh-chi monarch did not record passages from his autobiography as Asoka did, and when we are informed in the pages of a pious tract that his conversion was due to remorse for the blood shed during his wars, it is impossible to check the statement. Probably it is merely an echo of the story of Asoka, as told by himself.

Just as the writers of edifying books sought to enhance the glory of Asoka's conversion to the creed of the mild Sakya sage by blood-curdling tales of his

NAGA PEOPLE WORSHIPPING THE TRISUL EMBLEM OF BUDDHA, ON A FIERY PILLAR.
From a bas-relief at Amaravati.

fiendish cruelty during the days of his unbelief, so Kanishka was alleged to have had no faith either in right or wrong, and to have lightly esteemed the law of Buddha during his earlier life. The most authentic evidence on the subject of his changes of faith is afforded by the long and varied series of his coins, which, like all ancient coinages, reflect the religious ideas of the monarch in whose name they were struck. The finest, and presumably the earliest, pieces bear legends,

Greek both in script and language, with effigies of the sun and moon personified under their Greek names, Helios and Selene. On later issues the Greek script is retained, but the language is a form of old Persian, while the deities depicted are a strange medley of the gods worshipped by Greeks, Persians, and Indians. The rare coins exhibiting images of Buddha Sakyamuni with his name in Greek letters are usually considered to be among the latest of the reign, but they are well executed and may be earlier in date than is generally supposed. It is impossible to fix the exact date of Kanishka's conversion, but the event evidently did not occur until he had been for some years on the throne.

The appearance of the Buddha among a crowd of heterogeneous deities would have appeared strange, in fact would have been inconceivable to Asoka, while it seemed quite natural to Kanishka. The newer Buddhism of his day, designated as the Mahayana, or Great Vehicle, was largely of foreign origin, and developed as the result of the complex interaction of Indian, Zoroastrian, Christian, Gnostic, and Hellenic elements, which was made possible by the conquests of Alexander, the formation of the Maurya empire in India, and, above all, by the unification of the Roman world under the sway of the earlier emperors. In this newer Buddhism the sage Gautama became in practice, if not in theory, a god, with his ears open to the prayers of the faithful, and served by a hierarchy of Bodhisattvas and other beings acting as mediators between him and sinful men. Such a Buddha rightly took a place among the gods of the nations comprised in Kanishka's wide-spread empire, and the monarch, even after his "con-

EXTERNAL ELEVATION OF THE GREAT RAIL AT AMARAVATI.

version," probably continued to honour both the old and the new gods, as, in a later age, Harsha did alternate reverence to Siva and Buddha.

The celebrated Gandhara sculptures, of which the best examples date from the time of Kanishka and his proximate successors, give vivid expression in classical forms of considerable artistic merit to this modified Buddhism, a religion with a complicated mythology and well-filled pantheon. The florid Corinthian capitals and many other characteristic features of the style prove that the Gandhara school was merely a branch of the cosmopolitan Græco-Roman art of the early empire.

In Buddhist ecclesiastical history the reign of Kanishka is specially celebrated for the convocation of a council, organized on the model of that supposed to have been summoned by Asoka. Kanishka's council, which is ignored by the Ceylonese chroniclers, who probably never heard of it, is known only from the traditions of Northern India, as preserved by Tibetan, Chinese, and Mongolian writers. The accounts of this assembly, like those of the earlier councils, are discrepant, and the place of meeting is named variously as the Kundalavana Vihara, somewhere in Kashmir, the Kuvana monastery at Jalandhar in the north of the Panjab, or Kandahar.

According to some authorities, the assembly, like its predecessors, was concerned with the compilation and expurgation of the scriptures purporting to be the very words of Buddha, while, according to others, its business was restricted to the preparation of elaborate commentaries on all the three *pitakas*, or main divisions, of the pre-existing canon. Comparison of the different authorities may be held to justify the conclusion that the council was a reality; that it met first somewhere in Kashmir, and adjourned to Jalandhar (or, possibly, met first in Jalandhar, and adjourned to Kashmir), where it completed its sittings; and that it set the stamp of its approval on certain commentaries prepared in accordance with the teaching of the Sarvastivadin school, and its derivative, the Vaibashika. If it be true, as Hiuen Tsang was told, that the works authorized by the council were engraved on copper plates and deposited in a *stupa*, it is possible that they may yet be revealed by some lucky chance. But the vagueness of the statements concerning the locality of the council precludes the possibility of deliberate search for the alleged records of its decisions. The assembly is said to have been convened by the king on the advice of a saint named Parsvika, and to have sat under the presidency of Vasumitra.

The legends published by M. Sylvain Lévi include a strange tale professing to relate the end of Kanishka, which may possibly be founded on fact.

"The king," so runs the story, "had a minister named Mathara, of unusual intelligence. He addressed Kanishka in these words: 'Sire, if you wish to follow the advice of your servant, your power will assuredly bring the whole world into subjection. All will submit to you, and the eight regions will take refuge in your merit. Think over what your servant has said, but do not divulge it.' The king replied: 'Very well, it shall be as you say.' Then the minister called together the able generals and equipped a force of the four arms. Wherever the king turned, all men bowed before him like herbage under hail. The peoples of three regions came in to make their submission; under the hoofs of the horse ridden by King Kanishka everything either bent or broke. The king said: 'I have subjugated three regions; all men have taken refuge with me; the region of the north alone has not come in to make its submission. If I subjugate it, I shall never again take advantage of an opportunity against any one, be he who he may; but I do not yet know the best way to succeed in this undertaking.' The king's people, having heard these words, took counsel together and said: 'The king is greedy, cruel, and unreasonable; his campaigns and continued conquests have wearied the mass of his servants. He knows not how to be content, but wants to reign over the four quarters. The garrisons are stationed on distant frontiers, and our relatives are far from us. Such being the situation, we must agree among ourselves, and get rid of him. After that we may be happy.' As he was ill, they covered him with a quilt, a man sat on top of him, and the king died on the spot."

The reign of Kanishka appears to have lasted some twenty-five or thirty years, and may be assumed to have terminated about 150 A. D.

Very little is known about the successors of Kanishka. He was immediately followed by Huvishka, or Hushka, who was probably his son, and appears to have retained undiminished the great empire to which he succeeded. His dominions certainly included Kabul, Kashmir, Gaya, and Mathura. At the last named city, a splendid Buddhist monastery bore his name and no doubt owed its existence to his munificence, for, like Kanishka, he was a liberal patron of Buddhist ecclesiastical institutions. But he also resembled his more famous predecessor in an eclectic taste for a strange medley of Greek, Indian, and Persian deities. The types on the coins of Huvishka include Heracles, Sarapis, Skanda with his son Visakha, Pharro, the fire-god, and many others, but the figure and name of Buddha are wanting. It would seem that the Buddhist convictions of these old Turkish kings were not very deeply seated, and it is probably justifiable to hold that the royal favour was granted to the powerful monastic organization of the Buddhists as much as to their creed. No prudent monarch in those days could afford to neglect the wealthy and influential order, which had spread its ramifications all over the empire.

The town of Hushkapura, founded by Huvishka in Kashmir, occupied a position of exceptional importance just inside the Baramula Pass, then known as the "western gate" of the valley, and continued for centuries to be a place of note. When Hiuen Tsang visited Kashmir about 631 A.D., he enjoyed the liberal hospitality of the Hushkapura monastery for several days, and was escorted thence with all honour to the capital, where he found numerous religious institutions, attended by some five thousand monks. The town of Hushkapura is now represented by the small village of Ushkür, at which the ruins of an ancient *stupa* are visible.

The reign of Huvishka was undoubtedly prolonged, but all memory of its political events has perished. His abundant and varied coinage is little inferior in interest or artistic merit to that of Kanishka, with which it is constantly associated, and, like the contemporary sculpture, testifies to the continuance of Hellenistic influence. A few specimens of the gold coinage present well executed and characteristic portraits of the king, who was a determined-looking man, with strongly marked features, large, deep-set eyes, and an aquiline nose. So far as appears, the Kushan power suffered no diminution during his reign.

Huvishka was succeeded by Vasudeva, whose thoroughly Indian name is a proof of the rapidity with which the foreign invaders had succumbed to the influence of their environment. Testimony to the same fact is borne by his coins, almost all of which exhibit on the reverse the figure of the Indian god Siva, attended by his bull Nandi, and accompanied by the noose, trident, and other insignia of Hindu iconography. The inscriptions of Vasudeva, found chiefly at Mathura, certainly range in date from the year 74 to the year 98 of the era used in the Kushan age, and indicate a reign of not less than twenty-five years. If the Sanchi inscription bears the date 68, the reign would have lasted about thirty-five years.

It is evident that the Kushan power must have been decadent during the latter part of the long reign of Vasudeva, and apparently before its close, or immediately after that event, the vast empire of Kanishka obeyed the usual law governing Oriental monarchies, and broke up into fragments, after a brief period of splendid unity. Coins bearing the name of Vasudeva continued to be struck long after he had passed away, and ultimately present the royal figure clad in the garb of Persia, and manifestly imitated from the effigy of Sapor (Shahpur) I, the Sasanian monarch who ruled Persia from 238 to 269 A. D.

Absolutely nothing is known positively concerning the means by which this renewed Persian influence made itself felt in the interior of India. Bahram (Varahran) II is known to have conducted a campaign in Sistan at some time between 277 and 294, but there is no record of any Sasanian invasion of India in the third century, during which period all the ordinary sources of historical information dry up. No inscriptions certainly referable to that time have been discovered, and the coinage, issued by merely local rulers, gives little help. Certain it is that two great paramount dynasties, the Kushan in Northern India, and the Andhra in the table-land of the Deccan, disappear together almost at the moment when the Arsakidan dynasty of Persia was superseded by the Sasanian. It is impossible to avoid hazarding the conjecture that the three events were in some way connected, and that the Persianizing of the Kushan coinage of Northern India should be explained by the occurrence of an unrecorded Persian invasion. But the conjecture is unsupported by direct evidence, and the invasion, if it really took place, would seem to have been the work of predatory tribes subject to Iranian influence, rather than a regular attack by a Persian king.

So much, however, is clear that Vasudeva was the last Kushan king who continued to hold extensive territories in India. After his death there is no indication of the existence of a paramount power in Northern India. Probably numerous rajas asserted their independence and formed a number of short-lived states, such as commonly arise from the ruins of a great Oriental monarchy; but historical material for the third century is so completely lacking that it is impossible to say what or how many those states were.

The period was evidently one of extreme confusion, associated with foreign invasions from the northwest, which is reflected in the muddled statements of the *Vishnu Purana* concerning the Abhiras, Gardabhilas, Sakas, Yavanas, Bahlikas, and other outlandish dynasties named as the successors of the Andhras. The dynasties thus enumerated were clearly to a large extent contemporary, not consecutive, and none of them could claim paramount rank. It seems to be quite hopeless to attempt to reduce to order the Puranic accounts of this anarchical period, and nothing would be gained by quoting a long list of names, the very forms of which are uncertain.

Coins indicate that the Kushans held their own in the Panjab and Kabul for a long time. It is certain that the Kushan Kings of Kabul continued to be a considerable power until the fifth century, when they were overthrown by the White Huns. At the beginning of the fourth century one of them gave a daughter in marriage to Hormazd II, the Sasanian King of Persia, and when Sapor II besieged Amida, in 360 A.D., his victory over the Roman garrison was won with the aid of Indian elephants and Kushan troops under the command of their aged king, Grumbates, who occupied the place of honour and was supported by the Sakas of Sistan.

INDIAN PALMS.

It is difficult to judge how far the foreign chiefs who ruled the Panjab during the third century and struck coins similar to those of Vasudeva, yet with a difference, were Kushans, and how far they belonged to other Asiatic tribes. The marginal legends of the coins of this class, which are written in a modified Greek script, preserve the name either of Kanishka or Vasu[deva] Kushan, King of Kings, and so recognize the Kushan supremacy; but the name in Indian letters placed by the side of the spear is frequently monosyllabic, like a Chinese name, *Bha*, *Ga*, *Vi*, and so forth. These monosyllabic names seem to belong to chiefs of various Central Asian tribes who invaded India and acknowledged the supremacy of the Kushan or Shahi Kings of Kabul. One coin with the modified Kushan obverse, and the names *Bashana*, *Nu*, *Pakaldhi* (?) in Indian Brahmi characters in various parts of the field, has on the reverse a fire altar of the type found on the coins of the earliest Sasanian kings. It is thus clear that in some way or other, during the third century, the Panjab renewed its ancient connection with Persia.

Nothing definite is recorded concerning the dynasties of Northern India, excluding the Panjab, during the third century, and the early part of the fourth. The imperial city of Pataliputra is known to have continued to be a place of importance as late as the fifth century, but there is not even the slightest indication of the nature of the dynasty which ruled there during the third. The only intelligible dynastic list for the period is that of the Saka satraps of Western India, whose history will be more conveniently noticed in the next chapter in connection with that of the Gupta emperors.

CHAPTER XI

THE GUPTA EMPIRE AND THE WESTERN SATRAPS: CHANDRAGUPTA I TO KUMARAGUPTA I

FROM 320 TO 455 A.D.

THE period between the extinction of the Kushan and Andhra dynasties, about 220 or 230 A.D., and the rise of the imperial Gupta dynasty, nearly a century later, is one of the darkest in the whole range of Indian history. In the fourth century light again dawns, the veil of oblivion is lifted, and the history of India regains unity and interest.

A local raja at or near Pataliputra, bearing the famous name of Chandragupta, wedded, in or about the year 308, a princess named Kumara Devi, who belonged to the ancient Lichchhavi clan, celebrated ages before in the early annals of Buddhism. During the long period of about eight centuries which intervened between the reign of Ajatasatru and the marriage of Kumara Devi the history of the Lichchhavis has been lost. They now come suddenly into notice again in connection with this marriage, which proved to be an event of the highest political importance, being the foundation of the fortunes of a dynasty destined to rival the glories of the Mauryas.

Kumara Devi evidently brought to her husband as her dowry valuable influence, which in the course of a few years secured to him a paramount position in Magadha and the neighbouring countries. It seems probable that at the time of this fateful union the Lichchhavis were masters of the ancient imperial city, and that Chandragupta by means of his matrimonial alliance succeeded to the power previously held by his wife's relatives. In the olden days the Lichchhavis had been the rivals of the Kings of Pataliputra, and apparently, during the disturbed times which followed the reign of Pushyamitra, they paid off old scores by taking possession of the city, which had been built and fortified many centuries earlier for the express purpose of curbing their restless spirit.

Certain it is that Chandragupta was raised by his Lichchhavi connection from the rank of a local chief, as enjoyed by his father and grandfather, to such dignity that he felt justified in assuming the lofty title of "sovereign of Maharajas," usually associated with a claim to the rank of lord paramount. He struck coins in the joint names of himself, his queen, and the Lichchhavis, and his son and successor habitually described himself with pride as the son of the daughter of the Lichchhavis.

Chandragupta, designated as the First, to distinguish him from his grandson of the same name, extended his dominion along the Ganges valley as far as the junction of the Ganges and the Jumna, where Allahabad now stands, and ruled during his brief tenure of the throne a populous and fertile territory, which included Tirhut, Bihar, Oudh, and certain adjoining districts. His political importance was sufficient to warrant him in establishing, after the Oriental manner, a new era dating from his formal consecration, or coronation, when he was proclaimed as heir to the imperial power associated by venerable tradition with the possession of Pataliputra. The first year of the Gupta era, which continued in use for several centuries, ran from February 26, 320 A. D. to March 13, 321, of which dates the former may be taken as that of the coronation of Chandragupta I.

Before his death, which occurred five or six years later, Chandragupta selected as his successor the crown prince, Samudragupta, his son by the Lichchhavi princess. The paternal preference was abundantly justified by the young king, who displayed a degree of skill in the arts of both peace and war which entitles him to high rank among the most illustrious sovereigns of India.

From the moment of his accession, Samudragupta assumed the part of an aggressively ambitious monarch and resolved to increase his dominions at the expense of his neighbours. Wars of aggression have never been condemned by such public opinion as exists in the East, and no king who cared for his reputation could venture to rest contented within his own borders. Samudragupta had no hesitation in acting on the principle that "kingdom-taking" is the business of kings, and immediately after his succession to the throne plunged into war, which occupied many years of his unusually protracted reign.

When his fighting days were over, he employed a learned poet, skilled in the technicalities of Sanskrit verse, to compose a panegyric of his achievements, which he caused to be engraved on one of the stone pillars set up six centuries before by Asoka and incised with his edicts. Samudragupta, an orthodox Hindu, learned in all the wisdom of the Brahmans, and an ambitious soldier full of the joy of battle, who cared nothing for preachings of the monk Asoka recorded in an antique script and an unfamiliar dialect, made no scruple about setting his own ruthless boasts of sanguinary wars by the side of the quietest moralizings of him who deemed "the chiefest conquest" to be the conquest of piety.

Samudragupta's anxiety to provide for the remembrance of his deeds was not in vain. The record composed by his poet-laureate survives to this day practically complete, and furnishes a detailed contemporary account of the events of the reign, probably superior to anything else of the kind in the multitude of Indian inscriptions. Unfortunately the document is not dated, but it may be assigned with a very near approach to accuracy to the year 360 A. D., or a little earlier or later, and it is thus, apart from its value as history, of great interest as an important Sanskrit composition, partly in verse and partly in prose, of ascertained age and origin.

The value as dated literature of the great historical inscriptions, although emphasized by Bühler, is still, perhaps, not fully recognized by scholars who occupy themselves primarily with the literature preserved in libraries. But our concern at present in the elaborate composition of Harishena is with its contents as a historical document, rather than with its place in the evolution of Sanskrit.

The author of the panegyric classifies his lord's opponents geographically under four heads: eleven kings of the south; nine named Kings of Aryavarta, or the Ganges plain, besides many others not specified; the chiefs of the wild forest tribes; and the rulers of the frontier kingdoms and republics. He also explains Samudragupta's relations with certain foreign powers, too remote to come within the power of his arm. Although it is at present impossible to identify every one of the countries, kings, and peoples enumerated by the poet, enough is known to enable the historian to form a clear idea of the extent of the dominions and the range of the alliances of the most brilliant of the Gupta emperors. Since the matter of the record is arranged on literary rather than on historical principles, it is not possible to narrate the events of the reign in strict chronological order.

We may feel assured that this Indian Napoleon first turned his arms against the powers nearest him, and that he thoroughly subjugated the rajas of the Ganges plain, the wide region now known as Hindustan, before he embarked on his perilous adventures in the remote south. His treatment of the rajas of the north was drastic, for we are told that they were "forcibly rooted up," a process which necessarily involved the incorporation of their territories in the dominions of the victor. Among the nine names mentioned, only one can be recognized with certainty, that of Ganapati Naga, whose capital was at Padmavati, or Narwar, a famous city, which still exists in the territories of the Maharaja Sindia.

The greater part of these northern conquests must have been completed, and the subjugated territories absorbed, before Samudragupta ventured to undertake the invasion of the kingdoms of the south—a task which demanded uncommon boldness in design and masterly powers of organization and execution.

The invader, marching due south from the capital, through Chutia Nagpur, directed his first attack against the kingdom of South Kosala in the valley of the Mahanadi, and overthrew its king, Mahendra. Passing on, he subdued all the chiefs of the forest countries, which still retain their ancient wildness, and constitute the tributary states of Orissa and the more backward parts of the Central Provinces. The principal of those chiefs, who bore the appropriate name of Vyaghra Raja, or the Tiger King, is not otherwise known to history. At this stage of the campaign, the main difficulties must have been those of transport and supply, for the ill-armed forest tribes could not have offered serious military resistance to a well equipped army.

Still advancing southwards, by the east coast road,

Samudragupta vanquished the chieftain who held Pishtapura, now Pithapuram in the Godavari District, as well as the hill-forts of Mahendragiri and Kottura in Ganjam; King Mantaraja, whose territory lay on the banks of the Kolleru (Colair) Lake; the neighbouring Pallava King of Vengi between the Krishna and Godavari Rivers; and Vishnugopa, the Pallava King of Kanchi, or Conjevaram, to the southwest of Madras. Then turning westwards, he subjugated a third Pallava chieftain, named Ugrasena, King of Palakka, the modern Palghatcherry, situated in Malabar at the great gap in the Western Ghats.

This place, distant some twelve hundred miles in a direct line from Pataliputra, seems to have marked the southern limit of Samudragupta's audacious raid. He returned homewards through the western parts of the Deccan, subduing on his way the kingdom of Devarashtra, or the modern Mahratta country, and Erandapalla, or Khandesh.

This wonderful campaign, which involved more than three thousand miles of marching through difficult country, must have occupied about three years at least, and its conclusion may be dated approximately in 340 A. D.

No attempt was made to effect the permanent annexation of these southern states, and the triumphant victor admitted that he exacted only temporary submission and then withdrew. But beyond doubt he despoiled the rich treasuries of the south, and came back laden with golden booty, like the Mohammedan adventurer who performed the same military exploit nearly a thousand years later. Malik Kafur, the general of Ala-ud-din, Sultan of Delhi, in the years 1309 and 1310 repeated the performance of Samudragupta, operating, however, chiefly on the eastern side of the peninsula, and penetrating even farther south than his Hindu predecessor. He forced his way to Ramesvara, or Adam's Bridge, opposite Ceylon, where he built a mosque, which was still standing when Firishta wrote his history in the sixteenth century.

The enumeration by the courtly panegyrist of the frontier kingdoms and republics whose rulers did homage and paid tribute to the emperor, a title fairly earned by Samudragupta, enables the historians to define the boundaries of his dominions with sufficient accuracy, and to realize the nature of the political divisions of India in the fourth century.

On the eastern side of the continent the tributary kingdoms were Samatata, or the delta of the Ganges and Brahmaputra, including the site on which Calcutta now stands; Kamarupa, or Assam; and Davaka, which seems to have corresponded with the Bogra (Bagraha), Dinajpur, and Rajshahi Districts to the north of the Ganges, lying between Samatata and Kamarupa. Farther west, the mountain kingdom of Nepal, then, as now, retained its autonomy under the suzerainty of the paramount power, and the direct jurisdiction of the imperial government extended only to the foot of the mountains. The kingdom of Kartripura occupied the lower ranges of the Western Himalayas, including probably Kumaon, Almora, Garhwal, and Kangra.

The Panjab, Eastern Rajputana, and Malwa for the most part were in possession of tribes or clans living under republican institutions. The Yaudheya tribe occupied both banks of the Sutlaj, while the Madrakas held the central parts of the Panjab. The reader may remember that in Alexander's time these regions were similarly occupied by autonomous tribes, then called the Malloi, Kathaioi, and so forth. The Jumna probably formed the northwestern frontier of the Gupta empire. The Arjunayanas, Malavas, and Abhiras were settled in Eastern Rajputana and Malwa, and in this direction the river Chambal may be regarded as the imperial boundary. The line next turned in an easterly direction along the territories of minor nations whose position cannot be exactly determined, passing probably through Bhopal, until it struck the Narmada River, which formed the southern frontier.

VIEW OF BOTANICAL GARDENS, CALCUTTA.

The dominion under the direct government of Samudragupta in the middle of the fourth century thus comprised all the most populous and fertile countries of Northern India. It extended from the Hooghly on the east to the Jumna and Chambal on the west, and from the foot of the Himalayas on the north to the Narmada on the south.

Beyond these wide limits, the frontier kingdoms of Assam and the Ganges delta, as well as those on the southern slopes of the Himalayas, and the free tribes of Rajputana and Malwa, were attached to the empire by bonds of subordinate alliance, while almost all the kingdoms of the south had been overrun by the emperor's armies and compelled to acknowledge his irresistible might.

The empire thus defined was by far the greatest that had been seen in India since the days of Asoka, six centuries before, and its possession naturally entitled Samudragupta to the respect of foreign powers. We are not, therefore, surprised to learn that he maintained diplomatic relations with the Kushan King of Gandhar and Kabul, and the greater sovereign of the same race who ruled on the banks of the Oxus, as well as with Ceylon and other distant islands.

Communication between the King of Ceylon and Samudragupta had been established accidentally at a very early period in the reign of the latter, about 330 A.D. Meghavarna, the Buddhist King of Ceylon, had sent two monks, one of whom is said to have been his brother, to do homage to the Diamond Throne and visit the monastery built by Asoka to the east of the sacred tree at Bodh Gaya. The strangers, perhaps by reason of sectarian rancour, met with scant hospitality, and on their return to the island complained to the king that they could not find any place in India where they could stay in comfort. King Meghavarna recognized the justice of the complaint, and resolved to remedy the grievance by founding a monastery at which

TEMPLE AT BODH GAYA WITH BO-TREE.

his subjects, when on pilgrimage to the holy places, should find adequate and suitable accommodation. He accordingly despatched a mission to Samudragupta laden with the gems for which Ceylon has always been renowned, and other valuable gifts, and requested permission to found a monastery on Indian soil. Samudragupta, flattered at receiving such attentions from a distant power, was pleased to consider the gifts as tribute, and gave the required permission.

The envoy returned home, and, after due deliberation, King Meghavarna decided to build his monastery near the holy tree. His purpose was solemnly recorded on a copper plate and carried out by the erection of a splendid convent to the north of the tree. This building, which was three stories in height, included six halls, was adorned with three towers, and surrounded by a strong wall thirty or forty feet high. The decorations were executed in the richest colours with the highest artistic skill, and the statue of Buddha, cast in gold and silver, was studded with gems. The subsidiary *stupas*, enshrining relics of Buddha himself, were worthy of the principal edifice. In the seventh century, when Hiuen Tsang visited it, this magnificent establishment was occupied by a thousand monks of the Sthavira school of the Mahayana, and afforded ample hospitality to pilgrims from Ceylon. The site is now marked by an extensive mound.

It was presumably after his return from the south that Samudragupta determined to celebrate his manifold victories and proclaim the universality of his dominion by reviving the ancient rite of the horse-sacrifice (*asvamedha*), which had remained long in abeyance and probably had not been performed in Northern India since the days of Pushyamitra. The ceremony was duly carried out with appropriate splendour and accompanied with lavish gifts to Brahmans, comprising, it is said, millions of coins and gold pieces. Specimens of the gold medals struck for this purpose, bearing a suitable legend and the effigy of the doomed horse standing before the altar, have been found in small numbers. Another memorial of the event seems to exist in the rudely carved stone figure of a horse which was found in Northern Oudh and now stands at the entrance to the Lucknow Museum with a brief dedicatory inscription incised upon it, which apparently refers to Samudragupta.

Although the courtly phrases of the official eulogist cannot be accepted without a certain amount of reservation, it is clear that Samudragupta was a ruler of exceptional capacity and unusually varied gifts. The laureate's commemoration of his hero's proficiency in song and music is curiously confirmed by the existence of a few rare gold coins which depict his Majesty comfortably seated on a high-backed couch, engaged in playing the Indian lyre. The allied art of poetry was also reckoned among the accomplishments of this versatile monarch, who is said to have been reputed a king of poets and to have composed numerous metrical works worthy of the reputation of a professional author. We are further informed that the king took much delight in the society of the learned, and loved to employ his acute and polished intellect in the study and defence of the sacred scriptures, as well as in the lighter arts of music and poetry. The picture of Samudragupta as painted by his official panegyrist reminds the reader of that of Akbar as depicted by his no less partial biographer, Abul Fazl.

By a strange irony of fate this great king—warrior, poet, and musician—who conquered all India, and whose alliance extended from the Oxus to Ceylon, is unknown even by name to the earlier historians of India. His lost fame has been slowly recovered by the minute and laborious study of inscriptions and coins during the last seventy years, and the fact that it is now possible to write a long narrative of the events of his memorable reign is perhaps the most conspicuous illustration of the success gained by patient archæological research in piecing together the fragments, from which alone the chart of the authentic early history of India can be constructed.

The exact year of Samudragupta's death is not known, but he certainly lived to an advanced age, and enjoyed a reign of uninterrupted prosperity for about half a century. Before he passed away, he secured the peaceful transmission of the crown by nominating as his successor, from among many sons, the offspring of his queen, Datta Devi, whom he rightly deemed worthy to inherit a magnificent empire.

The son thus selected, who had probably been associated as crown prince (*yuvaraja*) with his father in the cares of government, assumed the name of his grandfather, in accordance with Hindu custom, and is therefore distinguished in the dynastic list as Chandragupta II. He also took the title of Vikramaditya (" sun of power "), and has a better claim than any other

The Iron Pillar of Delhi

The Iron Pillar is a solid mass of malleable iron weighing over six tons. It was not cast, but was constructed by a welding process and was originally surmounted by a statue, which was probably removed by the Mohammedans. The pillar was set up by Chandragupta II, at the close of his reign, and was dedicated in honour of Vishnu, his favourite divinity, but was not inscribed by the king. An inscription was added by Kumaragupta I, his son and successor, about 415 A.D. The column appears to have stood originally on a mound known as Vishnupada in the town of Mathura, but was removed to Delhi about 1050 A.D. by a prince named Anango Pala, who founded or refounded the city where it now stands.

sovereign to be regarded as the original of the mythical king of that name who figures so largely in Indian legends. The precise date of his accession is not recorded, but it cannot be far removed from 375 A.D., and, pending the discovery of some coin or inscription to settle the matter, that date may be assumed as approximately correct.

So far as appears, the succession to the throne was accomplished peacefully without contest, and the new emperor, who must have been a man of mature age at the time of his accession, found himself in a position to undertake the extension of the wide dominion bequeathed to him by his ever victorious father. He did not renew Samudragupta's southern adventures, but preferred to seek room for expansion toward the east, northwest, and southwest. Our knowledge of his campaign in Bengal is confined to the assertion made in the elegant poetical inscription on the celebrated Iron Pillar of Delhi that, "when warring in the Vanga countries, he breasted and destroyed the enemies confederate against him;" and the language of the poet may refer to the suppression of a rebellion rather than to a war of aggression. The same document is the only authority for the fact that he crossed the "seven mouths of the Indus" and vanquished in battle a nation called Vahlika, which has not been identified.

But the great military achievement of Chandragupta Vikramaditya was his advance to the Arabian Sea through Malwa and Gujarat, and his subjugation of the peninsula of Surashtra, or Kathiawar, which had been ruled for centuries by the Saka dynasty, known to European scholars as the western satraps. The campaigns which added these remote provinces to the empire must have occupied several years, and are known to have taken place between 388 and 401 A.D.

A HILL-TOP PAGODA.

The year 395 may be assumed as a mean date for the completion of the conquest, which involved the incorporation in the empire of the territory held by the Malavas and other tribes, who had remained outside the limits of Samudragupta's dominion. The annexation of Surashtra and Malwa not only added to the empire provinces of exceptional wealth and fertility, but opened up to the paramount power free access to the ports of the western coast, and thus placed Chandragupta II in direct touch with the sea-borne commerce with Europe through Egypt, and brought his court and subjects under the influence of the European ideas which travelled with the goods of the Alexandrian merchants.

The Saka dynasty, which was overthrown in 395 A. D., had been founded in the first century of the Christian era, probably by a chief named Bhumaka Kshaharata. He was followed by Nahapana, a member of the same clan. When the latter was destroyed by the Andhra king, as related in Chapter VIII, the local government passed into the hands of Chashtana and his descendants. In the middle of the second century the satrap Rudradaman, having decisively defeated his Andhra rival, had firmly established his own power not only over the peninsula of Surashtra, but also over Malwa, Cutch (Kachchh), Sind, the Konkan, and other districts—in short, over Western India. The capital of Chashtana and his successors was Ujjain, one of the most ancient cities of India, the principal depot for the commerce between the ports of the west and the interior, famous as a seat of learning and civilization, and also notable as the Indian Greenwich from which longitudes were reckoned. The place, which is still a considerable town with many relics of its past greatness, retains its ancient name, and was for a time the capital of Maharaja Sindia.

Samudragupṭa, although not able to undertake the

conquest of the west, had received an embassy from the satrap Rudrasena, son of Rudradaman, who was doubtless deeply impressed by the emperor's triumphant march through India. Chandragupta II, strong in the possession of the territory and treasure acquired by his father, resolved to crush his western rival and to annex the valuable provinces which owned the satrap's sway. The motives of an ambitious king in undertaking an aggressive war against a rich neighbour are not far to seek, but we may feel assured that differences of race, creed, and manners supplied the Gupta monarch with special reasons for desiring to suppress the impure foreign rulers of the west.

Chandragupta Vikramaditya, although tolerant of Buddhism and Jainism, was himself an orthodox Hindu, specially devoted to the cult of Vishnu, and as such cannot but have experienced peculiar satisfaction in "violently uprooting" foreign chieftains who cared little for caste rules. Whatever his motives may have been, he attacked, dethroned, and slew the satrap Rudrasinha, son of Satyasinha, and annexed his dominions. Scandalous tradition affirmed that "in his enemy's city the king of the Sakas, while courting another man's wife, was butchered by Chandragupta, concealed in his mistress's dress," but the tale does not sound like genuine history. The last notice of the satraps refers to the year 388 A.D., and the incorporation of their dominions in the Gupta empire must have been effected soon after that date.

The Gupta kings, excepting the founder of the

dynasty, all enjoyed long reigns, like the Moguls in later times. Chandragupta Vikramaditya occupied the throne for nearly forty years, and survived until 413 A.D. Little is known concerning his personal character, but the ascertained facts of his career suffice to prove that he was a strong and vigorous ruler, well qualified to govern and augment an extensive empire. He loved sounding titles which proclaimed his martial prowess, and was fond of depicting himself, after the old Persian fashion, as engaged in successful personal combat with a lion, and he had literary and artistic talents like his father.

There are indications that Pataliputra, although it may have been still regarded as the official capital, ceased to be the ordinary residence of the Gupta sovereigns after the completion of the extensive conquests effected by Samudragupta. The Maurya emperors, it is true, had managed to control a dominion considerably larger than that of the Guptas from the ancient imperial city, but, even in their time, its remoteness in the extreme east must have caused inconvenience, and a more central position for the court had obvious advantages. Ajodhya, the legendary abode of the hero Rama, the ruins of which have supplied materials for the building of the modern city of Fyzabad in Southern Oudh, enjoyed a more favourable situation, and appears to have been at times the headquarters of the government of both Samudragupta and his son, the latter of whom probably had a mint for copper coins there.

The Asoka pillar on which Samudragupta recorded

the history of his reign is supposed to have been erected originally at the celebrated city of Kausambi, which stood on the highroad between Ujjain and Northern India and was no doubt at times honoured by the residence of the monarch. The real capital of an Oriental despotism is the seat of the despot's court for the time being.

Pataliputra, however, although necessarily considerably neglected by warrior kings like Samudragupta and Vikramaditya, continued to be a magnificent and populous city throughout the reign of the latter, and was not finally ruined until the time of the Hun invasion in the sixth century, from which date it practically disappeared until it was rebuilt a thousand years later by Sher Shah. Since his time the venerable city, under the names of Patna and Bankipur, has regained much of its ancient importance and has played a part in many notable events.

We are fortunate enough to possess in the work of Fa-hien, the earliest Chinese pilgrim, a contemporary account of the administration of Chandragupta Vikramaditya, as it appeared to an intelligent foreigner at the beginning of the fifth century. The worthy pilgrim, it is true, was so absorbed in his search for Buddhist books, legends, and miracles that he had little care for the things of this world, and did not trouble even to mention the name of the mighty monarch in whose territories he spent six studious years. But now and then he allowed his pen to note some of the facts of ordinary life, and in more than one passage he has recorded particulars which, although insufficient to gratify the curiosity of the twentieth century, yet suffice to give a tolerably vivid picture of the state of the country. The picture is a very pleasing one on the whole, and proves that Vikramaditya was capable of bestowing on his people the benefits of orderly government in sufficient measure to allow them to grow rich in peace and prosper abundantly.

On the occasion of his first visit to Pataliputra the traveller was deeply impressed by the sight of Asoka's palace, which was at that time still in existence, and so cunningly constructed of stone that the work clearly appeared to be beyond the skill of mortal hands, and was believed to have been executed by spirits in the service of the emperor. Near a great *stupa*, also ascribed to Asoka, stood two monasteries, one occupied by followers of the Mahayana, and the other by those of the Hinayana sect. The monks resident in both establishments together numbered six or seven hundred, and were so famous for learning that their lectures were frequented by students and inquirers from all quarters.

Fa-hien spent three years here studying Sanskrit, and was made happy by obtaining certain works on monastic discipline as taught by various schools, for which he had sought elsewhere in vain. He describes with great admiration the splendid procession of images, carried on some twenty huge cars richly decorated, which annually paraded through the city on the eighth day of the second month, attended by singers and musicians, and notes that similar processions were common in other parts of the country.

The towns of Magadha were the largest in the Ganges plain, which Fa-hien calls by the name of Central India or the Middle Kingdom; the people were rich and prosperous, and seemed to him to emulate each other in the practice of virtue. Charitable institutions were numerous, rest-houses for travellers were provided on the highways, and the capital possessed an excellent free hospital endowed by benevolent and educated citizens.

"Hither come," we are told, "all poor or helpless patients suffering from all kinds of infirmities. They are well taken care of, and a doctor attends them, food and medicine being supplied according to their wants. Thus they are made quite comfortable, and, when they are well, they may go away."

No such foundation was to be seen elsewhere in the world at that date, and its existence, anticipating the deeds of modern Christian charity, speaks well both for the character of the citizens who endowed it, and for the genius of the great Asoka, whose teaching still bore such wholesome fruit many centuries after his decease. The earliest hospital in Europe is said to have been opened in the tenth century.

In the course of a journey of some five hundred miles from the Indus to Mathura on the Jumna, Fa-hien passed a succession of Buddhist monasteries tenanted by thousands of monks, and in the neighbourhood of Mathura found twenty of these buildings occupied by three thousand residents. Buddhism was growing in favour in this part of the country.

The region to the south of Mathura, that is to say, Malwa, specially excited the admiration of the traveller, who was delighted alike with the natural advantages of the country, the disposition of the people, and the moderation of the government. The climate seemed to him very agreeable, being temperate and free from the discomforts of frost and snow with which he was familiar at home and in the course of his journey. The large population lived happily under a sensible government which did not worry. With a glance at Chinese institutions, Fa-hien congratulates the Indians that "they have not to register their households, or attend to any magistrates and rules." They were not troubled with passport regulations, or, as the pilgrim bluntly puts it: "Those who want to go away, may go; those who want to stop, may stop."

BUDDHIST SCULPTURE ON THE BHARAHAT STUPA, SHOWING THE ERECTION OF THE JETAVANA MONASTERY.

(After Cunningham.)

The administration of the criminal law seemed to him mild in comparison with the Chinese system. Most crimes were punished only by fines, varying in amount according to the gravity of the offence, and capital punishment would seem to have been unknown. Persons guilty of repeated rebellion, an expression which probably includes brigandage, suffered amputation of the right hand; but such a penalty was exceptional, and judicial torture was not practised. The revenue was mainly derived from the rents of the Crown lands, and the royal officers, being provided with fixed salaries, had no occasion to live on the people.

The Buddhist rule of life was generally observed. "Throughout the country," we are told, "no one kills any living thing, or drinks wine, or eats onions or garlic. . . . They do not keep pigs or fowls, there are no dealings in cattle, no butchers' shops or distilleries in their market-places." The Chandala, or outcast tribes, who dwelt apart like lepers, and were required when entering a city or bazaar to strike a piece of wood as a warning of their approach, in order that other folk might not be polluted by contact with them, were the only offenders against the laws of piety (*dharma*), and the only hunters, fishermen, and butchers. Cowrie shells formed the ordinary currency. The Buddhist monasteries were liberally endowed by royal grants, and the monks received alms without stint,—houses, beds, mattresses, food, and clothes were never lacking to them wherever they might go.

These particulars, as collected and narrated by the earliest Chinese traveller in India, permit of no doubt that the dominions of Chandragupta Vikramaditya were well governed. The authorities interfered as little as possible with the subject, and left him free to prosper and grow rich in his own way. The devout pilgrim pursued his Sanskrit studies for three years at Pataliputra, and for two years at the port of Tamralipti (Tamluk), without let or hindrance, and it is clear that the roads were safe for travellers. Fa-hien never has occasion to complain of being stripped by brigands, a misfortune which befell his successor, Hiuen Tsang, more than once in the seventh century.

THE GOD BRAHMA.
From Moor's Hindu Pantheon.

Probably India has never been governed better, after the Oriental manner, than it was during the reign of Vikramaditya. The government did not attempt to do too much, but let the people alone, and was accordingly popular. The merciful teachings of Buddhism influenced the lives of all classes, except the most degraded, while, inasmuch as the sovereign was a Brahmanical Hindu, the tendency to the harassing kind of persecution, which a Buddhist or Jain government is apt to display, was kept in check, and liberty of conscience was assured. Fa-hien, as a pious devotee, necessarily saw everything through Buddhist spectacles, but it is evident that, with a Brahmanical supreme government, Hinduism of the orthodox kind must have been far more prominent than his account would lead the reader to suppose, and sacrifices must have been permitted. In fact, the Brahmanical reaction against Buddhism had begun at a time considerably earlier than that of Fa-hien's travels, and Indian Buddhism was already upon the downward path, although the pilgrim could not discern the signs of decadence.

While the general prosperity and tranquillity of the empire under the rule of Chandragupta Vikramaditya are abundantly proved by the express testimony of Fa-hien and by his unobstructed movements in all directions during many years, certain districts did not share in the general well-being, and had retrograded in population and wealth. The city of Gaya, we are informed, was empty and desolate; the holy places of Bodh Gaya, six miles to the south, were surrounded by jungle; and an extensive tract of country near the foot of the mountains, which had been the seat of a large population in the fifth century B.C., was now sparsely inhabited. The great city of Sravasti, on the upper course of the Rapti, was occupied by only two hundred families, and the holy towns of Kapilavastu and Kusinagara were waste and deserted, save for a scanty remnant of monks and their lay attendants.

The son of Vikramaditya, who ascended the throne in 413 A.D., is known to history as Kumaragupta I, in order to distinguish him from his great-grandson of the same name. The events of this king's reign, which exceeded forty years, are not known in detail, but the distribution of the numerous contemporary inscriptions and coins permits of no doubt that, during the greater part of his unusually prolonged rule, the empire suffered no diminution. On the contrary, it probably gained certain additions, for Kumara, like his grandfather, celebrated the horse-sacrifice as an assertion of his paramount sovereignty, and it is not likely that he

SCENE NEAR BODH GAYA.
From a photograph.

would have indulged in this vaunt, unless to some extent justified by successful warfare.

The extant records furnish the information that at the close of his reign, in the middle of the fifth century, Kumara's dominions suffered severely from the irruption of the Hun hordes, who had burst through the northwestern passes, and spread in a destructive flood all over Northern India. Before entering upon the discussion of the Hun invasion and the consequent break-up of the Gupta empire, it is desirable to pause, in order to record a few brief observations on the significance of the rule of the great Gupta sovereigns in the evolution of Indian language, literature, art, and religion.

BUDDHIST SCULPTURE.

CHAPTER XII

THE GUPTA EMPIRE AND THE WHITE HUNS

FROM 455 TO 606 A. D.

THE general prevalence of Buddhism in Northern India, including Kashmir, Afghanistan, and Suwat, during the two centuries immediately preceding, and the two next following the Christian era, is amply attested by the numerous remains of Buddhist monuments erected during that period and a multitude of inscriptions, which are almost all either Buddhist or Jain. The Jain cult, which was closely related to the Buddhist, does not appear to have gained very wide popularity, although it was practised with great devotion at certain localities, of which Mathura was one.

But the orthodox Hindu worship, conducted under the guidance of Brahmans, and associated with sacrificial rites abhorrent to Jain and Buddhist sentiment, had never become extinct, and had at all times retained a large share of both popular and royal favour. Kadphises II, the Kushan conqueror, was himself conquered by captive India, and adopted with such zeal the worship of Siva as practised by his new subjects, that he constantly placed the image of that Indian god upon his coins and described himself as his devotee. Many other facts concur to prove the continued worship of the old Hindu gods during the period in which Buddhism was unquestionably the most popular and generally received creed.

In some respects, Buddhism in its Mahayana form was better fitted than the Brahmanical system to attract the reverence of casteless foreign chieftains, and it would not be unreasonable to expect that they should have shown a decided tendency to favour Buddhism rather than Brahmanism; but the facts do not indicate any clearly marked general preference for the Buddhist creed on the part of the foreigners. The only distinctively Buddhist coins are the few rare pieces of that kind struck by Kanishka, who undoubtedly, in his later years, liberally patronized the ecclesiastics of the Buddhist Church, as did his successor, Huvishka; but the next king, Vasudeva, reverted to the devotion for Siva, as displayed by Kadphises II. So the later Saka satraps of Surashtra seem to have inclined personally much more to the Brahmanical than to the Buddhist cult, and they certainly bestowed their patronage upon the Sanskrit of the Brahmans rather than upon the vernacular literature.

The development of the Mahayana school of Buddhism, which became prominent and fashionable from the time of Kanishka in the second century, was in itself a testimony to the reviving power of Brahmanical Hinduism. The newer form of Buddhism had much in common with the older Hinduism, and the relation is so close that even an expert often feels a difficulty in deciding to which system a particular image should be assigned.

Brahmanical Hinduism was the religion of the pandits, whose sacred language was Sanskrit, a highly artificial literary modification of the vernacular speech of the Panjab. As the influence of the pandits upon prince and peasant waxed greater in matters of religion and social observance, the use of their special vehicle of expression became more widely diffused, and gradually superseded the vernacular in all documents of a formal or official character. In the third century B.C. Asoka had been content to address his commands to his people in language easy to be understood by the vulgar, but in the middle of the second century A.D. the western satrap Rudradaman felt that his achievements could be adequately commemorated only in elaborate Sanskrit. It is impossible to go more deeply into the subject in these pages, but it is certain that the revival of the Brahmanical religion was accompanied by the diffusion and extension of Sanskrit, the sacred language of the Brahmans.

Whatever may have been the causes, the fact is abundantly established that the restoration of the Brahmanical religion to popular favour, and the associated revival of the Sanskrit language, first became noticeable in the second century, were fostered by the western satraps during the third, and made a success by the Gupta emperors in the fourth century. These princes, although apparently perfectly tolerant both of Buddhism and Jainism, were themselves beyond question zealous Hindus, guided by Brahman advisers, and skilled in Sanskrit, the language of the pandits.

An early stage in the reaction against Buddhist condemnation of sacrifice had been marked by Pushyamitra's celebration of the horse-sacrifice toward the close of the second century. In the fourth, Samudragupta revived the same ancient rite with added splendour, and in the fifth, his grandson repeated the solemnity. Without going further into detail, the matter may be summed up in the remark that coins, inscriptions, and monuments agree in furnishing abundant evidence of the recrudescence during the Gupta period of Brahmanical Hinduism at the expense of Buddhism, and of the favour shown by the ruling powers to "classical" Sanskrit at the expense of the more popular literary dialects, which had enjoyed the patronage of the Andhra kings.

Good reasons can be adduced for the belief that Chandragupta II Vikramaditya, who reigned at the close of the fourth and the beginning of the fifth century and conquered Ujjain, should be regarded as the original of the Raja Bikram of Ujjain, famed in popular legend, at whose court the Nine Gems of Sanskrit literature are supposed to have flourished. Whether Kalidasa, poet and dramatist, the most celebrated of these authors, actually graced the durbar of Chandragupta Vikramaditya at Ujjain, or lived under the protection of his son or grandson, is a question still open, and it is even possible that he was a courtier of one of Chandragupta's satrap predecessors; but popular tradition certainly appears to be right in placing the greatest of Indian poets in the age of which Vikramaditya is the most conspicuous political figure.

To the same age probably should be assigned the principal Puranas in their present form, the metrical legal treatises, of which the so-called Code of Manu is the most familiar example, and, in short, the mass of the "classical" Sanskrit literature. The patronage of the great Gupta emperors gave, as Professor Bhandarkar observes, "a general literary impulse," which extended to every department and gradually raised Sanskrit to the position which it long retained as the sole literary language of Northern India. The decline of Buddhism and the diffusion of Sanskrit proceeded side by side, with the result that, by the end of the Gupta period, the force of Buddhism on Indian soil had been nearly spent and India, with certain local exceptions, had again become the land of the Brahmans.

BATHING-PLACE AT UJJAIN.

The literary revolution was necessarily accompanied by corresponding changes in the art of architecture. The forms of buildings specially adapted for the purposes of Buddhist ritual dropped out of use, and remarkable developments in the design of the Hindu temple were elaborated, which ultimately culminated in the marvellously ornate styles of the mediæval period, extending from the ninth to the end of the twelfth century.

BRAHMAN PRIESTS AT SECUNDRA — INDIA.
From stereograph, copyright 1903, by Underwood & Underwood, New York.

The golden age of the Guptas, glorious in literary, as in political, history, comprised a period of a century and a quarter (330 - 455 A. D.), and was covered by three reigns of exceptional length. The death of Kumara, early in 455, marks the beginning of the decline and fall of the empire. Even before his death, he had become involved, about the year 450, in serious distress by a war with a rich and powerful nation named Pushyamitra, otherwise unknown to history. The imperial armies were defeated, and the shock of military disaster had endangered the stability of the dynasty, which was "tottering" to its fall, when the energy and ability of Skandagupta, the crown prince, restored the fortunes of his family by effecting the overthrow of the enemy.

When Skandagupta came to the throne in the spring of 455, he encountered a sea of troubles. The Pushyamitra danger had been averted, but one more formidable closely followed it, an irruption of the savage Huns, who had poured down from the steppes of Central Asia through the northwestern passes, and carried devastation over the smiling plains and crowded cities of India. Skandagupta, who was probably a man of mature years and ripe experience, proved equal to the need, and inflicted upon the barbarians a defeat so decisive that India was saved for a time.

It is evident that this great victory over the Huns must have been gained at the very beginning of the new reign, because another inscription, executed in the year 457, recites Skandagupta's defeat of the barbarians, and recognizes his undisputed possession of the peninsula of Surashtra (Kathiawar), at the extreme western extremity of the empire. The dedication, three years afterward, by a private Jain donor of a sculptured column at a village in the east of the Gorakhpur District, distant about ninety miles from Patna, testifies to the fact that Skandagupta's rule at this early period of his reign included the eastern as well as the western provinces, and the record expressly characterizes the rule of the reigning sovereign as being "tranquil."

Five years later, in the year 465, a pious Brahman in the country between the Ganges and Jumna, which is now known as the Bulandshahr District, when endowing a temple to the Sun, felt justified in describing the rule of his king in the central parts of the empire as "augmenting and victorious." The conclusion is, therefore, legitimate that the victory over the barbarian invaders was gained at the beginning of the reign, and was sufficiently decisive to secure the tranquillity of all parts of the empire for a considerable number of years.

But, about 465 A.D., a fresh swarm of nomads poured across the frontier, and occupied Gandhara, or the Northwestern Panjab, where a "cruel and vindictive" chieftain usurped the throne of the Kushans and "practised the most barbarous atrocities." A little later, about 470, the Huns advanced into the interior and again attacked Skandagupta in the heart of his dominions. He was unable to continue the successful resistance which he had offered in the earlier days of his rule, and was forced at last to succumb to the repeated attacks of the foreigners. The financial distress of his administration is very plainly indicated by the abrupt debasement of the coinage in his later years.

The death of Skandagupta may be assumed to have occurred in or about the year 480. When he passed away, the empire perished, but the dynasty remained, and was continued in the eastern provinces for many generations. Skanda left no heir male capable of undertaking the cares of government in a time of such stress, and was accordingly succeeded on the throne of Magadha and the adjacent districts by his half-brother, Puragupta, the son of Kumaragupta I by Queen Ananda.

The reign of this prince was apparently very brief,

and the only event which can be assigned to it is a bold attempt to restore the purity of the coinage. The rare gold coins, bearing on the reverse the title Prakasaditya, which are generally ascribed to Puragupta, although retaining the gross weight of the heavy *suvarna*, each contain 121 grains of pure gold, and are thus equal in value to the *aurei* of Augustus, and superior in intrinsic value to the best Kushan or early Gupta coins.

Puragupta was succeeded by his son Narasimhagupta Baladitya, who was followed by his son, Kumaragupta II. Although these kings continued to assume the high-sounding titles borne by their imperial ancestors, their power was very circumscribed, and confined to the eastern portions of what had been the Gupta empire.

The imperial line passes by an obscure transition into a dynasty comprising eleven princes, who appear to have been for the most part merely local rulers of Magadha. The last of them, Jivitagupta II, was in power at the beginning of the eighth century. The most considerable member of this local dynasty was Adityasena in the seventh century, who asserted a claim to paramount rank, and even ventured to celebrate the horse-sacrifice.

In the western province of Malwa we find the names of rajas named Budhagupta and Bhanugupta, who cover the period from 484 to 510, and were evidently the heirs of Skandagupta in that region. But the latter of these two princes, at all events, occupied a dependent position, and was presumably subordinate to the Hun chieftains.

Toward the close of the fifth century, a chief named Bhatarka, who belonged to a clan called Maitraka, probably of foreign origin, established himself at Valabhi in the east of the peninsula of Surashtra (Kathiawar), and founded a dynasty which lasted until about 770 A.D., when it was overthrown by Arab invaders from Sind. The earlier Kings of Valabhi do not appear to have been independent, and were doubtless obliged to pay tribute to the Huns; but, after the destruction of the Hun domination, the Kings of Valabhi asserted their independence, and made themselves a considerable power in the west of India, both on the mainland and in the peninsula of Surashtra.

The city was a place of great wealth when visited by Hiuen Tsang in the seventh century, and was famous in Buddhist Church history as the residence of two distinguished teachers, Gunamati and Sthiramati, in the sixth century. After the overthrow of Valabhi, its place as the chief city of Western India was taken by Anhilwara (Nahrwalah, or Patan), which retained that honour until the fifteenth century, when it was superseded by Ahmadabad. The above observations will, perhaps, give the reader all the information that he is likely to want concerning the principal native dynasties which inherited the fragments of the Gupta empire.

But the Huns, the foreign savages who shattered that empire, merit more explicit notice. The nomad Mongol tribes known as Huns, when they moved westwards from the steppes of Asia to seek subsistence for their growing multitudes in other climes, divided into two main streams, one directed toward the valley of the Oxus, and the other to that of the Volga.

The latter poured into Eastern Europe in 375 A. D., forcing the Goths to the south of the Danube, and thus indirectly causing the sanguinary Gothic war, which cost the Emperor Valens his life in 378 A. D. The Huns quickly spread over the lands between the Volga and the Danube, but, owing to chronic disunion and the lack of a great leader, failed to make full use of their advantageous position, until Attila appeared and for a few years welded the savage mass into an instrument of such power that he was "able to send equal defiance to the courts of Ravenna and Constantinople."

His death in 453 A. D. severed the only bond which held together the jealous factions of the horde, and within a space of twenty years after that event the Hunnic empire in Europe was extinguished by a fresh torrent of barbarians from Northern Asia.

The Asiatic domination of the Huns lasted longer. The section of the horde which settled in the Oxus valley became known as the Ephthalites, or White Huns, and gradually overcame the resistance of Persia, which ceased when King Firoz was killed in 484 A. D. Swarms of these White Huns also assailed the Kushan kingdom of Kabul, and thence poured into India. The attack repelled by Skandagupta in 455 A. D. must have been delivered by a comparatively weak body, which arrived early and failed to effect a lodgment in the interior.

About ten years later the nomads appeared in greater force and overwhelmed the kingdom of Gandhara, or Peshawar, and starting from that base, as already related, penetrated into the heart of the Ganges provinces, and overthrew the Gupta empire. The collapse of Persian opposition in 484 must have greatly facilitated the eastern movement of the horde, and allowed immense multitudes to cross the Indian frontier. The leader in this invasion of India, which, no doubt, continued for years, was a chieftain named Toramana, who is known to have been established as ruler of Malwa in Central India prior to 500 A. D. He assumed the style and titles of an Indian "sovereign of *maharajas*," and Bhanugupta, as well as the King of Valabhi and many other local princes, must have been his tributaries.

When Toramana died, about 510 A. D., the Indian dominion which he had acquired was consolidated sufficiently to pass to his son Mihiragula, whose capital in India was Sakala in the Panjab, which should be identified apparently with either Chuniot or Shahkot in the Jhang District.

But India at this time was only one province of the Hun empire. The headquarters of the horde were at Bamyin in Badhaghis near Herat, and the ancient city of Balkh served as a secondary capital. The Hun king, whose court, whether at Bamyin or Herat cannot be determined, was visited by Song-Yun, the Chinese pilgrim-envoy in 519 A. D., was a powerful monarch levying tribute from forty countries, extending from the frontier of Persia on the west, to Khotan on the borders of China in the east. This king was either Mihiragula himself, or his contemporary overlord, most probably the latter. The local Hun king of Gandhara, to whom Song-Yun paid his respects in the following year, 520 A. D., must be identified with Mihiragula. He was then engaged in a war with the King of Kashmir (Ki-pin), which had already lasted for three years.

All Indian traditions agree in representing Mihiragula as a bloodthirsty tyrant, stained to a more than ordinary degree with the "implacable cruelty" noted by historians as characteristic of the Hun temperament. Indian authors having omitted to give any detailed description of the savage invaders who ruthlessly oppressed their country for three-quarters of a century, recourse must be had to European writers to obtain a picture of the devastation wrought and the terror caused to settled communities by the fierce barbarians.

The original accounts are well summarized by Gibbon:—

"The numbers, the strength, the rapid motions, and the implacable cruelty of the Huns were felt and dreaded and magnified by the astonished Goths, who beheld their fields and villages consumed with flames and deluged with indiscriminate slaughter. To these real terrors they added the surprise and abhorrence which were excited by the shrill voice, the uncouth gestures, and the strange deformity of the Huns. . . . They were distinguished from the rest of the human species by their broad shoulders, flat noses, and small black eyes, deeply buried in the head; and, as they were almost destitute of beards, they never enjoyed the manly graces of youth or the venerable aspect of age."

The Indians, like the Goths, experienced to the full the miseries of savage warfare, and suffered an added horror by reason of the special disgust felt by fastidi-

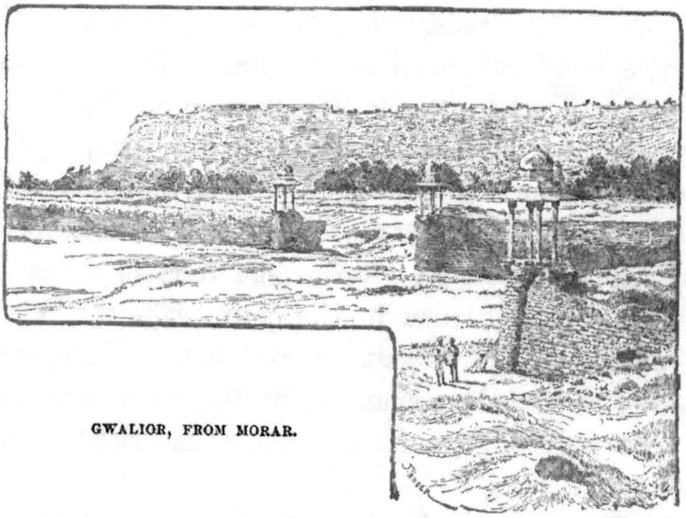

GWALIOR, FROM MORAR.

ous caste-bound Hindus at the repulsive habits of barbarians to whom nothing was sacred.

The cruelty practised by Mihiragula became so unbearable that the native princes, under the leadership of Baladitya, King of Magadha (probably the same as Narasimhagupta), and Yasodharman, a raja of Central India, formed a confederacy against the foreign tyrant. About the year 528 A. D., they accomplished the delivery of their country from oppression by inflicting a decisive defeat on Mihiragula, who was taken prisoner and would have forfeited his life deservedly but for the magnanimity of Baladitya, who spared the captive and sent him to his home in the north with all honour.

But Mihiragula's younger brother had taken advantage of the misfortunes of the head of the family to usurp the throne of Sakala, which he was unwilling to surrender. Mihiragula, after spending some time in concealment, took refuge in Kashmir, where he was kindly received by the king, who placed him in charge of a small territory. The exile submitted to this enforced retirement for a few years, and then took an opportunity to rebel and seize the throne of his benefactor. Having succeeded in this enterprise, he attacked the neighbouring kingdom of Gandhara. The king, perhaps himself a Hun, was treacherously surprised and slain, the royal family was exterminated, and multitudes of people were slaughtered on the banks of the Indus. The savage invader, who worshipped as his patron deity Siva, the god of destruction, exhibited ferocious hostility against the peaceful Buddhist cult, and remorselessly overthrew the *stupas* and monasteries, which he plundered of their treasures.

But he did not long enjoy his ill-gotten gains. Before the year was out he died, and "at the time of his death there were thunder and hail and a thick darkness, and the earth shook, and a mighty tempest raged. And the holy saints said in pity: 'For having killed countless victims and overthrown the law of Buddha, he has now fallen into the lowest hell, where he shall pass endless ages of revolution.'" Thus the tyrant met the just reward of his evil deeds in another world, if not in this. The date of his death is not known exactly, but the event must have occurred in or about the year 540, just a century before Hiuen Tsang was on his travels. The rapidity of the growth of the legend concerning the portents attending the tyrant's death is good evidence of the depth of the impression made by his outlandish cruelty, which is further attested by the Kashmir tale of the fiendish pleasure which he is believed to have taken in rolling elephants down a precipice.

Yasodharman, the Central Indian raja, who has been mentioned as having taken an active part in the confederacy formed to obtain deliverance from the tyranny of Mihiragula, is known from three inscriptions only, and is not mentioned by Hiuen Tsang, who gives the credit for the victory over the Huns to Baladitya, King of Magadha. Yasodharman took the honour to himself, and erected two columns of victory inscribed with boasting words to commemorate the defeat of the foreign invaders. Nothing whatever is known about either his ancestry or his successors; his name stands absolutely alone and unrelated. The belief is therefore warranted that his reign was short and of much less importance than that claimed for it by his magniloquent inscriptions.

The dominion of the White Huns in the Oxus valley did not long survive the defeat and death of Mihiragula in India. The arrival of the Turks in the middle of the sixth century changed the situation completely. The Turkish tribes, having vanquished a rival horde called Joan-joan, made an alliance with Khusru Anushirvan, King of Persia, grandson of Firoz, who had been killed by the Huns in 484 A. D., and at some date between 563 and 567 the allies destroyed the White Huns. For a short time the Persians held Balkh and other portions of the Hun territory, but the gradual weakening of the Sasanian power soon enabled the Turks to extend their authority toward the south as far as Kapisa and to annex the whole of the countries which had been included in the Hun empire.

In later Sanskrit literature the term "Hun" (*Huna*) is employed in a very indeterminate sense to denote a foreigner from the northwest, in the same way as the *Yavana* had been employed in ancient times, and as *Wilayati* is now understood. One of the thirty-six so-called "royal" Rajput clans was actually given the name of Huna. This vagueness of connotation raises some doubt as to the exact meaning of the term Huna as applied to the clans on the northwestern frontier against whom Harsha of Thanesar and his father waged incessant war at the close of the sixth and the beginning of the seventh century. But it is unlikely that within fifty years of Mihiragula's defeat the true meaning of Huna should have been forgotten, and the opponents of Harsha may be regarded as having been outlying colonies of real Huns, who had settled among the hills on the frontier. After Harsha's time they are not again heard of, and were presumably either destroyed or absorbed into the surrounding population.

The extinction of the Ephthalite power on the Oxus necessarily dried up the stream of Hun immigration into India, which enjoyed immunity from foreign attack for nearly five centuries after the defeat of Mihiragula. The following chapters will tell how India made use, or failed to make use, of the opportunity thus afforded for internal development unchecked by foreign aggression.

Very little is known about the history of India during the second half of the sixth century. It is certain that no paramount power existed, and that all the states of the Ganges plain had suffered severely from the ravages of the Huns, but, excepting bare catalogues of names in certain local dynastic lists, no facts of general interest have been recorded. The king called Siladitya of Mo-la-po by the Chinese traveller, Hiuen Tsang, has no political connection with Harsha-Siladitya of Kanauj and Thanesar, as has been commonly supposed, or with the history of Northern India.

CHAPTER XIII

THE REIGN OF HARSHA

FROM 606 TO 648 A. D.

THE deficiency of material which embarrasses the historian when dealing with the latter half of the sixth century is no longer experienced when he enters upon the seventh. For this period he is fortunate enough to possess, in addition to the ordinary epigraphic and numismatic sources, two contemporary literary works, which shed much light upon the political condition of India generally, and supply, in particular, abundant and trustworthy information concerning the reign of Harsha, who ruled the North as paramount sovereign for more than forty years.

The first of these works is the invaluable book of travels compiled by the Chinese pilgrim Hiuen Tsang, who visited almost every part of India between 630 and 645 A. D. and recorded observations more or less minute about each state and province. The narrative in the *Travels* is supplemented by the pilgrim's biography, written by his friend, Hwui-li, which supplies many additional details. The second work alluded to is the historical romance entitled the "Deeds of Harsha" (*Harsha-charita*), composed by Bana, a Brahman author who lived at the court and enjoyed the patronage of the hero of his tale. Further information of much interest and importance is given by the official Chinese histories, and when all sources are utilized, our knowledge of the events of the reign of Harsha far surpasses in precision that which we possess respecting any other early Indian king, except Chandragupta Maurya and Asoka.

From remote ages the country surrounding the city of Thanesar (Sthanvisvara) has been holy ground, known as the "Land of Kuru," and famous as the battle-field of legendary heroes. In the latter part of the sixth century, the Raja of Thanesar, Prabhakara-vardhana by name, had raised himself to considerable eminence by successful wars against his neighbours, including the Hun settlements in the Northwestern Panjab, and the clans of Gurjara, or the country of Gujarat, between the Chinab and Jihlam Rivers.[1] The fact that his mother was a princess of Gupta lineage no doubt both stimulated his ambition and aided its realization.

In the year 604, this energetic raja had despatched his elder son, Rajya-vardhana, a youth just entering upon manhood, with a large army to attack the Huns on the northwestern frontier, while his younger and favourite son, Harsha, four years junior to the crown prince, followed his brother with a cavalry force at a

[1] Not to be confounded with the Western province of Gujarat.

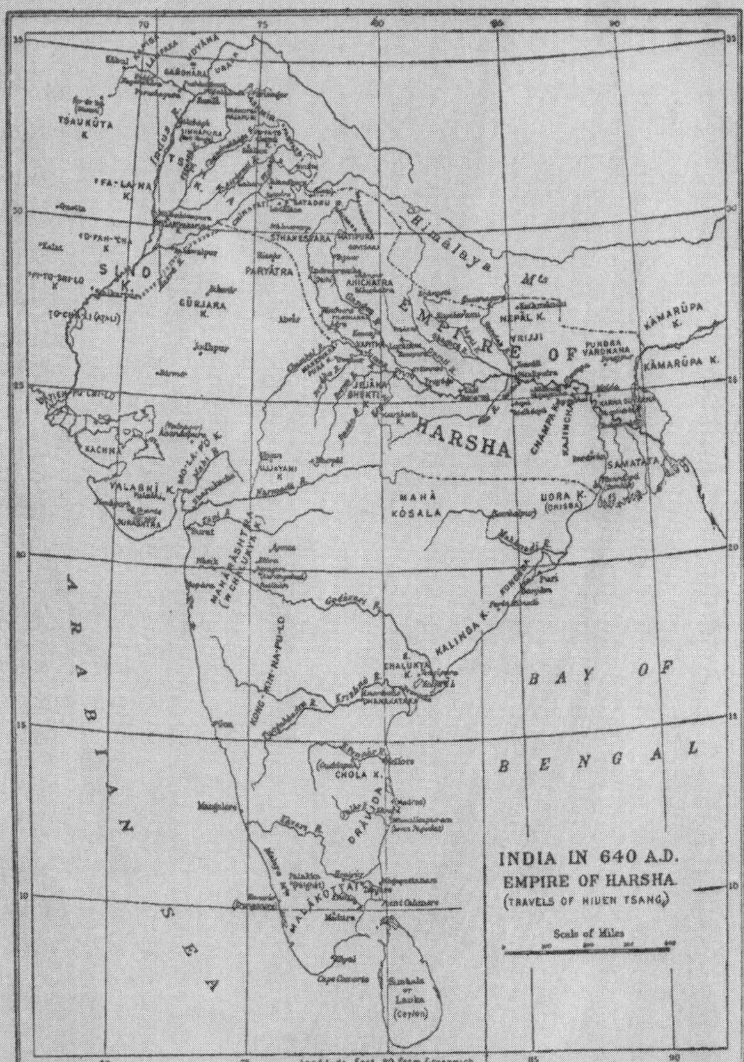

EMPIRE OF HARSHA, KING OF NORTHERN INDIA.

considerable interval. The elder prince advanced into the hills to seek the enemy, while the younger lingered in the forests at the foot of the mountains to enjoy the sport of all kinds which they offered in abundance.

While thus pleasantly employed, Harsha, who was then a lad fifteen years of age, received news that his father lay dangerously ill with a violent fever. He returned to the capital with all speed, where he found the king in a hopeless condition. The disease quickly ran its course, and all was over long before the elder son, who had been victorious in his campaign, could return to claim his birthright. There are indications that a party at court inclined to favour the succession of the younger prince, but all intrigues were frustrated by the return of Rajya-vardhana, who ascended the throne in due course. He had hardly seated himself when news arrived which compelled him again to take the field.

A courier brought the distressing intelligence that Grahavarman, King of Kanauj, and husband of Rajyasri, sister of the princes, had been slain by the King of Malwa, who cruelly misused the princess, "confining her like a brigand's wife, with a pair of iron fetters kissing her feet." The young king, resolute to avenge his sister's wrongs, started at once with a mobile force of ten thousand cavalry, leaving the elephants and heavy troops behind in his brother's charge. The King of Malwa was defeated with little effort, but the joy of victory was turned into sorrow when the victor was treacherously slain by an ally of the Malwan king,

Sasanka, King of Central Bengal, who had inveigled Rajya-vardhana to a conference by fair promises, and

GREAT TEMPLE, MADURA.

had assassinated him when off his guard. Harsha was further informed that his widowed sister had escaped from confinement and fled to the Vindhya forests for refuge, but no certain news of her hiding-place could be obtained.

The murdered king was too young to leave a son capable of assuming the cares of government, and the nobles seem to have hesitated before offering the crown to his youthful brother. Acting on the advice of Bhandi, a slightly senior cousin, who had been educated with the young princes, they ultimately resolved to invite Harsha to undertake the responsibilities of the royal office. For some reason which is not apparent on the face of the story, he hesitated to express his consent, and it is said that he consulted a Buddhist oracle before accepting the invitation. Even when his reluctance, whether sincere or pretended, had been overcome by the favourable response of the oracle, he still sought to propitiate Nemesis by abstaining at first from the assumption of the kingly style, modestly designating himself as Prince Siladitya. There is reason to suppose that Harsha did not boldly stand forth as avowed king until the spring of 612 A. D., when he had been five and a half years on the throne, and that his formal coronation, or consecration, took place in that year. The era called after his name, of which the year 1 was 606 - 7 A. D., dated from the time of his accession in October, 606.

The immediate duties incumbent upon him obviously were the pursuit of his brother's murderer and the recovery of his widowed sister. The latter task, being the more urgent, was undertaken in all haste, even at the cost of permitting the assassin's escape. The haste shown was none too great, for the princess, despairing of rescue, was on the point of burning herself alive with her attendants, when her brother, guided by aboriginal chiefs, succeeded in tracing her in the depths of the Vindhya jungles. The details of the campaign against Sasanka have not been recorded, and it seems clear that he escaped with little loss. He is known to have been still in power as late as the year 619, but his kingdom probably became subject to Harsha at a later date.

Harsha, having recovered his sister—a young lady of exceptional attainments, learned in the doctrines of the Sammitiya school of Buddhism—devoted his signal ability and energy to the prosecution of a methodical scheme of conquest, with the deliberate purpose of bringing all India "under one umbrella." He possessed at this stage of his career a force of five thousand elephants, twenty thousand cavalry, and fifty thousand infantry. Apparently he discarded as useless the chariots, which constituted, according to ancient tradition, the fourth arm of a regularly organized Indian host.

With this mobile and formidable force Harsha overran Northern India, and, in the picturesque language of his contemporary, the Chinese pilgrim, "he went from east to west subduing all who were not obedient; the elephants were not unharnessed, nor the soldiers unhelmeted." By the end of five and a half years the conquest of the northwestern regions, and probably also of a large portion of Bengal, was completed, and his military resources were so increased that he was able to put in the field sixty thousand war elephants and one hundred thousand cavalry. But he continued fighting for thirty years longer, and, as late as 643 A. D., was engaged in his last campaign, an attack upon the sturdy inhabitants of Ganjam on the coast of the Bay of Bengal.

His long career of victory was broken by one failure. Pulikesin II, the greatest of the Chalukya dynasty, whose achievements will be noticed more fully in a later chapter, vied with Harsha in the extent of his conquests, and had raised himself to the rank of lord paramount of the south, as Harsha was of the north. The northern king could not willingly endure the existence of so powerful a rival, and essayed to overthrow him, advancing in person to the attack, with "troops from the five Indies and the best generals from all countries." But the effort failed. The King of the Deccan guarded the passes on the Narmada so effectually that Harsha was constrained to retire discomfited, and to accept that river as his frontier. This campaign may be dated about the year 620 A. D.

In the latter years of his reign the sway of Harsha over the whole of the basin of the Ganges (including Nepal), from the Himalaya to the Narmada, was undisputed. Detailed administration of course remained in the hands of the local rajas, but even the king of distant Assam (Kamarupa) in the east obeyed the orders of the suzerain, and the King of Valabhi in the extreme west attended in his train.

For the control of his extensive empire, Harsha relied upon his personal supervision exercised with untiring energy rather than upon the services of a trained bureaucracy. Except during the rainy season, when travelling with a huge camp was impracticable, he was incessantly on the move, punishing evil-doers and rewarding the meritorious. Luxurious tents, such as were used by the Mogul emperors, and still form the movable habitations of high Anglo-Indian officials, had not then been invented, and Harsha was obliged to be content with a "travelling palace" made of boughs and reeds, which was erected at each halting-place and burned at his departure.

Hiuen Tsang, like his predecessor, Fa-hien, more than two centuries earlier, was favourably impressed by the character of the civil administration, which he considered to be founded on benign principles. The principal source of revenue was the rent of the Crown lands, amounting, in theory at all events, to one-sixth of the produce. The officials were remunerated by grants of land; compulsory labour upon public works was paid for; taxes were light; the personal services exacted from the subject were moderate in amount; and liberal provision was made for charity to various religious communities.

Violent crime was rare, but the roads and river routes were evidently less safe than in Fa-hien's time, as Hiuen Tsang was stopped and robbed by brigands more than once. Imprisonment was now the ordinary penalty, and it was of the cruel Tibetan type; the prisoners, we are told, "are simply left to live or die, and are not counted among men." The other punishments were more sanguinary than in the Gupta period: mutilation of the nose, ears, hands, or feet being inflicted as the penalty of serious offences, and even for failure in filial piety; but this penalty was sometimes commuted for banishment. Minor offences were visited with fines. Ordeals by water, fire, weighment, or poison were much esteemed as efficient instruments for the ascertainment of truth and are described with approval by the Chinese pilgrim.

Official records of public events were kept in every province by special officers, whose duty it was to register "good and evil events, with calamities and fortunate occurrences." Such records were, no doubt, consulted by the writers of the great historical inscriptions, but no specimen of them has survived.

Education evidently was diffused widely, especially among the Brahmans and numerous Buddhist monks, and learning was honoured by the government. King Harsha was not only a liberal patron of literary merit, but was himself an accomplished calligraphist and an author of reputation. Besides a grammatical work, three extant Sanskrit plays are ascribed to his pen, and there is no reason for hesitating to believe that he had at least a large share in their composition, for royal authors were not uncommon in ancient India. One of these plays, the *Nagananda,* which has an edifying Buddhist legend for its subject, is considered to rank among the best works of the Indian theatre, and the other dramas, the *Ratnavali*, or "Necklace," and the *Priyadarsika*, or "Gracious Lady," although lacking in originality, are praised highly for their simplicity both of thought and expression.

The greatest ornament of the literary circle at Harsha's court was the Brahman Bana, author of the historical romance devoted to a panegyrical account of the deeds of his patron, which is an amazingly clever, but irritating, performance, executed in the worst possible taste, and yet containing passages of admirable and vivid description. The man who attributes to the commander-in-chief, Skandagupta, "a nose as long as his sovereign's pedigree," may fairly be accused of having perpetrated the most grotesque simile in all literature. But the same man could do better, and shows no lack of power when depicting the death-agony of the king. "Helplessness had taken him in hand; pain had made him its province, wasting its domain, lassitude its lair. . . . He was on the confines of doom, on the verge of the last gasp, at the outset of the Great Undertaking, at the portal of the Long Sleep, on the tip of death's tongue; broken in utterance, unhinged in mind, tortured in body, waning in life, babbling in speech, ceaseless in sighs; vanquished by yawning, swayed by suffering, in the bondage of racking pains." Such writing, although not in perfect good taste, unmistakably bears the stamp of power.

One campaign sated Asoka's thirst for blood; thirty-seven years of warfare were needed by Harsha before he could be content to sheathe the sword. His last

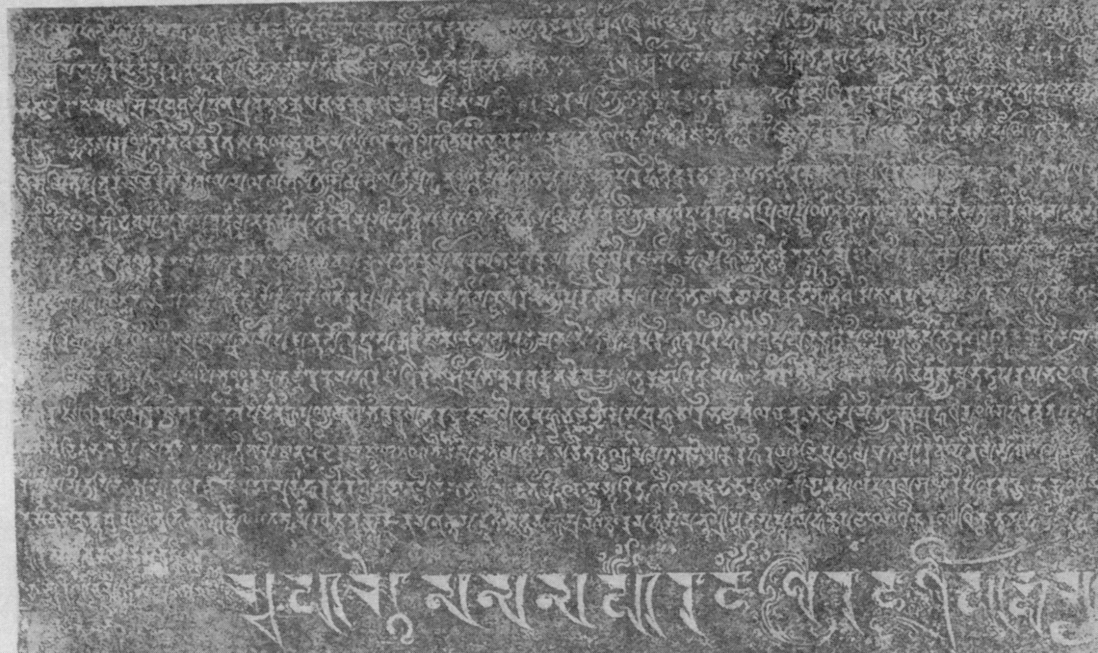

King Harsha's Autograph on the Banskhera Inscription.
"My own hand. Sri Harsha, Lord Paramount." (Svahasto mama maharajadhiraja sri Harshasya.) From Epigraphia Indica.

campaign was fought against the people of Ganjam (Kongoda) in 643 A.D., and then at last this king of many wars doffed his armour and devoted himself to the arts of peace and the practice of piety, as understood by an Indian despot. He obviously set himself to imitate Asoka, and the narrative of the doings in the latter years of Harsha's reign reads like a copy of the history of the great Maurya.

At this period the king began to show marked favour to the quietist teachings of Buddhism, first in its Hinayana, and afterward in its Mahayana form. He led the life of a devotee, and enforced the Buddhist prohibitions against the destruction of animal life with the utmost strictness and scant regard for the sanctity of human life. "He sought," we are told, "to plant the tree of religious merit to such an extent that he forgot to sleep and eat," and forbade the slaughter of any living thing, or the use of flesh as food throughout the "Five Indies," under pain of death without hope of pardon.

Benevolent institutions on the Asokan model, for the benefit of travellers, the poor, and the sick, were established throughout the empire. Rest-houses (*dharmsala*) were built in both the towns and rural parts, and provided with food and drink. Physicians were stationed at them to supply medicines without stint to those who needed them. The king also imitated his prototype in the foundation of numerous religious establishments devoted to the service both of the Hindu gods and the Buddhist ritual.

In his closing years the latter received the chief share of the royal favour, and numerous monasteries were erected, as well as several thousand *stupas*, each about a hundred feet high, built along the banks of the sacred Ganges. These latter structures doubtless were of a flimsy character, built chiefly of timber and bamboo, and so have left no trace; but the mere multiplication of *stupas*, however perishable the materials might be, was always a work of merit. Although Buddhism was visibly waning in the days of Harsha and Hiuen Tsang, the monks of the order were still numerous, and the occupants of the monasteries enumerated by the pilgrims numbered nearly two hundred thousand. A monastic population of such magnitude offered abundant opportunities for the exercise of princely liberality.

The picture of the state of religious belief and practice in India during the seventh century, as drawn by the contemporary authors, is filled with curious and interesting details. The members of the royal family to which Harsha belonged freely acted on their individual preferences in the matter of religion. His remote ancestor, Pushyabhuti, is recorded to have entertained from boyhood an ardent devotion toward Siva, and to have turned away from all other gods. Harsha's father was equally devoted to the worship of the Sun, and daily offered to that luminary "a bunch of red lotuses set in a pure vessel of ruby, and tinged, like his own heart, with the same hue." The elder brother and sister of Harsha were faithful Buddhists, while Harsha himself distributed his devotions among the three deities of the family, Siva, the Sun, and Buddha, and erected costly temples for the service of all three. But, in his later years, the Buddhist doctrines held the chief place in his affections, and the eloquence of the Chinese Master of the Law induced him to prefer the advanced teaching of the Mahayana sect to the more primitive Hinayana doctrine of the Sammitiya school with which he had previously been familiar.

The religious eclecticism of the royal family was the reflection and result of the state of popular religion at the time. Buddhism, although it had certainly lost the dominant position in the Ganges plain which it had once held, was still a powerful force, and largely influenced the public mind. The Jain system, which had never been very widely spread or aggressive in the north, retained its hold on certain localities, especially at Vaisali and in Eastern Bengal, but could not pretend to rival the general popularity of either Buddhism or Puranic Hinduism.

The last-named modification of the Hindu system was now firmly established, and the earlier Puranas were already revered as ancient and sacred writings. The bulk of the population in most provinces was then, as now, devoted to the service of the Puranic gods, each man and woman being, of course, free to select a particular deity, Siva, the Sun, Vishnu, or another, for special adoration according to personal predilection. As a rule, the followers of the various religions lived peaceably together, and no doubt many people besides the king sought to make certain of some divine support by doing honour to all the principal objects of popular worship in turn.

But, while toleration and concord were the rule, exceptions occurred. The King of Central Bengal, Sasanka, who has been mentioned as the treacherous murderer of Harsha's brother, and who was probably a scion of the Gupta dynasty, was a worshipper of Siva, and hated Buddhism, which he did his best to destroy. He dug up and burned the holy Bodhi tree at Bodh Gaya, on which, according to legend, Asoka had lavished inordinate devotion; he broke the stone marked with the footprints of Buddha at Pataliputra; and he destroyed the convents, and scattered the monks, carrying his persecutions to the foot of the Nepalese hills. These events must have happened about 600 A. D. The Bodhi tree was replanted after a short time by Purnavarman, King of Magadha, who is described as being the last descendant of Asoka, and as such was specially bound to honour the object venerated by his great ancestor.

THE SACRED BO-TREE.
From the Buddhist Stupa at Sanchi.
(After Hardy, Asoka.)

Harsha himself sometimes offended against the

principle of perfect religious toleration and equality. Like Akbar, he was fond of listening to the expositions of rival doctors, and he heard with great pleasure the arguments adduced by the learned Chinese traveller in favour of the Mahayana form of Buddhism, with the doctrines of which he does not seem to have been familiar. An interesting illustration of the freedom of ancient Hindu society from the trammels of the system of female seclusion introduced by the Mohammedans is afforded by the fact that his widowed sister sat by the king's side to hear the lecture by the Master of the Law, and frankly expressed the pleasure which she received from the discourse.

The king, however, was determined that his favourite should not be defeated in controversy, and when opponents were invited to dispute the propositions of the Chinese scholar, the terms of the contest were not quite fair. Harsha, having heard a report that Hiuen Tsang's life was in danger at the hands of his theological rivals, issued a proclamation concluding with the announcement that "if any one should touch or hurt the Master of the Law, he shall be forthwith beheaded; and whoever speaks against him, his tongue shall be cut out; but all those who desire to profit by his instructions, relying on my good-will, need not fear this manifesto."

The pilgrim's biographer naïvely adds that "from this time the followers of error withdrew and disappeared, so that, when eighteen days had passed, there had been no one to enter on the discussion."

A curious legend, narrated by Taranath, the Tibetan historian of Buddhism, if founded on fact, as it may be, indicates that Harsha's toleration did not extend to foreign religions. The story runs that the king built near Multan a great monastery constructed of timber after the foreign fashion, in which he entertained the strange teachers hospitably for several months, and that at the close of the entertainment he set fire to the building, and consumed along with it twelve thousand followers of the outlandish system, with all their books. This drastic measure is said to have reduced the religion of the Persians and Sakas to very narrow limits for a century, and it is alleged that their doctrine, presumably Zoroastrianism, was kept alive only by a single weaver in Khorasan.

King Harsha was so delighted with the discourse of Hiuen Tsang, whom he had met while in camp in Bengal, that he resolved to hold a special assembly at Kanauj, which was then his capital, for the purpose of giving the utmost publicity to the Master's teaching. The king marched along the southern bank of the Ganges, attended by an enormous multitude, while his vassal Kumara, King of Kamarupa, with a large but less numerous following, kept pace with him on the opposite bank. Advancing slowly in this way, Harsha, Kumara, and the attendant host reached Kanauj in the course of ninety days, and there encamped, in February or March, 644 A.D. The sovereign was received by Kumara, the Raja of Kamarupa, who had accompanied him on the march, the Raja of Valabhi in Western

India, who was connected with him by marriage, and eighteen other tributary rajas, as well as by four thousand learned Buddhist monks, including a thousand from the Nalanda monastery in Bihar, and some three thousand Jains and orthodox Brahmans.

The centre of attraction was a great monastery and shrine specially erected upon the bank of the Ganges, where a golden image of Buddha, equal to the king in stature, was kept in a tower a hundred feet high. A similar but smaller image, three feet in height, was carried daily in solemn procession, escorted by the twenty rajas and a train of three hundred elephants. The canopy was borne by Harsha in person, attired as the god Sakra, while his vassal, Raja Kumara, the most important of the princes in attendance, was clad as the god Brahma, and had the honour of waving a white fly-whisk. The sovereign, as he moved along, scattered on every side pearls, golden flowers, and other precious substances, in honour of the "Three Jewels,"—Buddha, the Religion, and the Order,—and having with his own hands washed the image at the altar prepared for the purpose, bore it on his shoulder to the western tower, and there offered to it thousands of silken robes embroidered with gems. Dinner was succeeded by a public disputation of the one-sided kind already described, and in the evening the monarch returned to his "travelling palace," a mile distant.

These ceremonies, which lasted for many days, were terminated by startling incidents. The temporary monastery, which had been erected at vast cost, suddenly took fire, and was in great part destroyed; but when the king intervened in person, the flames were stayed, and pious hearts recognized a miracle.

Harsha, attended by his princely train, had ascended the great *stupa* to survey the scene, and was coming down the steps, when a fanatic, armed with a dagger, rushed upon him and attempted to stab him. The assassin, having been captured instantly, was closely interrogated by the king in person, and confessed that he had been instigated to commit the crime by certain "heretics," who resented the excessive royal favour shown to the Buddhists. Five hundred Brahmans of note were then arrested, and, being "straitly questioned," were induced to confess that, in order to gratify their jealousy, they had fired the tower by means of burning arrows, and had hoped to slay the king during the resulting confusion. This confession, which was no doubt extorted by torture, was probably wholly false; but, whether true or not, it was accepted, and on the strength of it the alleged principals in the plot were executed, and some five hundred Brahmans were sent into exile.

After the close of the proceedings at Kanauj, Harsha invited his Chinese guest to accompany him to Prayaga (Allahabad), at the confluence of the Ganges and Jumna, to witness another imposing ceremonial. The Master of the Law, although anxious to start on his toilsome homeward journey, could not refuse the invitation, and accompanied his royal host to the scene of the intended display. Harsha explained that it had been his practice for thirty years past, in accordance with the custom of his ancestors, to hold a great quinquennial assembly on the sands where the rivers meet, and there to distribute his accumulated treasures to the poor and needy, as well as to the religious of all denominations. The present occasion was the sixth of the series (644 A.D.), which evidently had not been begun until Harsha had consolidated his power in the north.

The assembly was attended by all the vassal kings and a vast concourse of humbler folk estimated to number half a million, including poor, orphans, and destitute persons, besides specially invited Brahmans and ascetics of every sect from all parts of Northern India. The proceedings lasted for seventy-five days, terminating apparently about the end of April, and were opened by an imposing procession of all the rajas with their retinues. The religious services were of the curiously eclectic kind characteristic of the times.

On the first day an image of Buddha was set up in one of the temporary thatched buildings upon the sands, and vast quantities of costly clothing and other articles of value were distributed. On the second and third days, respectively, the images of the Sun and Siva were similarly honoured, but the accompanying distribution in each case was only half the amount of that consecrated to Buddha. The fourth day was devoted to the bestowal of gifts on ten thousand selected religious persons of the Buddhist order, who each received one hundred gold coins, a pearl, and a cotton garment, besides choice food, drink, flowers, and perfumes. During the next following twenty days, the great multitude of Brahmans were the recipients of the royal bounty. They were succeeded by the people whom the Chinese author calls "heretics," that is to say, Jains and members of sundry sects, who received gifts for the space of ten days. A like period was allotted for the bestowal of alms upon mendicants from distant regions, and a month was occupied in the distribution of charitable aid to poor, orphaned, and destitute persons.

"By this time the accumulation of five years was exhausted. Except the horses, elephants, and military accoutrements, which were necessary for maintaining order and protecting the royal estate, nothing remained. Besides these the king freely gave away his gems and goods, his clothing and necklaces, ear-rings, bracelets, chaplets, neck-jewel, and bright head-jewel; all these he freely gave without stint. All being given away, he begged from his sister [Rajyasri] an ordinary second-hand garment, and, having put it on, he paid worship to the 'Buddhas of the ten regions,' and rejoiced that his treasure had been bestowed in the field of religious merit."

The strange assembly, which in general appearance must have much resembled the crowded fair still held annually on the same ground, then broke up, and, after a further detention of ten days, Hiuen Tsang was permitted to depart. The king and Kumara Raja offered him abundance of gold pieces and other precious things, none of which he would accept, save a fur-lined cape, the gift of Kumara. But although the Master of the Law uniformly declined gifts intended to serve his personal use, he did not disdain to accept money for the necessary expenses of his arduous journey overland to China. These were provided on a liberal scale by the grant of three thousand gold and ten thousand silver pieces carried on an elephant.

A raja named Udhita was placed in command of a mounted escort, and charged to conduct the pilgrim in safety to the frontier. In the course of about six months of leisurely progress, interrupted by frequent halts, the raja completed his task, and brought his sovereign's guest in safety to Jalandhar in the north of the Panjab, where Hiuen Tsang stayed for a month. He then started with a fresh escort, and, penetrating with difficulty the defiles of the Salt Range, crossed the Indus, and ultimately reached his home in distant China by the route over the Pamirs and through Khotan, in the spring of 646 A. D.

The pages of Hiuen Tsang and his biographer give the latest information about King Harsha, who died at the end of 647, or the beginning of 648, not long after his distinguished guest's departure. During his lifetime he maintained diplomatic intercourse with the Chinese empire. A Brahman envoy, whom he had sent to the Emperor of China, returned in 643 A. D., accompanied by a Chinese mission bearing a reply to Harsha's despatch. The mission remained for a considerable time in India, and did not go back to China until 645 A. D. The next year, Wang-hiuen-tse, who had been the second in command of the earlier embassy, was sent by his sovereign as head of a new Indian mission, with an escort of thirty horsemen. Before the envoys reached Magadha in 648 A. D., King Harsha had died, and the withdrawal of his strong arm had plunged the country into disorder, which was aggravated by famine.

Arjuna, a minister of the late king, usurped the throne, and gave a hostile reception to the Chinese mission. The members of the escort were massacred, and the property of the mission plundered, but the envoys, Wang-hiuen-tse and his colleague, were fortunate enough to escape into Nepal by night.

The reigning King of Tibet, the famous Srong-tsan Gampo, who was married to a Chinese princess, succoured the fugitives, and supplied them with a force of a thousand horsemen, which co-operated with a Nepalese contingent of seven thousand men. With this small army Wang-hiuen-tse descended into the plains, and, after a three days' siege, succeeded in storming the chief city of Tirhut. Three thousand of the garrison were beheaded, and ten thousand persons were drowned in the neighbouring river. Arjuna fled, and, having collected a fresh force, offered battle. He was again disastrously defeated and taken prisoner. The victor promptly beheaded a thousand prisoners, and in a later action captured the entire royal family, took twelve thousand prisoners, and obtained thirty thousand head of cattle. Five hundred and eighty walled towns made their submission, and Kumara, the King of Eastern India, who had attended Harsha's assemblies a few years earlier, sent in abundant supplies of cattle, horses, and accoutrements for the victorious army. Wang-hiuen-tse brought the usurper Arjuna as a prisoner to China, and was promoted for his services. Thus ended this strange episode, which, although known to antiquaries for many years, has hitherto escaped the notice of the historians of India.

The observations of Hiuen Tsang throw considerable light upon the political arrangements of India in the regions beyond the limits of Harsha's empire during the seventh century A.D. In the north, Kashmir was the predominant power, and had reduced the kingdoms of Taxila and the Salt Range (Simhapura), as well as the minor principalities of the lower hills, to the rank of dependencies.

The greater part of the Panjab between the Indus and the Bias Rivers was comprised in the kingdom called Tseh-kia by the pilgrim, the capital of which was an unnamed city situated close to Sakala, where the tyrant Mihiragula had held his court. The province of Multan, where the Sun-god was held in special honour, and a country called Po-fa-to, to the northeast of Multan, were dependencies of this kingdom.

Sind was remarkable for being under the government of a king belonging to the Sudra caste, and for the large number of Buddhist monks which the country supported, estimated at ten thousand. But the quality was not in proportion to the quantity, as most of the ten thousand were denounced as idle fellows given over to self-indulgence and debauchery. The Indus delta, to which the pilgrim gives the name of O-tien-po-chi-lo, was a province of the kingdom of Sind.

The Kings of Ujjain in Central India and of Pundra-vardhana in Bengal, both of which kingdoms were more or less subject to Harsha's control, belonged to the Brahman caste. The Ujjain country supported a dense population, which included few Buddhists. Most of the monasteries were in ruins, and only three or four, occupied by some three hundred monks, were in use. The early decay of Buddhism in this region, which was sanctified by the traditions of Asoka, and included the magnificent buildings at Sanchi, is a very curious fact.

SURYA, THE SUN.

Bhaskara-varman, or Kumara Raja, the King of Kamarupa, or Assam, who played such a prominent part in Harsha's ceremonials, was also by caste a Brahman, and without faith in Buddha, although well disposed toward learned men of all religions. He was so far subject to the sovereign of Northern India that he could not afford to disobey Harsha's commands.

Kalinga, the conquest of which had cost Asoka such

bitter remorse nine hundred years earlier, was depopulated, and mostly covered with jungle. The pilgrim observes in picturesque language that "in old days the kingdom of Kalinga had a very dense population. Their shoulders rubbed one with the other, and the axles of their chariot-wheels grided together, and when they raised their arm-sleeves a perfect tent was formed." Legend sought to explain the change by the curse of an angry saint.

Harsha was the last native monarch prior to the Mohammedan conquest who held the position of paramount power in the North. His death loosened the bonds which restrained the disruptive forces always ready to operate in India, and allowed them to produce their normal result, a medley of petty states, with ever varying boundaries, and engaged in unceasing internecine war. Such was India when first disclosed to European observation in the fourth century B.C., and such it always has been, except during the comparatively brief periods in which a vigorous central government has compelled the mutually repellent molecules of the body politic to check their gyrations, and submit to the grasp of a superior controlling force.

Excepting the purely local incursions of the Arabs in Sind and Gujarat during the eighth century, India was exempt from foreign aggression for nearly five hundred years, from the defeat of Mihiragula in 528 A.D. until the raids of Mahmud of Ghazni at the beginning of the eleventh century, and was left free to work out her destiny in her own fashion. She cannot claim to have achieved success. The three following chapters, which attempt to give an outline of the salient features in the bewildering annals of Indian petty states when left to their own devices for several centuries, may perhaps serve to give the reader a notion of what India always has been when released from the control of a supreme authority.

CHAPTER XIV

THE MEDIÆVAL KINGDOMS OF THE NORTH

648 TO 1200 A. D.

I—RELATIONS WITH CHINA AND TIBET

THE tenacity of the Chinese government in holding on to the most distant possessions of the empire has been exemplified in recent times by the recovery of Kashgaria and Yunnan from Mohammedan powers, and of Kuldja from the Russians. The history of the seventh and eight centuries offers many illustrations of the same characteristic, and exhibits China as making the most determined efforts to exercise influence in, and assert suzerainty over, the countries on the northern frontier of India.

In the first half of the sixth century the power of China in the " Western Countries " had vanished, and the Ephthalites, or White Huns, ruled a vast empire, which included Kashgaria (the " Four Garrisons " of Chinese writers), Kashmir, and Gandhara, the region near Peshawar.

About the year 565 (" between 563 and 567 ") the

Ephthalite dominion passed into the hands of the Western Turks and Persians; but the grasp of the latter power on the provinces south of the Oxus soon relaxed, and the Turks became the heirs of the Ephthalites in the whole of their territory as far as the Indus. Accordingly, in 630 A. D., when Hiuen Tsang was on his way to India, his safety was assured by passports granted by Tong-she-hu, the "Kazan," or supreme chief of the Western Turks, which guaranteed him protection as far as Kapisa. In the same year the pilgrim's powerful protector was assassinated, and the Chinese, under the guidance of the Emperor Tai-tsong, the second prince of the Tang dynasty, inflicted upon the Northern or Eastern Turks a defeat so decisive that the vanquished became slaves to the Chinese for fifty years.

When relieved from fear of the Northern Turks, the Chinese were able to turn their arms against the western tribes, and in the years 640-8 succeeded in occupying Turfan, Korashar, and Kucha, thus securing the northern road of communication between the East and West.

At this time Tibet was on amicable terms with the Middle Kingdom. In 641 the Chinese Princess Wencheng had been given in marriage to Srong-tsan-Gam-po, King of Tibet, and in the years 643-5 the Chinese envoys to Harsha had been able to reach India through the friendly states of Tibet and Nepal, both of which sent troops to rescue Wang-Hiuen-tse from the troubles into which he fell after Harsha's death.

The work of subduing the Turks, begun by the Emperor Tai-tsong, was continued by his successor, Kao-tsong (650-83), and, by the year 659, China was nominally mistress of the entire territory of the Western Turks, which was then formally annexed. In 661-5 China enjoyed unparalleled prestige, and had reached a height of glory never again attained. Kapisa was a province of the empire, and the imperial retinue included ambassadors from Udyana, or the Suwat valley, and from all the countries extending from Persia to Korea. But this magnificent extension of the empire did not last long. A terrible defeat inflicted by the Tibetans in 670 deprived China of Kashgaria, or the "Four Garrisons," which remained in the hands of the victors until 692 A. D., when the province was recovered by the Chinese.

Between 682 and 691 the Northern Turks had regained a good deal of the power which had been shattered by the defeat of 630, and even exercised a certain amount of control over the western tribes. But internal dissension was at all times the bane of the Central Asian nations, and the Chinese well knew how to take advantage of the national failing. They intervened in the tribal quarrels, with the support of the Uigurs and Karluks, with such effect that in 744 the Uigurs established themselves on the Orkhon in the eastern part of the Turkish territory, while on the west the Karluks gradually occupied the country of the Ten Tribes, and took possession of Tokmak and Talas, the former residences of the Turkish chiefs.

Between 665 and 715 the government of China was unable to interfere effectually in the affairs of the countries between the Jaxartes (Syr Darya) and the Indus, since the southern route to the west through Kashgaria had been closed by the Tibetans, and the roads over the Hindu Kush were blocked by the conquests of Kotaiba, the Arab general.

The accession of the Emperor Hiuen-tsong in 713 marks a revival of Chinese activity; and determined efforts were made by means both of diplomacy and arms to keep open the Pamir passes and to check the ambition of the Arabs and Tibetans, who sometimes combined. In 719, Samarkand and other kingdoms invoked the aid of China against the armies of Islam, while the Arab leaders sought to obtain the co-operation of the minor states on the Indian borderland. The chiefs of Udyana (Suwat), Khottal (west of Badakshan), and Chitral, having refused to listen to Moslem blandishments, were rewarded by the Emperor of China with letters patent conferring on each the title of king, and a similar honour was bestowed upon the rulers of Yasin (Little Po-lu), Zabulistan (Ghazni), Kapisa, and Kashmir, received investiture as king from the emperor in kingdoms, so as to form an effective barrier against both Arabs and Tibetans. Chandrapida, King of Kashmir, received investiture as king from the emperor in 720, and his brother Muktapida-Lalitaditya was similarly honoured in 733.

A few years later—in 744 and 747—Chinese influence had been so far extended that the emperor granted titles to the King of Tabaristan, south of the Caspian. In the latter year a Chinese army crossed the Pamirs, in spite of all difficulties, and reduced the King of Yasin to subjection.

But, as in the seventh century, so in the eighth, the Chinese dominion over the western countries was short-lived, and was shattered by a disastrous defeat inflicted in 751 on the Chinese general Sien-chi by the Arabs, who were aided by the Karluk tribes. Indirectly this disaster had an important consequence for European civilization. The art of making paper, up to that time a monopoly of remote China, was introduced into Samarkand by Chinese prisoners, and so became known to Europe, with results familiar to all.

AN INDIAN SCENE.

From the middle of the eighth century, contact between the politics of India and China ceased, and was not renewed until the English conquest of Upper Burma in 1885. In these latter days, Tibet, which has been a dependency of China since the close of the thirteenth century, has again come within the purview of the Indian government, and its affairs are again the subject of Indo-Chinese diplomacy.

II—NEPAL

The kingdom of Nepal, the most valuable portion of which is the enclosed valley in which Kathmandu and other towns are situated, although it has remained generally outside the ordinary range of Indian politics, has maintained sufficient connection with India to require brief mention in a history of that country. In Asoka's time Nepal was an integral part of the empire, and was probably administered directly from the capital as one of the home provinces. In the days of Samudragupta, in the fourth century A.D., when we next hear of the Nepalese kingdom it was an autonomous tributary frontier state, but, after the fall of the Gupta empire in the following century, it became independent.

Harsha again reduced the kingdom to the position of a tributary state about 638 A.D., and ten years later, when he died, the Nepalese recovered their independence, subject, perhaps, to some slight control from China. They were able to give valuable assistance to the envoy Wang-Hiuen-tse in 648 A.D., when he was expelled from India by Harsha's usurping successor. At the beginning of the eighth century, before the revival of Chinese activity in the reign of the Emperor Hiuen-tsong, Nepal was for a time a dependency of Tibet.

The establishment of the Nepalese era, which dates from October 20, 879 A.D., in the reign of Raghava-deva, probably marks some important event in local history, the exact nature of which is not known. The kingdom was never subjugated by any of the Mohammedan dynasties, and has retained its autonomy to this day. The conquest of the country by the Gurkhas took place in 1768. A corrupt and decaying form of Buddhism still survives in the country.

III—KASHMIR

A detailed account of the history of Kashmir would fill a volume; in this place a brief notice of some of the leading passages will suffice. The valley had been included in the Maurya empire in the time of Asoka, and again in the Kushan dominion in the days of Kanishka and Huvishka. Harsha, although not strong enough to annex Kashmir, was yet able to compel the king to surrender a cherished relic, an alleged tooth of Buddha, which was carried off to Kanauj. The authentic chronicles of the kingdom begin with the Karkota dynasty, which was founded by Durlabhavardhana during Harsha's lifetime. This prince and his son Durlabhaka are credited with long reigns.

The latter was succeeded by his three sons in order, the eldest of whom, Chandrapida, received investiture as king from the Emperor of China in 720, by whom the third son, Muktapida, also known as Lalitaditya, was similarly honoured in 733. This prince, who is said to have reigned for thirty-six years, extended the power of Kashmir far beyond its normal mountain limits, and about the year 740 inflicted a crushing defeat upon Yasovarman, King of Kanauj. He also vanquished the Tibetans, Bhutias, and the Turks on the Indus. His memory has been perpetuated by the famous Martanda temple, which was built by him, and still exists. The acts of this king, and all that he did, and something more, are set forth at large in Kalhana's chronicle.

The reign of Avantivarman in the latter part of the ninth century was notable for his enlightened patronage of literature, and for the beneficent schemes of drainage and irrigation carried out by Suyya, his minister of public works. The next king, Sankaravarman, distinguished himself in war, but is chiefly remembered as the author of an ingenious system of fiscal oppression, and the plunderer of temple treasures. The details of his exactions are worth reading as proving the capacity of an Oriental despot without a conscience for unlimited and ruthless extortion. During his reign, the last of the Turki Shahiya Kings of Kabul, the descendants of Kanishka, was overthrown by the Brahman Lalliya, who founded a dynasty which lasted until 1021, when it was extirpated by the Mohammedans.

During the latter half of the tenth century, power was in the hands of an unscrupulous queen named Didda, the granddaughter of a Shahiya king, who, first as queen-consort, then as regent, and ultimately as sovereign for twenty-three years, misgoverned the unhappy state for half a century. In the reign of her nephew, Sangrama, the kingdom suffered an attack from Mahmud of Ghazni, and, although its troops were defeated by the invader, preserved its independence, which was protected by the inaccessibility of the mountain barriers.

During the eleventh century, Kashmir, which has

been generally unfortunate in its rulers, endured unspeakable miseries at the hands of the tyrants Kalasa and Harsha. The latter, who was evidently insane, imitated Sankaravarman in the practice of plundering temples, and rightly came to a miserable end.

A local Mohammedan dynasty obtained power in 1339, and the religion of Islam gradually spread in the valley during the fourteenth century; but the natural defences of the kingdom effectually guarded it against the ambition of the sovereigns of India, until Akbar conquered it in 1587 and incorporated it in the Mogul empire.

IV—DELHI, KANAUJ, AJMIR, AND GWALIOR

Europeans are so accustomed to associate the name of Delhi with the sovereignty of India that they do not easily realize the fact that Delhi is among the most modern of the great Indian cities. Vague legends, it is true, irradiate the lands along the bank of the Jumna near the village of Indarpat with the traditional glories of the prehistoric Indraprastha, and these stories may or may not have some substantial basis. But, as an historical city, Delhi dates only from the middle of the eleventh century, when Anangapala, a Rajput chief of the Tomara clan, built the Red Fort, where the Kutb mosque now stands, and founded a town. The celebrated iron pillar on which the eulogy of Chandragupta Vikramaditya is incised, was removed by him from its original position, probably Mathura, and set up in 1052 A.D. as an adjunct to a group of temples, from the materials of which the Mohammedans afterward constructed the great mosque.

Anangapala, who seems to have come from Kanauj, ruled a principality of modest dimensions, extending to Agra on the south, Ajmir on the west, Hansi on the north, and the Ganges on the east. His dynasty lasted for just a century, until 1151 A. D., when it was supplanted by the Chauhan chief, Visala-deva of Ajmir.

The grandson of Visala-deva was Prithivi Raja, or Rai Pithora, famous in song and legend as a chivalrous lover and doughty champion, in whose person the lordships of Ajmir and Delhi were united. His fame as a bold lover rests upon his daring abduction of the not unwilling daughter of Jayachchandra (Jaichand), the Gaharwar Raja of Kanauj, which occurred in or about 1175. His reputation as a warrior is securely founded upon the story of his defeat of the Chandella raja and the capture of Mahoba in 1182, as well as upon gallant resistance to the flood of Mohammedan invasion. Rai Pithora may indeed be fairly described as the popular hero of Northern India, and his exploits in love and war are to this day the subject of rude epics and bardic lays.

The dread of the victorious Mussulman host led by Shihab-ud-din, who was now undisputed master of the Panjab, constrained the jarring states of Upper India to lay aside their quarrels and combine for a moment against the common foe. At first fortune favoured the Hindus, and in 1191 Prithivi Raja succeeded in inflicting a severe defeat upon the invaders at Tirauri, between Thanesar and Karnal, which forced them to retire beyond the Indus. Two years later, in 1193, Shihab-ud-din, having returned with a fresh force, again encountered Prithivi Raja, who was in command of an immense host, swollen by contingents from numerous confederate princes. A vigorous charge by twelve thousand well-armed Mussulman horsemen repeated the lesson given by Alexander long ages before, and demonstrated the incapacity of a mob of Indian militia to stand the onset of trained cavalry. To use the graphic language of the Mohammedan historian, "this prodigious army, once shaken, like a great building, tottered to its fall, and was lost in its own ruins." Prithivi Raja, who was taken prisoner, was executed in cold blood, and the wretched inhabitants of his capital, Ajmir, were either put to the sword or sold into slavery.

In the same year, 1193 A. D. (A. H. 589), Delhi fell, and Shihab-ud-din marched against Kanauj and took that city, which had been for several centuries the most splendid of the cities of Northern India. The raja, Jayachchandra, retired toward Benares, but was overtaken by his adversary, routed, and slain. The holy citadel of Hinduism fell into the hands of the victors, who could now feel assured that the triumph of Islam was secure.

The surrender of Gwalior by its Parihar raja in 1196, the capture of Nahrwalah in 1197, and the capitulation of Kalinjar in 1203 completed the reduction of Upper India, and when Shihab-ud-din died in 1206, Elphinstone says he "held, in different degrees of subjection, the whole of Hindustan Proper, except Malwa and some contiguous districts. Sind and Bengal were either entirely subdued, or in rapid course of reduction. On Gujarat he had no hold, except what is implied in the possession of the capital (Nahrwalah, or Anhalwara). Much of Hindustan was immediately under his officers, and the rest under dependent or at least tributary princes. The desert and some of the mountains were left independent from neglect."

An important consequence of the capture of Kanauj was the migration of the bulk of the Gaharwar clan to the deserts of Marwar in Rajputana, where they settled, and became known as Rathors. The state so founded, now generally designated by the name of its capital, Jodhpur, is one of the most important principalities of Rajputana. Similar clan movements, necessitated by the pressure of Mohammedan armies, were frequent at this period, and to a large extent account for the existing distribution of the Rajput clans.

V—THE CHANDELLAS OF JEJAKABHUKTI AND THE KALACHURIS OF CHEDI

The ancient name of the province between the Jumna and Narmada, now known as Bundelkhand, was Jejakabhukti, and the extensive region farther to the south, which is now under the administration of the Chief Commissioner of the Central Provinces, nearly corresponds with the old kingdom of Chedi. In the mediæval history of these countries two dynasties, the Chandellas and the Kalachuris, which occasionally were

The Fort, Gwalior.
From a Photograph.

SAS BAHU TEMPLE, GWALIOR.

connected by marriage, and constantly were in contact whether as friends or as enemies, are conspicuous.

The Chandellas, like several other dynasties, first come into notice early in the ninth century, when Nannuka Chandella, about 831 A. D., overthrew a Parihar chieftain, and became lord of Jejakabhukti. The Parihar capital had been at Mau-Sahaniya between Nowgong (Naugaon) and Chhatarpur. The predecessors of the Parihars were Gaharwar Rajas, members of the clan which afterward gave Kanauj the line of kings commonly miscalled Rathors.

The Chandella princes were great builders, and beautified their chief towns, Mahoba, Kalinjar, and Khajuraho, with many magnificent temples and lovely lakes, formed by throwing massive dams across the openings between the hills. In this practice of building embankments and constructing lakes the Chandellas were imitators of the Gaharwars, who are credited with the formation of some of the most charming lakes in Bundelkhand.

King Dhanga (950 - 99 A. D.), who lived to an age of more than a hundred years, was the most notable of his family. Some of the grandest temples at Khajuraho are due to his munificence, and he took an active part in the politics of his time. In 978 A. D. he joined the league formed by Jaipal to resist Sabuktigin, and shared with the Rajas of Ajmir and Kanauj in the disastrous defeat which the allies suffered from the invaders at Lamghan on the Kabul River.

When Mahmud of Ghazni threatened to overrun

India, Dhanga's son, Ganda (999-1025), joined the new confederacy of Hindu princes organized by Ananga Pala of Lahore in 1008, which also failed to stay the hand of the invader. Twelve years later Ganda attacked Kanauj and killed the raja, who had made terms with the Mohammedans, but in 1022 or 1023 he was himself compelled to surrender the strong fortress of Kalinjar to Mahmud.

Gangeyadeva Kalachuri of Chedi (*cir.* 1015-40), the contemporary of Ganda and his successors, was an able and ambitious prince, who seems to have aimed at attaining the position of paramount power in Upper India. In 1019 his suzerainty was recognized in distant Tirhut, and his projects of aggrandizement were taken up and proceeded with by his son Karnadeva (*cir.* 1040-70), who joined Bhima, King of Gujarat, in crushing Bhoja, the learned King of Malwa, about 1053 A. D.

But some years later, Karnadeva was taught the lesson of the mutability of fortune by suffering a severe defeat at the hands of Kirttivarman Chandella (1049-1100), who widely extended the dominion of his house. Kirttivarman is also memorable in literary history as the patron of the curious allegorical play entitled the *Prabodhachandrodaya*, or "Rise of the Moon of Intellect," which was performed at his court, and gives in dramatic form a very clever exposition of the Vedanta system of philosophy.

The last Chandella king to play any considerable part upon the stage of history was Paramardi, or Parmal (1165-1203), whose reign is memorable for his

TEMPLE OF MAHADEVA, KAJURAHO.

defeat in 1182 by Prithivi Raja Chauhan, and for the capture of Kalinjar in 1203 (A. H. 599) by Kutb-ud-din Ibak. The Chauhan and Chandella war occupies a large space in the popular Hindi epic, the Chand-Raisa, which is familiar to the people of Upper India.

The account of the death of Parmal and the capture of Kalinjar, as told by the contemporary Mohammedan historian, may be quoted as a good illustration of the process by which the Hindu kingdoms passed under the rule of their new Moslem masters.

" 'The accursed Parmar,' the Rai of Kalinjar, fled into the fort after a desperate resistance in the field, and afterward surrendered himself, and placed 'the collar of subjection' round his neck, and, on his promise of allegiance, was admitted to the same favours as his ancestor had experienced from Mahmud Sabuktigin, and engaged to make a payment of tribute and elephants, but he died a natural death before he could execute any of his engagements. His Diwan, or Mahtea, by name Aj Deo, was not disposed to surrender so easily as his master, and gave his enemies much trouble, until he was compelled to capitulate, in consequence of severe drought which dried up all the reservoirs of water in the forts. 'On Monday, the 20th of Rajab, the garrison, in an extreme state of weakness and distraction, came out of the fort, and by compulsion left their native place empty; . . . and the fort of Kalinjar, which was celebrated throughout the world for being as strong as the wall of Alexander,' was taken. 'The temples were converted into mosques and abodes of goodness, and the ejaculations of the bead-counters and the voices of the summoners to prayer ascended to the highest heaven, and the very name of idolatry was annihilated. . . . Fifty thousand men came under the collar of slavery, and the plain became black as pitch with Hindus.' Elephants and cattle, and countless arms also, became the spoil of the victors.

"The reins of victory were then directed toward Mahoba, and the government of Kalinjar was conferred on Hazabbar-ud-din Hasan Arnal. When Kutb-ud-din was satisfied with all the arrangements made in that quarter, he went toward Badaun, 'which is one of the mothers of cities, and one of the chiefest of the country of Hind.'"

Chandella rajas lingered on as purely local chiefs until the sixteenth century, but their affairs are of no general interest. The Chandella clan was scattered, and its most notable modern representative is the Raja of Gidhaur, near Mungir (Monghyr) in Bengal.

The Kalachuri or Haihaya Rajas of Chedi are last mentioned in an inscription of the year 1181 A.D., and the manner of their disappearance is not exactly known, but there is reason to believe that they were supplanted by the Baghels of Rewa. The Hayobans Rajputs of the Baliya District in the United Provinces claim descent from the Rajas of Ratanpur in the Central Provinces, and are probably really an offshoot of the ancient Haihaya race. The Kings of Chedi used a special era, according to which the year 1 was equivalent to 249 - 50 A. D., and it is possible that the dynasty may have been established at that early date, but nothing substantial is known about it before the ninth century.

VI—PARAMARAS OF MALWA

The Paramara dynasty of Malwa, the region north of the Narmada, anciently known as the kingdom of Ujjain, is specially memorable by reason of its association with many eminent names in the history of later Sanskrit literature. The dynasty was founded by a chief named Upendra, or Krishnaraja, at the beginning of the ninth century, when so many ruling families attract notice for the first time, and lasted for about four centuries.

The seventh raja, named Munja, who was famous for his learning and eloquence, was not only a patron of poets, but was himself a poet of no small reputation, and the anthologies include various compositions attributed to his pen. The authors Dhanamjaya, Dhanika, and Halayudha were among the distinguished scholars who graced his court. His energies were not solely devoted to the peaceful pursuit of literature, however, as the Chalukya King Taila II was defeated by him sixteen times. The seventeenth attack failed, and Munja, who had crossed the Godavari, Taila's northern boundary, was defeated, captured, and executed about 995 A. D.

The nephew of Munja, the famous Bhoja, ascended the throne of Dhara, which was in those days the capital of Malwa, about 1010 A. D., and reigned gloriously for more than forty years. Although his fights with the neighbouring powers, including one of the Mohammedan armies of Mahmud of Ghazni, are now forgotten, his fame as an enlightened patron of learning and a skilled author remains undimmed, and his name has

RUINS OF THE TEMPLE OF BHOJPUR.

become proverbial as that of the model king. Works on astronomy, architecture, the art of poetry, and other subjects are credibly attributed to him, and there is no doubt that he was a prince, like Samudragupta, of very uncommon ability.

The great Bhojpur Lake, a beautiful sheet of water to the southeast of Bhopal, covering an area of 250 square miles, formed by massive embankments closing the outlets in a circle of hills, was his noblest monument, and continued to testify to the skill of his engineers until the fifteenth century, when the dam was cut by order of a Mohammedan king, and the water drained off. The bed of the lake is now a fertile plain intersected by the Indian Midland Railway.

About 1053 A. D. this accomplished prince succumbed to an attack by the confederate Kings of Gujarat and Chedi, and the glory of his house departed.[1] His dynasty lasted as a purely local power until the beginning of the thirteenth century, when it was superseded by chiefs of the Tomara clan, who were in their turn followed by Chauhan rajas, from whom the crown passed to Mohammedan kings in 1401. Akbar suppressed the local dynasty in 1569, and incorporated Malwa into the Mogul empire.

VII—PALA AND SENA DYNASTIES OF BIHAR AND BENGAL

Harsha, when at the height of his power, exercised a certain amount of control as suzerain over the whole of Bengal, even as far east as the distant kingdom of Kamarupa, or Assam, and seems to have possessed full sovereign authority over Western and Central Bengal. After his death, the local rajas no doubt asserted their independence; but, except for the strange story of Arjuna and Wang-Hiuen-tse, related in the thirteenth

[1] Bhoja Paramara of Dhara must not be confounded with the numerous distinct rajas of the same name. Bhoja, a King of Kanauj late in the ninth century, was a specially notable personage.

chapter, no particulars are known concerning the history of Bengal during more than a century and a half.

Early in the ninth century (*cir.* 815 A.D.), approximately when the Chandella, Paramara, and other dynasties are first heard of, a chieftain named Gopala became ruler of Bengal. Toward the close of his life he extended his power westwards over Magadha or Bihar, and is said to have reigned forty-five years. He was a pious Buddhist, and was credited with the foundation of a great monastery at his capital, the town of Bihar (Udandapura, or Otantapuri), which had taken the place of Pataliputra, then in ruins. Inasmuch as the word *pala* was an element in the personal names of the founder of the family and his successors, the dynasty is commonly and conveniently designated as that of the "Pala Kings of Bengal."

The third king, Devapala (*cir.* 853-93 A.D.), is alleged to have conquered Kamarupa and Orissa. The ninth king, Mahipala, is known to have been on the throne in 1026 A.D., and is believed to have reigned for fifty years, until about 1060. Like all the members of his dynasty, he was a devout Buddhist, and the revival of Buddhism in Tibet, effected in 1013 A.D. by Dharmapala of Magadha and his three pupils, may be attributed to this king's missionary zeal.

At about the time of Mahipala's death, a raja named Vijayasena founded a rival dynasty in Bengal commonly called that of the "Sena kings," which seems to have wrested the eastern provinces for a time from the hands of the Pala dynasty, the power of which was then much circumscribed. Gangeyadeva of Chedi, as has been already mentioned, was recognized as the sovereign of Tirhut in 1076 A.D. But his supremacy did not last long, and an independent local dynasty of Northern Tirhut was established at Simraon early in the thirteenth century.

In Bihar and Bengal both "Palas" and "Senas" were swept away by the torrent of Mohammedan invasion at the end of the twelfth century, when Kutb-ud-din's general, Mohammed, the son of Bakhtiyar, stormed Bihar in 1193 A.D. (A.H. 589), and surprised Nudiah (*vulgo* Nuddea) in the following year. The name of the last Hindu ruler of Bihar is given by tradition as Indradyumna, who is supposed, but not proved, to have belonged to the Pala line.

The Mussulman general, who had already made his name a terror by repeated plundering expeditions in Bihar, seized the capital by a daring stroke. The almost contemporary historian met one of the survivors of the attacking party in 1243 A.D., and learned from him that the fort of Bihar was seized by a party of only two hundred horsemen, who boldly rushed the postern gate and gained possession of the place. Great quantities of plunder were obtained, and the slaughter of the "shaven-headed Brahmans," that is to say, the Buddhist monks, was so thoroughly completed that, when the victor sought for some one capable of explaining the contents of the books in the libraries of the monasteries, not a living man could be found who was able to read them. "It was discovered," we are told, "that the whole fort and city was a place of study."

This crushing blow, followed up, of course, by similar acts of violence, destroyed the vitality of Buddhism in its ancient home. No doubt a few devout though disheartened adherents of the system lingered round the desecrated shrines for a few years longer, and even to this day traces of the religion once so proudly dominant may be discerned in the practices of obscure sects; but Buddhism as a popular religion in Bihar, its last abode in Upper India south of the Himalaya, was destroyed once and for all by the sword of a single Mussulman adventurer. Many monks who escaped death fled to Tibet, Nepal, and Southern India.

The overthrow of the "Sena" dynasty was accomplished with equal or even greater ease. The ruler of Eastern Bengal in those days was an aged king, called Rai Lakhmaniya by the Mohammedan writer, and was reputed to have occupied the throne for eighty years. His family, we are told, was respected by all the Rais, or chiefs, of Hindustan, and he was considered to hold the rank of khalif (caliph), or sovereign. Trustworthy persons affirmed that no one, great or small, ever suffered injustice at his hands, and his generosity was proverbial.

This much-respected sovereign held his court at Nudiah, situated in the upper delta of the Ganges, on the Bhagirathi River, about sixty miles north of the site of Calcutta. The town still gives its name to a

British district, and is renowned as the seat of a Hindu college organized after the ancient manner.

The year after his facile conquest of Bihar, Mohammed, the son of Bakhtiyar, equipped an army for the subjugation of Bengal. Riding in advance, he suddenly appeared before Nudiah with a slender following of eighteen horsemen, and boldly entered the city. The people supposed him to be a horse-dealer, but when he reached the gate of the Rai's palace, he drew his sword and attacked the unsuspecting household. The Rai, who was at his dinner, was completely taken by surprise, "and fled barefooted by the rear of the palace; and his whole treasure, and all his wives, maid-servants, attendants, and women, fell into the hands of the invader. Numerous elephants were taken, and such booty was obtained by the Mohammedans as is beyond all compute. When his (Mohammed's) army arrived, the whole city was brought under subjection, and he fixed his headquarters there."

Rai Lakhmaniya fled to the shrine of Jagannath (Juggernaut) in Orissa, where he died. The conqueror presently destroyed the city of Nudiah, and established the seat of his government at Lakhnauti. Mosques, colleges, and Mohammedan monasteries were endowed by him and his officers in all parts of the kingdom, and a great portion of the spoil was judiciously sent to his distant chief, Kutb-ud-din.

Such was the dishonoured end of the last Hindu kingdoms of Bengal and Bihar, which would have made a better fight for life if they had deserved to exist.

The administration of the aged Lakhmaniya must have been hopelessly inefficient to permit a foreign army to march unobserved across Bengal, and to allow of the surprise of the palace by an insignificant party of eighteen horsemen.

Notwithstanding the manifest rottenness of their system of government, the "Sena" kings were sufficiently conceited to establish a special era of their own, which they called by the name of Lakshmana-sena. The first current year, according to this computation, corresponded with 1119-20 A.D., and the epoch was apparently the date of either the accession or coronation of Lakshmana-sena, who seems to have been identical with the aged Rai Lakhmaniya of the Mohammedan historians. One form of the tradition represents this king as having come to the throne in 510 A.H., equivalent to 1116-17 A.D., just eighty lunar years previous to the easy victory of the Moslem invader, and the era was invented presumably to mark the date of Lakshmana-sena's coronation in October, 1119 A.D.

View of Saswar, in the Deccan, Southeast of Poona

CHAPTER XV

THE KINGDOMS OF THE DECCAN

THE term Deccan, a convenient and familiar corruption of the Sanskrit word meaning the south, may be, and sometimes is, extended so as to cover the whole of India south of the Narmada, but is more usually understood as designating a more limited territory, in which Malabar and the Tamil countries of the extreme south are not included. Thus limited, the term connotes the whole region occupied by the Telugu-speaking populations, as well as Maharashtra, or the Maratha country. With reference to modern political divisions, the greater part of the Deccan in this restricted sense is occupied by the territories of the Nizam of Hyderabad.

Physically, the country is for the most part a hot, hilly table-land, watered by two great rivers, the Godavari and the Krishna (Kistna), the latter of which receives on the south an important affluent, the Tungabhadra.

In this region the dominant power for four centuries and a half, up to about 230 A. D., was the Andhra, the history of which has already been discussed. For some three centuries after the extinction of the Andhra dynasty, "we have," as remarked by Professor Bhandarkar, "no specific information about the dynasties that ruled over the country;" but there is reason to

GLIMPSE OF HYDERABAD.
From stereograph, copyright 1903, by Underwood & Underwood, New York.

believe that the western territory, or Maharashtra, was governed by princes belonging to the Rashtrakuta, or Ratta, clan, which long afterward, in the middle of the eighth century, became for a time the leading power of the Deccan.

Practically the political history of the Deccan begins in the middle of the sixth century with the rise of the

Chalukya dynasty. The Chalukyas appear to have been a race of Rajputs from the north, who imposed their rule upon the Dravidian inhabitants of the Deccan tableland. The dynasty was founded by a chieftain named Pulikesin I, who made himself master of the town of Vatapi, the modern Badami in the Bijapur District, about 550 A. D., and established a principality of modest dimensions. He aimed, however, at more extended power, and is said to have asserted his claim to a paramount position by celebrating an *asvamedha*, or horse-sacrifice.

His sons, Kirttivarman and Mangalesa, extended the possessions of the family both eastward and westward. The clans more or less completely subjugated by the former include the Mauryas of the Konkan, the strip of coast between the Western Ghats and the sea, who claimed descent from the ancient imperial Maurya dynasty.

The succession to Mangalesa was disputed between his son and one of the sons of Kirttivarman. The latter, having overcome his rival, ascended the throne of Vatapi as Pulikesin II in 608 A. D., and was formally crowned in the following year. For the space of twenty years or more this able prince devoted himself to a career of aggression directed against all the neighbouring states. On the west and north, the Kings of Lata (Southern Gujarat), Gurjara (Northern Gujarat and Rajputana), Malwa, and the Mauryas of the Konkan felt the weight of Pulikesin's arm.

In the east he drove the Pallavas from Vengi, between the Krishna and Godavari, and established his brother Kubja Vishnuvardhana there as viceroy in 609 A.D. A few years later, about 620 A.D., while Pulikesin was fully occupied by the war with Harsha of Kanauj, this prince set up as an independent sovereign, and founded the line of the Eastern Chalukyas.

All the southern kingdoms, the Chola, Pandya, and Kerala, as well as the Pallava, were forced into conflict with the ambitious King of Vatapi, who was undoubtedly the most powerful monarch to the south of the Narmada in 630 A.D. Ten years before that date he had successfully repelled the attack on his dominions led in person by Harsha, the lord paramount of the north, who aspired to the sovereignty of all India.

The fame of the King of the Deccan spread beyond the limits of India, and reached the ears of Khusru II, King of Persia, who, in the thirty-sixth year of his reign, 625-6 A.D., received a complimentary embassy from Pulikesin. The courtesy was reciprocated by a return embassy sent from Persia, which was received with due honour at the Indian court. A large fresco painting in Cave No. 1 at Ajanta, although unhappily mutilated, is still easily recognizable as a vivid representation of the ceremonial attending the presentation of their credentials by the Persian envoys.

This picture, in addition to its interest as a contemporary record of unusual political relations between India and Persia, is of the highest value as a landmark in the history of art. It not only fixes the date of some of the most important paintings at Ajanta, but also

Pulikesin II Receives the Envoys from the Persian King, Khusru II.
From an Ajanta Cave Painting. (After Griffiths.)

proves, or goes a long way toward proving, that the Ajanta school of pictorial art was derived directly from Persia, and ultimately from Greece.

The wonderful caves in the Ajanta valley were duly admired by Hiuen Tsang, who visited the court of Pulikesin II, probably in the year 640 A. D. The pilgrim was profoundly impressed by the military power of Pulikesin, who was obeyed by his numerous subjects with "perfect submission."

But his prosperity was not destined to last much longer. In 642 A. D., the long-continued war, which, since the year 609 A. D., had been generally disastrous to the Pallavas of Kanchi, took a new turn, and brought ruin and death upon Pulikesin. The Pallava king took and plundered his capital, and presumably put him to death. For thirteen years the Chalukya power, which Pulikesin had laboured so hard to exalt, was in abeyance, while the Pallavas dominated Southern India.

In 655 A. D. Vikramaditya I, a son of Pulikesin, restored the fallen fortunes of his family by inflicting a severe defeat upon the Pallavas, whose strongly fortified capital, Kanchi, was captured. Victory inclined now to one side, and now to the other. During this reign a branch of the Chalukya dynasty succeeded in establishing itself in Gujarat, where in the next century it offered vigorous opposition to the Arabs.

The main feature of the succeeding reigns was the never ending conflict with the Pallavas, whose capital was again taken by Vikramaditya II about 740 A. D.

In the middle of the eighth century, Dantidurga,

a chieftain of the ancient Rashtrakuta family, fought his way to the front, and overthrew Kirttivarman II Chalukya. The main branch of the Chalukyas now became extinct, and the sovereignty of the Deccan passed to the Rashtrakutas, in whose hands it remained for two centuries and a quarter.

During the two centuries of the rule of the early Chalukya dynasty of Vatapi, great changes in the religious state of the country were in progress. Buddhism, although still influential, was slowly declining, and suffering gradual supersession by its rivals, Jainism and Brahmanical Hinduism. The sacrificial form of the Hindu religion received special attention, and was made the subject of a multitude of formal treatises. The Puranic forms of Hinduism also grew in popularity, and everywhere elaborate temples dedicated to Vishnu, Siva, or other members of the Puranic pantheon, were erected. The orthodox Hindus borrowed from their Buddhist rivals the practice of excavating cave-temples, and one of the earliest Hindu works of this class is that made in honour of Vishnu by Mangalesa Chalukya, at the close of the sixth century. Jainism was specially popular in the Southern Maratha country.

Dantidurga Rashtrakuta, after his occupation of Vatapi, effected other conquests, but, becoming unpopular, was deposed by his uncle, Krishna I, who completed the establishment of Rashtrakuta supremacy over the dominions formerly held by the Chalukyas, while a branch of his family founded a principality in

Gujarat. The reign of Krishna I is memorable for the execution of the most marvellous architectural freak in India, the Kailasa temple at Elura (Ellora), which is by far the most extensive and sumptuous of the rock-cut shrines.

Krishna I was succeeded by his son Dhruva, an able and warlike prince, who continued with success the aggressive wars so dear to the heart of an Indian raja. Govinda III, son of Dhruva, may justly claim to be the most remarkable prince of his vigorous dynasty. He transferred his capital from Nasik to Manyakheta, generally identified with Malkhed in the Nizam's dominions, and extended his power from the Vindhya Mountains and Malwa on the north to Kanchi on the south, while his direct rule was carried at least as far as the Tungabhadra. He created his brother Viceroy of Lata, or Southern Gujarat.

THE GOD KRISHNA.

The long reign of the next king, Amoghavarsha, who occupied the throne for at least sixty-two years, was largely spent in constant wars with the Eastern Chalukya Rajas of Vengi. The Digambara, or naked, sect of the Jains was liberally patronized by this prince. The rapid progress made by Digambara Jainism late in the ninth, and early in the tenth century, under the guidance of various notable leaders, including Jinasena and Gunabhadra, who enjoyed the favour of more than one monarch, had much to do with the marked decay of Buddhism, which daily lost ground, until it finally disappeared from the Deccan in the twelfth century.

The war with the Cholas in the reign of Krishna III, Rashtrakuta, was remarkable for the death of the Chola king on the field of battle in 949 A. D. Much bitterness was introduced into the wars of this period by the hostility between the rival religions, Jainism and orthodox Hinduism.

The last of the Rashtrakuta kings, Kakka II, was overthrown in 973 A. D. by Taila II, a scion of the old Chalukya stock. He restored the family of his ancestors to its former glory, and founded the dynasty known as that of the Chalukyas of Kalyani, which lasted, like that which it followed, for nearly two centuries and a quarter. The impression made upon their contemporaries by the Rashtrakutas was evidently considerable, and was justified by the achievements of their period. Although the art displayed at Ellora is not of the highest kind, the Kailasa temple is one of the wonders of the world, a work of which any nation might be proud. Many other temples were the outcome of the royal munificence, and literature of the type then in fashion was liberally encouraged.

Taila, the restorer of the Chalukya name, reigned for twenty-four years, and during that time succeeded in recovering all the ancient territory of his race, with the exception of the Gujarat province. Much of his time was spent in fighting Munja, the Paramara Raja

Temple of Kailasa, Ellora.
From a Photograph.

of Dhara, who claimed the victory in sixteen conflicts. But toward the close of his reign Taila enjoyed the luxury of revenge. His enemy, having crossed the Godavari, which then formed the boundary between the two kingdoms, was defeated, taken captive, and for a time treated with the courtesy due to his rank. But an attempt to escape was visited with cruel indignities to the captive raja, who was ultimately beheaded, 995 A. D.

Two years later Taila died, and transmitted the crown to his son Satyasraya, during whose reign the Chalukya kingdom suffered severely from invasion by the Chola king, Rajaraja the Great, who overran the country with a vast host, said to number nine hundred thousand men, pillaging and slaughtering in so merciless a fashion that even the women, children, and Brahmans were not spared.

In 1059 A. D., Somesvara I, who was called Ahavamalla, fought a battle at Koppam in Mysore, in which Rajadhiraja, the then reigning Chola king, lost his life. Somesvara also claims the honour of having stormed both Dhara in Malwa and Kanchi in the south, and of having defeated Karna, the valiant King of Chedi. In 1068 A. D., Somesvara, seized by an incurable fever, put an end to his sufferings by drowning himself in the Tungabhadra River, while reciting his faith in Siva. Suicide in such circumstances is authorized by Hindu custom, and more than one instance is on record of rajas having terminated their existence in a similar manner.

Vikramaditya VI, or Vikramanka, the hero of Bilhana's historical poem, who came to the throne in 1076 A. D., reigned for half a century in tolerable, though not unbroken, peace. He is recorded to have captured Kanchi, and late in his reign was engaged in a serious struggle with Vishnu, the Hoysala King of Dorasamudra in Mysore. His capital Kalyana, probably the modern Kalyani in the Nizam's dominions, was the residence of the celebrated jurist, Vijnanesvara, author of the *Mitakshara*, the chief authority on Hindu law outside of Bengal.

SIVA PUJA, OR WORSHIP OF SIVA.

After the death of Vikramanka, the Chalukya power declined, and in the course of the years 1156-62 A. D., during the reign of Taila III, the commander-in-chief, Bijjala, or Vijjana, Kalachurya, revolted and obtained possession of the kingdom. This was held by him and his sons until 1183 A. D., when the Chalukya prince, Somesvara IV, succeeded in recovering a portion of his ancestral dominions. But he was not strong enough to resist the attacks of encroaching neighbours, and in the course of a few years the greater part of his kingdom had been absorbed by the Yadavas of Devagiri on the west, and the Hoysalas of Dorasamudra on the south. The end of the Chalukya dynasty of Kalyana may be dated in 1190 A. D., after which time the rajas of the line ranked merely as petty chiefs.

The brief intrusive reign of Bijjala, the usurping rebel, was marked by a religious revolution effected by a revival of the cult of Siva and the foundation of a new sect, the Vira Saivas, or Lingayats, which is a power to this day. Bijjala was a Jain. According to one version of the legend, he wantonly blinded two holy men of the Lingayat sect, and was assassinated in consequence in the year 1167 A. D. The blood of the saints proved, as usual, to be the seed of the Church, which had been founded by Basava, the Brahman minister of Bijjala.

In other legends the tale is told quite differently. There is, however, no doubt that the rise of the Lingayats dates from the time of Bijjala. The members of the sect, who are especially numerous in the Kanarese Districts, worship Siva in his phallic form, reject the authority of the Vedas, and cherish an intense aversion to Brahmans, notwithstanding the fact that the founder of their religion was himself a Brahman.

The growth of this new sect, which secured numerous adherents among the trading classes, up to that time the main strength of both Buddhism and Jainism, checked the progress of the latter religion, and drove another nail into the coffin of Buddhism, the existence of which in the Deccan cannot be traced later than the first half of the twelfth century.

During the twelfth and thirteenth centuries, chiefs belonging to a family or clan named Hoysala attained considerable power in the Mysore country. The first notable prince of this line was Vishnu, or Bittiga (1117 A.D.), who established his capital at Dorasamudra, the modern Halebid, famous for the fine temple which excited Mr. Fergusson's enthusiastic admiration. During Vishnu's reign the Jain religion enjoyed high favour under the protection of his minister Gangaraja, and the Jain temples, which had been destroyed by the orthodox Chola invaders, were restored. Vishnu boasts in his records of numerous conquests, and claims to have defeated the rajas of the Chola, Pandya, and Chera kingdoms in the south. About the year 1223 A.D., one of his successors, Narasimha II, who was then in alliance with the Cholas, actually occupied Trichinopoli.

The dynasty lasted until 1310 A.D., when the Mohammedan generals, Malik Kafur and Khwaja Haji, entered the Hoysala kingdom, laid it waste, captured the reigning raja, and despoiled his capital, which was finally destroyed by a Moslem force in 1327 A.D.

The Yadava Kings of Devagiri who have been mentioned were descendants of feudatory nobles of the Chalukya kingdom. The territory which they acquired, lying between Devagiri (Daulatabad) and Nasik, was known as Sevana. The first of the Yadava line to attain a position of importance was Bhillama, who was killed in battle by the Hoysala chief in 1191 A. D. The most powerful raja was Singhana (*acc.* 1210 A. D.), who invaded Gujarat and other countries, and established a short-lived kingdom almost rivalling in extent the realms of the Chalukyas and Rashtrakutas.

The dynasty, like that of the Hoysalas, was destroyed by the Mohammedans. When Ala-ud-din, Sultan of Delhi, crossed the Narmada, the northern frontier of the Yadava kingdom, in 1294, the reigning raja, Ramachandra, was obliged to surrender, and to ransom his life by payment of an enormous amount of treasure, which is said to have included six hundred *maunds* of pearls, two *maunds* of diamonds, rubies, emeralds, and sapphires, and so forth.

When the Sultan's incursion was repeated by Malik Kafur in 1309 A. D., Ramachandra again refrained from opposition, and submitted to the invader. He was the last independent Hindu sovereign of the Deccan. After his death, his son-in-law, Harapala, stirred up a revolt against the foreigners in 1318, but, being defeated, was flayed alive and decapitated. Thus miserably ended the Yadava line.

The celebrated Sanskrit writer, Hemadri, popularly known as Hemadpant, flourished during the reigns of Ramachandra and his predecessor, Mahadeva. He devoted himself chiefly to the reduction to a system of Hindu religious practices and observances, and with this object compiled important works upon Hindu sacred law. He is said to have introduced a form of current script, the Modi, from Ceylon, and has given a valuable historical sketch of his patron's dynasty in the introduction to one of his books.

Specimen of Southern Indian Temple Sculpture

One of the characteristics of the Southern Indian temples, built in the Dravidian style of architecture, is the long pillared hall with massive sculptured figures on either side. Some of the best specimens of Indian carving are to be found in these corridors, or choultries, as they are called. They are deserving of the attention of the student as examples of Oriental sculpture.

CHAPTER XVI

THE KINGDOMS OF THE SOUTH

I—THE "THREE KINGDOMS"

ANCIENT tradition recognizes the "Kingdoms of the South" as three—the Pandya, the Chola, and the Chera. Of these three the Pandya kingdom occupied the extremity of the peninsula, south of Pudukottai, the Chola kingdom extended northwards to Nellore, while the Chera kingdom lay to the west, and included the Malabar coast.

In the third century B.C., the Chola and Pandya realms were well known to Asoka; but in lieu of the Chera state he specifies two kingdoms, those of Kerala and Satiyaputra. The former of these is undoubtedly the Malabar coast south of the Chandragiri River; the latter should probably be identified with the tract on the same coast to the north of that river, of which Mangalore is the centre, and in which the Tulu tongue, one of the Dravidian languages, is spoken. In the Kerala of Asoka, which may be regarded as synonymous with the Chera of tradition, the prevailing language is

Malayalam. The Chola and Pandya kingdoms both belong to the Tamil-speaking region. Thus all the kingdoms of the south were occupied by races speaking Dravidian languages, who are themselves generally spoken of as Dravidians.

No Aryan language had penetrated into those kingdoms, which lived their own life, completely secluded from Northern India, and in touch with the outer world only through the medium of maritime commerce, which had been conducted with success from very early times. The pearls of the Gulf of Manar, the beryls of Coimbatore, and the pepper of Malabar were not to be had elsewhere, and were eagerly sought by foreign merchants, probably as early as the seventh or eighth century before Christ.

But the ancient political history of Southern India is irretrievably lost, and the materials for tracing the development of the high degree of civilization unquestionably attained by the Dravidian races are lamentably scanty. Nor is it possible to define with any accuracy the time when Aryan ideas and the religion of the Brahmans penetrated to the kingdoms of the south, although there are reasons for assuming that 500 B.C. may be taken as a mean date.

The missionaries of Asoka introduced Buddhism, and his brother Mahendra built a monastery in the Chola country, but whether or not they found any form of the Brahman religion in possession it is impossible to say. The Jain religion also found great favour in the southern countries, but how or when it was introduced from the north, there is no good evidence to show.

The historical period begins much later in the south than in the north, and it is quite impossible to carry back the story of the south, like that of the north, to 600 B.C. As will appear in the following pages, the orderly history of the Chola and Pandya dynasties does not commence until the ninth and tenth centuries A.D. respectively, although both kingdoms existed in Asoka's time.

The earliest dynastic annals are those of the Pallavas, which begin in the second century A.D. The Pallava realm is not included in the three traditional "kingdoms of the south," the reason apparently being that the Pallavas were an intrusive foreign, non-Dravidian race, which lorded it over the ancient territorial Dravidian kingdoms in varying degrees from time to time.

II—THE PANDYA, CHERA, KERALA, AND SATIYAPUTRA KINGDOMS

The Pandya country, as defined by tradition, extended north and south from the Southern Vellaru River (Pudukottai) to Cape Comorin, and east and west from the sea to the "great highway," the Achchankovil Pass leading into Kerala or Travancore, and was thus nearly co-extensive with the present Districts of Madura and Tinnevelli. The kingdom was ordinarily divided into five principalities, known as the "five Pandyas." The capital of the premier chief was in early days at Korkai on the Tamraparni River in Tinnevelli.

Korkai, or Kolkai, the Greek Κόλχοι, now an insignificant village, was once a great city, and is indicated by all native traditions as the cradle of South Indian civilization, the home of the mythical three brothers, who were supposed to have founded the Pandya, Chera, and Chola kingdoms. In the days of its glory the city was a seaport, the headquarters of the pearl trade, which constituted the chief source of wealth enjoyed by the Pandya kings, whose special crest or cognizance was the battle-axe, often associated with the elephant. In the course of time, the silting up of the delta rendered Korkai inaccessible to ships, and the city gradually decayed, like the Cinque Ports in England.

Its commercial business was transferred to the new port, Kayal (Coel), which was founded three miles lower down the river, and continued to be for many centuries one of the greatest marts of the east. Here Marco Polo landed in the thirteenth century, and was much impressed by the wealth and magnificence of prince and people. But the same process which had ruined Korkai caused the abandonment of Kayal, and compelled the Portuguese to remove their trade to Tuticorin, where a sheltered roadstead, free from deposits of silt, offered superior convenience. The site of Kayal is now occupied by the huts of a few Mohammedans and native Christian fishermen.

Madura, which was regarded in later times as the Pandya capital, and the central seat of Tamil literature and learning, is also of high antiquity, and probably coexisted with Korkai from a very early date. The Kings of Madura adopted a fish, or a pair of fishes, as the family crest.

No continuous history of the Pandya dynasties prior to the twelfth century can be written. The scraps of information concerning them before that time are exceedingly meagre. The most ancient mention of the name Pandya is found in the commentary of the grammarian Katyayana, who may be assigned to the fourth century B.C. In Asoka's time the Pandya kingdom was independent, and lay altogether outside the limits of the northern empire, which extended to about the latitude of Madras.

A Pandya king sent an embassy to Augustus Cæsar, and the pearl fishery in his dominions was well known to the Greeks and Romans of the first century A.D. Pliny was aware that the king resided at Madura in the interior. Roman copper coins of the smallest value have been found in such numbers at Madura as to suggest that a Roman colony was settled at that place. They come down to the time of Arcadius and Honorius (400 A.D.).

Roman gold coins of the early empire have been discovered in such large quantities in Southern India that it is apparent that they served for the gold currency of the peninsula, as the English sovereign now does in many foreign countries. Five coolie loads of *aurei* were found in 1851 near Cannanore on the Malabar coast, mostly belonging to the mintage of Tiberius and Nero, and many other large hoards of Roman coins, gold, silver, and copper, have been discovered in various localities from time to time.

It is, therefore, certain that the Pandya state, during the early centuries of the Christian era, shared along with the Chera kingdom of Malabar a very lucrative trade with the Roman empire, and was in exclusive possession of the much prized pearl fishery, which had its headquarters first at Korkai, and afterward at Kayal.

From the fifth century onwards, occasional references to the Pandya dynasty and country are met with in literature and inscriptions. When Hiuen Tsang visited the south in 640 A. D., and stayed at Kanchi, the southern limit of his travels, he ascertained that the inhabitants of the region called by him Malakottai, which was equivalent to the Pandya state and the Malabar coast with a portion of the traditional Chola country, were reputed to care little for learning. In ancient times many Buddhist monasteries had existed, but these were in ruins at the time of his visit, only the bare walls remaining, though the country was studded with hundreds of Brahmanical temples and the adherents of the Jain sect were numerous.

The most ancient Pandya king to whom an approximate date can be assigned is Rajasimha, the contemporary of Parantaka I, Chola (907 - 47 A. D.), who claims to have defeated his southern neighbour, and "destroyed" Madura. A great-grandson of the same Chola king fought with a Pandya raja bearing the name of

Vira. The fact that many names or titles, Sundara, Vira, Kulasekhara, and others, recur over and over again, causes special difficulty in attempts to construct the Pandya dynastic list.

The Pandya state, in common with the other kingdoms of the south, undoubtedly was reduced to a condition of tributary dependence by Rajaraja the Great about the year 1000, and continued to be more or less under Chola control for a century and a half, or a little longer, although, of course, the local administration remained in the hands of the native rajas.

The Jain religion, which was popular in the days of Hiuen Tsang in the seventh century, and had continued to enjoy the favour of the Pandya kings, was odious to their Chola overlords, who were strict adherents of Siva. A credible tradition affirms that, apparently at some time in the eleventh century, a Pandya king named Sundara was married to a Chola princess, sister of King Rajendra, and was converted from Jainism to the Saiva faith by his consort. King Sundara displayed even more than the proverbial zeal of a convert, and persecuted his late co-religionists, who refused to apostatize, with the most savage cruelty inflicting on no less than eight thousand innocent persons a horrible death by impalement. Certain unpublished sculptures on the walls of a temple at Trivatur in Arcot are believed to record these executions.

The long duration of Chola supremacy suffices to explain in large measure the lack of early Pandya inscriptions. The series does not begin until near the end of the twelfth century, but, after that time, the records are so numerous that a dynastic list which seems to be almost complete for the thirteenth century has been constructed by Professor Kielhorn. The dynasty can be traced, with some breaks, up to the middle of the sixteenth century, but it lost most of its political importance after the sack of Madura by Malik Kafur's Mohammedan host in 1310 A. D. The maritime commerce of the kingdom, however, continued to exist on a considerable scale to a much later date.

The most conspicuous event in the political history of the Pandya kingdom is the invasion of the Sinhalese armies under the command of two generals of Parakrama-bahu, King of Ceylon, which occurred about 1175 A. D. Two detailed accounts of this incident, written from different points of view, are extant. The story, as told in the island chronicle, the *Mahavamsa*, naturally represents the victorious career of the invaders as unbroken by defeat; but the rival account, preserved in an inscription, proves that the invading army gained considerable success at first, but was ultimately obliged to retire in consequence of the vigorous resistance of a coalition of the southern princes. The occasion of the Sinhalese intervention was a disputed succession to the Pandya throne of Madura, contested by claimants bearing the oft-recurring names of Vira and Sundara.

Very little can be said about the southwestern kingdoms, known as Chera, Kerala, and Satiyaputra. The last-named is mentioned by Asoka only, and its exact position is unknown, but should probably be identified with that portion of the Konkans — or lowlands between the Western Ghats and the sea — where the Tulu language is spoken, and of which Mangalore is the centre.

The name of Kerala is still well remembered, and there is no doubt that the kingdom so called was equivalent to the Southern Konkans, or Malabar coast. The ancient capital was Vanji, also named Karur, or Karuvur, the Κάρουρα of Ptolemy, situated close to Cranganore. This represents Muziris, the port for the pepper trade, mentioned by Pliny and the author of the *Periplus* at the end of the first century A. D.

The etymological identity of the names Kerala and Chera is affirmed by philologists of high authority, but whether this theory be correct or not, it is certain that in early times the Chera kingdom included that of Kerala. According to an unverified tradition, the latter separated in 389 A. D., after which date the Chera realm was restricted to Coimbatore and the southern parts of Mysore and Salem.

The crest or cognizance of the Chera kings was a bow. Their coins are very rare, and only two types, characterized by the bow device, are known, which are found in Salem and Coimbatore. The existence of a native work, the *Keralolpati*, which professes to give the history of Kerala, raises hopes which are disappointed by perusal.

The authentic list of the Rajas of Travancore begins in 1335 A. D., and that of the rajas of the neighbouring state of Cochin, which is less complete, does not commence until more than two centuries later.

III—THE CHOLA KINGDOM

According to tradition, the Chola country (*Cholamandalam*) was bounded on the north by the Pennar, and on the south by the southern Vellaru River, or, in other words, it extended along the eastern coast from Nellore to Pudukottai, where it abutted on the Pandya territory. On the west it extended to the borders of Coorg. The limits thus defined include Madras, and several other British districts on the east, as well as the whole of the Mysore state. The most ancient capital was Uraiyur, or old Trichinopoli, so far as is known with certainty.

But the existence of well-known traditional boundaries must not be taken to justify the inference that they always agreed with the frontiers of the Chola kingdom, which, as a matter of fact, varied enormously. The limits of the Chola country, as determined by tradition, seem to mark ethnic rather than political frontiers, at least on the north and west, where they do not differ widely from the lines of demarcation between the Tamil and the other Dravidian languages. Tamil, however, is as much the vernacular of the Pandya as of the Chola region, and no clear ethnical distinction can be drawn between the peoples residing north and south of the Vellaru.

The kingdom of the Cholas, which, like that of the Pandyas, was unknown to Panini, was familiar by name to Katyayana, and was recognized by Asoka as independent. Inasmuch as the great Maurya's authority unquestionably extended to the south of Chitaldurg in Mysore, and down to at least the fourteenth degree

WATER-LILIES IN BOTANIC GARDEN, MADRAS
From stereograph, copyright 1903, by Underwood & Underwood, New York.

of latitude, the Chola kingdom of his time must have been of modest dimensions.

A passage in the work of Ptolemy, the geographer of the second century A.D., is usually interpreted as referring to the Chola kingdom, and intimating that Arcot was then the capital. But the language used is obscure, and the true meaning doubtful. Occasional references to the country throw little light upon its history.

From about the middle of the second century A. D. the lordship of the Chola country, as defined by tradition, was disputed by the intrusive Pallava clans of foreign origin. Chola rajas continued to exist throughout all political vicissitudes, and to take part in the unceasing internecine wars which characterize the early history of Southern India. It is clear, however, that these rajas were often reduced to a merely subordinate position, and were much circumscribed in authority.

The observations of Hiuen Tsang give an interesting notice of the Chola kingdom in the seventh century, the significance of which has not been fully appreciated. His visit to the south may be dated with almost absolute certainty in the year 640 A. D. At that time the kingdom of Chola (Chu-li-ye) was a restricted territory, estimated to be four or five hundred miles in circuit, with a small capital town barely two miles in circumference. The country was wild and mostly deserted, consisting of a succession of hot marshes and jungles, occupied by a scanty population of ferocious habits, addicted to open brigandage. The few Buddhist monasteries were ruinous, and the monks dwelling in them as dirty as the buildings. The prevailing religion was Jainism, but there were a few Brahmanical temples.

The position of the country is indicated as being some two hundred miles or less to the southwest of Amaravati. It must, therefore, be identified with a portion of the Ceded Districts, and more especially with the Cuddapah District, which possesses the hot climate and other characteristics noted by the pilgrim, and was still notorious for brigandage when annexed by the British in 1800. The pilgrim speaks merely of the "country" of Chola, and makes no mention of a king, doubtless for the reason that the local raja was a person of small importance, subordinate to the reigning Pallava King of Kanchi, the powerful Narasimha-varman, who two years later destroyed the Chalukya power.

In the ninth century, the Chola rajas seem to have begun to recover their authority, and at the beginning of the tenth century, an able and vigorous prince, Parantaka I (907 - 47 A. D.), succeeded in making himself formidable to his neighbours, with whom he was constantly at war during his long reign. He claims to have carried his victorious arms even to Ceylon. Inscriptions recorded in the North Arcot and Chingleput Districts prove the extension of his power into the heart of the Pallava dominions, and are of especial interest to students of village institutions by reason of the full details which they give of the manner in which local affairs were administered by committees, or panchayats, exercising their power under royal sanction.

Rajaditya, the son and successor of Parantaka, was killed in battle with Krishnaraja III, the Rashtrakuta king, in 949 A. D. His death was followed by a period of disturbance lasting for thirty-six years, during which the names of five obscure rajas are recorded.

The accession in A. D. 985 of a strong ruler, Rajaraja-deva the Great, put an end to dynastic intrigue, and placed at the head of the state a man qualified to make it the leading power in the south. In the course of a busy reign of some twenty-seven years, Rajaraja passed from victory to victory, and, when he died, was beyond dispute the lord paramount of Southern India, ruling a realm which included nearly the whole of the Madras Presidency, Ceylon, and a large part of Mysore.

His earliest recorded conquests were won on the mainland toward the north and west between the twelfth and fourteenth years of his reign, and comprised the Eastern Chalukya kingdom of Vengi, formerly held by the Pallavas, Coorg, and extensive regions in the table-land of the Deccan. During the next three years, Quilon (Kollam), on the Malabar coast, and the northern kingdom of Kalinga were added to his dominions. Protracted campaigns in Ceylon next occupied Rajaraja, and resulted in the annexation of the island in the twentieth year of his reign.

The ancient enmity between the Chalukyas and the Pallavas was inherited by the Chola power, and led to a four years' war which ended in the defeat of the Chalukyas, who had not long been freed from subjection to the Rashtrakutas. Rajaraja, moreover, did not confine his operations to the land. He possessed a powerful navy, and his last martial exploit was the acquisition of a large number of unspecified islands, meaning, perhaps, the Laccadives and Maldives.

The magnificent temple at his capital, Tanjore (Tanjuvur), built by his command, the walls of which are

VIEW OF THE GREAT TEMPLE AT BHUVANESWAR.

engraved with the story of his victories, stands to this day as a memorial of his victorious career.

Although himself a worshipper of Siva, he was sufficiently liberal-minded to endow a Burmese Buddhist temple at the port of Negapatam, where two such temples continued to be the object of foreign pilgrimages until the fifteenth century. One of them, probably that endowed by Rajaraja, survived in a ruinous condition until 1867, when the remains of it were pulled down by the Jesuit Fathers and utilized for the construction of Christian buildings.

Rajendra-Choladeva I, the son and successor of Rajaraja, continued his father's ambitious career, and added still more territory to the Chola dominions. He spent a long reign in war with his neighbours, as befitted a self-respecting king, and carried his arms far to the north, even into Orissa and Bengal. He did not neglect the navy, and sent an expedition by sea against a place called Kadaram, situated somewhere in Lower Burma or the Indo-Chinese peninsula.

His successor, Rajadhiraja, an equally vigorous fighter, emphasized his claim to paramount power by reviving the ancient and costly rite of the horse-sacrifice, or *asvamedha.* In the year 1059 A.D. he was killed at the battle of Koppam in Mysore, while fighting the Chalukyas. The war in which this battle occurred was waged with great bitterness, owing to the religious animosity between the combatants.

The next king worthy of notice was Rajendra-Choladeva II, son-in-law of the first of that name, and a member of the Eastern Chalukya dynasty of Vengi. That province, situated between the Krishna and Godavari Rivers, had been ruled, after its conquest in the time of Rajaraja, by the local kings as a fief of the Tanjore monarchy. In 1070 A. D., however, Rajendra-Choladeva II took advantage of internal dissensions to seize the throne of his lord, and thus to found a new line of Chola-Chalukya kings. His special achievement in war was his defeat of the Paramara King of Dhara in Central India.

Vikrama Chola, whose exploits are the subject of a Tamil poem of some merit, is remembered for a successful raid on Kalinga in 1120 A. D.

After the time of Vikrama, the Chola power gradually declined, and during the thirteenth century the Pandya Kings of Madura recovered their independence, and even reduced the Chola rajas to a position of inferiority. The Mohammedan invasion under Malik Kafur in 1310 deprived the Chola kingdom of its importance, but local chiefs of the old dynasty may be traced as late as the fifteenth and sixteenth centuries.

IV—THE PALLAVA CONFEDERACY

Although the Pallavas seem to have been the premier power in the south for more than four centuries, it is strange that no mention of them is to be found either in the vernacular historical legends or in the native dynastic lists. They had been forgotten, and remained unknown to European inquirers until the accidental discovery of a copper-plate grant in 1840 reminded the world that such a dynasty had existed. Sixty years of patient archæological research have elicited so many facts that it is now possible to write an outline of Pallava history, with some breaks, from the second century A. D. to the Chola conquest in 996, and for the last few centuries of that long period to write it almost continuously.

The origin of the Pallava clan or tribe is obscure. The name appears to be identical with Pahlava, the appellation of a foreign clan or tribe frequently mentioned in inscriptions and Sanskrit literature, and ultimately with Parthiva, or Parthian.

This apparently sound etymology naturally suggests the theory that the Pallavas, who became a ruling race in the south, must have come originally from the countries beyond the northwestern frontier of India, and gradually worked their way down to Malabar and the Coromandel coast. This theory is supported by the ascertained fact that Pahlavas formed a distinct and noticeable element in the population of Western India early in the second century, when they were classed by native writers with the Sakas and Yavanas as objects of hostility to native kings.

Vilivayakura II, the Andhra king (113 to 138 A. D.), prided himself on his prowess in expelling the Sakas, Yavanas, and Pahlavas from his dominions on the western coast; and it is reasonable to believe that some of the defeated clans retired into the interior toward the east and south. The Sakas retained the government of the peninsula of Surashtra until the closing years of the fourth century, but no Pahlava principality in Western India is mentioned, and it is quite credible that the Pahlavas may have sought their fortune in the south.

When first heard of in the second century A. D. the Pallavas are already a ruling race, and their king, Siva-skanda-varman, was lord of so many subordinate chiefs that he considered himself authorized to perform the *asvamedha*, or horse-sacrifice, a rite permissible only to a paramount sovereign.

On the whole, although positive evidence of the supposed migration is lacking, it is highly probable that the Pallavas were really identical with the Pahlavas, and were a foreign tribe which gradually fought its way across India and formed three principalities at Kanchi, Vengi, and Palakkada, which were known as "the three Pallava dominions." This movement from the west must have occupied a considerable time, and may be assumed to have ended before 150 A. D. The three Pallava chiefs seem to have belonged to different sections of the tribe, which had become thoroughly Hinduized, with a special leaning, occasionally to Buddhism and Vishnuism, but more often to the Saiva faith.

The home territories actually colonized and directly administered by the Pallavas do not seem to have been very extensive. The Pallava power was superimposed upon the ancient territorial states, much in the same way as the Mahratta power was in later times, and presumably was confined ordinarily to the levying of tribute and blackmail. This view of the nature of the Pallava government explains the fact that its existence was forgotten.

Every man could tell the position of the Chola country, but nobody could define the Pallava country, the extent of which depended on the relative strength of a predatory tribe. In fact, during the seventh century, almost the whole of the traditional "Chola country" was in subjection to the Pallavas, and the special Chola territory was limited to a small and unhealthy tract in the north. About the time (642 to 655 A.D.) the Pallavas succeeded in imposing their rule for a few years upon the whole of the Western Chalukya kingdom, and at an unspecified date they levied tribute even from the Kalinga territory in the north.

The three Pallava chiefs held their courts at Kanchi, or Conjevaram, a strongly fortified town, between Madras and Arcot; at Vengi, between the deltas of the Krishna and Godavari; and at Palakkada, or Palghat, in Malabar, situated at the gap in the Western Ghats. A town named Dasanapura, from which some grants were issued, does not seem to have been the capital of a principality, and may have been only a precinct of Kanchi, which was always the headquarters of the clan.

In religion the Pallavas were, so far as is known, orthodox Hindus, with the exception of one Buddhist chief, Simha-varman II, who is described as a lay worshipper of Buddha, and as having presented an image at Amaravati. Several of the princes were devoted to the worship of Vishnu, but in later times the rajas inclined to the cult of Siva, and adopted the figure of a bull as the family crest.

The celebrated rock-cut temples at Mamallaipuram near Madras, commonly called the "Seven Pagodas," were excavated under the orders of various kings of the dynasty during the sixth and seventh centuries, as were also the cave-temples at Mahendravadi and Mamandur in North Arcot. The temples at the former place, three Saiva and one Vaishnava, date from the reign of Mahendra-varman I, who came to the throne about A. D. 600.

The first Pallava king about whom anything substantial is known was Sivaskanda-varman, who lived in the second century A. D. His capital, although not expressly named, was doubtless Kanchi, and his power extended into the Telugu country as far as the Krishna River, over territory included at times in the Andhra kingdom. He had officers stationed at Amaravati (Dhanakataka), the famous Buddhist holy place, but he himself was an orthodox Hindu, with a special devotion for Siva. The king's boast that he had celebrated the *asvamedha*, or horse-sacrifice, is good evidence that he exercised jurisdiction over a considerable number of subordinate rajas. He confirmed a grant made by an ancestor named Bappa, possibly his father, who may be regarded as the founder of the dynasty.

The next glimpse of the Pallavas is obtained two centuries later from the record of the temporary conquests effected by the northern monarch, Samudra-

The Genesa Ratha at Mamallaipuram.
One of the Seven Pagodas.

gupta, who claims to have defeated eleven kings of the south. Among these rajas three seem to have been Pallavas, namely, Vishnugopa of Kanchi, Ugrasena of Palakka (=Palakkada), and Hasti-varman of Vengi.

The last-named prince may be reasonably identified with King Attivarma, who issued an undated grant in the Prakrit tongue, which was found in the Guntur District to the south of the Krishna River. It is possible that the Vishnugopa of Kanchi, conquered by Samudragupta, may be identical with the *yuvaraja*, or crown prince of the same name, who issued a grant in the Sanskrit language during the reign of his elder brother Simha-varman, but it is more probable that the author of the grant was distinct from and later than the foe of Samudragupta.

The grant made by the crown prince is but one of several illustrations of the Pallava custom, in virtue of which the heir apparent was associated in the government with his father or elder brother as colleague for years before he obtained the succession in natural course. Much confusion in chronology results when the years of office as crown prince are combined with the regnal years after accession. The Dravidian fashion of dating, which was also used in the early Andhra records, is peculiar, in that the division of the year into months is ignored, and the date is expressed by quoting the serial number of the fortnight in each of the three seasons—hot, rainy, and cold; as, for example, an inscription of Sivaskanda-varman is dated on the fifth day of the sixth fortnight of the rainy season in the eighth regnal year.

Several Pallava grants are known to have been issued from the court at Palakkada, and it is reasonable to assume that Ugrasena of Pạlakka was a Pallava, a kinsman and subordinate of the King of Kanchi, like Hasti-varman of Vengi. An early inscription of approximately the same period, found in Mysore, mentions a grant of land "on the shore of the western ocean" as having been made by the Pallava sovereign of Kanchi.

From all these particulars the conclusion may be drawn that in the fourth century three Pallava chiefs were established at Kanchi, Vengi, and Palakkada, the latter two being subordinate to the first, and that Pallava rule extended from the Godavari on the north to the Pandya boundary, or the Southern Vellaru River, on the south, while it stretched across Mysore from sea to sea.

A raja named Simha-varman II, son of the Crown Prince Vishnugopa previously mentioned, issued a grant in the eighth year of his reign from Dasanapura. His father's grant and this document, when read together, give a complete genealogy of the Kings of Kanchi for five generations and an equal number of reigns, covering a period of about a century, but, unfortunately, neither the initial nor the terminal year of this period can be fixed with precision.

Numerous documents executed by both Pallava and Chalukya kings during the sixth, seventh, and eighth centuries, furnished with copious genealogical details, supply sufficient material for the reconstruction of the outline of Pallava history during the period extending from about 575 to 770 A. D.

The Pallava dominion was evidently of wide extent during the reign of Simhavishnu, who claims to have defeated the King of Ceylon, as well as sundry continental kings, including the Chola, Pandya, and Kerala rajas. His successor, Mahendra-varman I, was contemporary with the earlier years of Pulikesin II, the greatest of the Western Chalukya sovereigns, who fought his way to the throne in 608 A. D. and was crowned in the following year. The ambition of this monarch naturally brought him into conflict with the Pallavas, at that time the leading power of the south.

About the year 609 or 610 A. D., Pulikesin defeated Mahendra-varman, and drove him to take shelter behind the walls of his capital, Kanchi. The seriousness of the defeat is proved by the fact that the province of Vengi, which had been in the possession of a Pallava chieftain for centuries, was annexed by the Chalukya king, who placed it in charge of Vishnuvardhana, his younger brother. After a few years, in or about 620 A. D., this prince established himself as an independent sovereign, and so founded the Eastern Chalukya line, which subsisted as a separate dynasty until 1070 A. D., when it was merged in the Chola dynasty.

Notwithstanding the loss of this important province, the Pallava king claimed to have gained a victory over the invader at Pullalura near Kanchi. This boast probably means that Pulikesin was repulsed in an attempt to seize the Pallava capital, and was compelled to retire to his own territory.

Hiuen Tsang, who visited Kanchi in the year 640 A. D., during the reign of Narasimha-varman I, and stayed there for a considerable time, calls the country

PAVILION, LITTLE CONJEVARAM.

of which Kanchi was the capital by the name of Dravida, and describes it as about a thousand miles in circuit. It corresponded, therefore, very closely with the traditional "Chola country" (*Chola-mandalam*) between the Pennar and Southern Vellaru Rivers. The soil was fertile and regularly cultivated, producing abundance of grain, flowers, and fruits. The capital was a large city, five or six miles in circumference.

The pilgrim had intended to proceed thence to Ceylon by sea, a three days' journey, but he learned that it was in a state of disorder, and abandoned the proposed visit. While staying at Kanchi he occupied himself in collecting from his informants the Buddhist legends current in the island, and in recording such particulars as interested him concerning the Indian kingdoms of the extreme south, which he was unable to visit personally. He then turned to the northwest, across Mysore, until he reached the kingdom of Kong-kin-na-pu-lo in the west, and so made his way into the kingdom of the Chalukya sovereign, Pulikesin II, which he calls Maharashtra.

In the Pallava realm of Kanchi he found some hundreds of Buddhist monasteries, occupied by a large number of monks, estimated at ten thousand, all attached, like the majority of the Ceylonese, to the Sthavira school of the Mahayana, as well as about eighty Brahmanical temples, and numerous adherents of the Jain or Nirgrantha sect, which had gained great vogue in Southern India from very early times. In the kingdom of Kong-kin-na-pu-lo, the exact situation of which is uncertain, there was a similar mixture of religions, and "several hundred temples, in which many sectaries dwell together," were to be seen.

The war between the Pallavas and Chalukyas, initiated by Pulikesin II, proved to be of long duration, and in its course fortune favoured sometimes one, and sometimes another combatant. Pulikesin himself experienced the full bitterness of the instability of fortune and in 642 A. D., at the close of his reign and life, suffered the mortification of seeing his kingdom overrun, and his capital, Vatapi (Badami), taken by the Pallava king, Narasimha-varman I. The Chalukya power then remained in abeyance for some thirteen years, during which the Pallavas governed the kingdom, doubtless through the agency of local rajas.

In or about 655 A. D., Vikramaditya I, a son of Pulikesin, retrieved the fortunes of his family, and recovered his father's dominions from Paramesvaravarman, who had succeeded to the Pallava throne. During this war Kanchi was taken and occupied for a time by the Chalukyas. On the other hand, the Pallavas claimed a victory gained at Peruvalanallur.

The perennial conflict continued during the succeeding reigns, and Kanchi was again taken by Vikramaditya II Chalukya, about 740 A. D., in the reign of Nandivarman Pallava, who may be considered the last of his line to enjoy extensive dominion.

When the Rashtrakutas supplanted the Chalukyas in the middle of the eighth century, the traditional hostility of the two powers was not abated, and the new rulers took up the old quarrel with the Pallavas. King Dhruva, cousin of Dantidurga, who had overthrown the Chalukya dynasty, inflicted a defeat on the Pallavas about 775 A. D., and his son, Govinda III, levied tribute from Dantiga, King of Kanchi, in 803 A. D.

During the tenth century we hear of wars between the Pallavas and the Ganga Kings of Gangavadi, or Mysore, who are now commonly known as the Western

Gangas, in order to distinguish them from the family of the same name which ruled Kalinga, and held court at Kalinganagara, the modern Mukhalingam in the Ganjam District.

Toward the close of the tenth century, Rajaraja the Great, the Chola king (985-1011 A.D.), succeeded in reducing to subjection all the kingdoms of the south, and in making himself lord paramount of Southern India. This able monarch annexed Vengi in 996 A.D., and in subsequent years brought under his sway both Kalinga and the territories of the Rashtrakutas, which had been recovered by Taila, the Chalukya king, in 973 A.D. The operations of Rajaraja put an end to the Pallava independent power, which had lasted for more than eight centuries.

The later Pallava chiefs sank into the position of mere feudatory nobles and officials in the service of the territorial kingdoms, and it is on record that the Pallava raja took the first place among the feudatories of King Vikrama Chola early in the twelfth century. The rajas can be traced as in possession of limited local power down to the thirteenth century, and Pallava nobles are mentioned as late as the close of the seventeenth century.

The raja of the Pudukottai tributary state, who is the recognized head of the Kallar tribe, still styles himself Raja Pallava, and claims descent from the ancient royal family. The Vellalas, who admittedly hold the first place among the Tamil-speaking agricultural classes, profess to be descended in the female line from the Pallava kings, with whom the Palli caste, as well as the Kallar, boasts a connection. The latter caste exercised, during the eighteenth century, a formidable control over the peaceable inhabitants of the Carnatic, from whom its members levied blackmail on a regular system, and so probably continued the practice which had made the Pallavas a terror to their neighbours in the early centuries of the Christian era.

CHRONOLOGICAL APPENDIXES

APPENDIX I

CHRONOLOGY (APPROXIMATE) OF SAISUNAGA AND NANDA DYNASTIES

Serial No.	King (Vayu Purana).	Length of Reign.		Probable date of Accession.	Remarks.
		Vayu P.	Assumed.		
	SAISUNAGA DYNASTY.			B. C.	
1	Sisunaga . . .	40 } 136	} 81	600	} Nothing known.
2	Sakavarna . .	36		...	
3	Kshemadharman	20		...	
4	Kshattraujas . .	40		...	
5	Bimbisara . . .	28	28	519	Built New Rajagriha; annexed Anga; contemporary with Mahavira and Gautama Buddha; voyage of Skylax, *cir.* 500.
6	Ajatasatru . .	25	32	491	Parricide; death of Mahavira, *cir.* 490; death of Buddha, 487; built fort of Pataliputra; wars with Kosala and Vaisali.
7	Darsaka (Harshaka) . . .	25	25	459	Nothing known.
8	Udaya	33	33	434	Built city of Pataliputra.
9	Nandivardhana .	42 } 85	} 40	401	} Nothing known.
10	Mahanandin . .	43		...	
	Total . .	332	239		
	Average .	33.2	23.9		
	NANDA DYNASTY.				
11 } 12 }	Mahapadma, etc. 9; 2 generations	} 100	} 40	361	
	MAURYA DYNASTY.				
13	Chandragupta .	24	24	321	
14	Bindusara . . .	25	25	297	
15	Asoka	36	40	272	Tibetan tradition reckons 10 reigns from No. 6, Ajatasatru, to No. 15, Asoka, inclusive; and places Asoka's accession in 234 A. B. (Rockhill, *Life of the Buddha*, pp. 33, 233). He is said to have visited Khotan in 250 and 254 A. B. (*J. A. S. B.* 1886, part 1, pp. 195, 197).
	Death of Asoka .			*cir.* 232	
	End of Maurya Dynasty.			*cir.* 184	

APPENDIX II

CHRONOLOGY OF THE INDIAN CAMPAIGN OF ALEXANDER THE GREAT

FROM MAY, 327, TO MAY, 324 B.C.

DATE B. C.	EVENT.
327	**The Advance.**
Early in May .	Passage of Hindu Kush mountains over the Khawak and Kaoshan passes.
June	From Nikaia (Jalalabad), Alexander with picked force proceeds to the subjugation of the mountains; Hephaistion with rest of army advancing to the Indus through the valley of the Kabul River.
August . . .	Capture of stronghold of Astes (Hasti) by Hephaistion after thirty days' siege.
September . .	Alexander subdivides his force, advancing in person against the Aspasians; he crosses the Gouraios (Panjkora) River, captures Massaga of the Assakenians (probably Manglaur on Suwat River), and massacres 7,000 Indian mercenaries.
November . .	Siege of Aornos (Mahaban).
December . .	Capture of Aornos (Mahaban).
326	
January . . .	Arrival of Alexander at bridge-head at Ohind.
February . .	Halt of army for thirty days.
March . . .	Passage of Indus "in beginning of spring;" halt at Taxila.
April	Advance eastward.
May	Arrival at the Hydaspes (Jihlam) River.
Beginning of July	Battle of the Hydaspes; defeat of Poros.
July	Foundation of Nikaia and Boukephala; passage of the Akesines (Chinab) River near the foot of the hills.
August . . .	Passage of the Hydraotes (Ravi) River, and conflict with the Kathæans.
September . .	Arrival at the Hyphasis (Bias) River; refusal of army to proceed farther.
	The Retreat.
Sept.–October .	Retirement to the Hydaspes (Jihlam) River.
End of October	Commencement of voyage down the rivers, and of march of army escorting the fleet.
325	
January . . .	Collapse of the Mallian power.
Till September	Voyage continued, fighting with the Sogdoi, Sambos, Mousikanos, etc.
Beginning of October	Departure of Alexander to march through Gedrosia.
End of October	Nearchos starts on voyage to the Persian Gulf.

DATE B. C.	EVENT.
324	
Early in Jan. .	Arrival of Alexander at Poura (Bampur), the Gedrosian capital, sixty days distant from Ora.
January . . .	Halt of army at Poura.
February . .	March through Karmania, about 300 miles.
End of April or beginning of May	Arrival at Susa in Persia, after about 500 miles of marching from western frontier of Karmania.
323	
June	Death of Alexander at Babylon.

NOTE.—The time spent by Alexander in India proper, from his passage of the Indus in March, 326, until his departure for Gedrosia in September, 325, was about nineteen months. The voyage down the river occupied about ten months out of this period, and the march from India to Susa was effected in about seven months. The march from the Bactrian frontier, that is to say, from the Hindu Kush to the Indus, and the subjugation of the mountain tribes on the northwestern frontier of India were completed in ten months.

I. May, 327, to February, 326, inclusive: march from Hindu Kush to Indus, ten months.

II. March, 326, to September, 325, inclusive: in India proper, nearly nineteen months.

III. October, 325, to April, 324, inclusive: march to Susa, seven months.

TOTAL DURATION OF EXPEDITION, THREE YEARS.

APPENDIX III

THE MAURYA DYNASTY

CHRONOLOGICAL TABLE

YEAR B.C.	EVENT.
326 or 325 .	Chandragupta Maurya in his youth met Alexander the Great.
Sept., 325 .	Alexander quitted India.
Feb., 324 . .	Alexander, while in Karmania, received news of the murder of his satrap Philippos, in India; and placed Eudamos and Ambhi, King of Taxila, in charge of the Indian provinces.
June, 323 .	Death of Alexander at Babylon.
Oct., 323–322	Revolt of Panjab under Chandragupta Maurya.
321. . . .	Destruction of Nanda dynasty of Magadha; **accession of Chandragupta Maurya as Emperor of India.**
321. . . .	Second partition of Alexander's empire at Triparadeisos.
315. . . .	Seleukos Nikator compelled by Antigonos to retire to Egypt.
312. . . .	Recovery of Babylon by Seleukos.
Oct. 1, 312 .	Establishment of Seleukidan era.
306. . . .	Assumption by Seleukos of title of king.
305 or 304 .	Invasion of India by Seleukos.
303. . . .	Defeat of Seleukos by Chandragupta; treaty of peace; cession of a large part of Ariana by Seleukos.
303–301 . .	March of Seleukos against Antigonos.
302. . . .	Megasthenes ambassador of Seleukos at Pataliputra.
301. . . .	Defeat and death of Antigonos at Ipsos in Phrygia.
297. . . .	**Accession of Bindusara Amitraghata as Emperor of India.**
circa 296 . .	Deïmachos ambassador of Seleukos at Pataliputra.
285. . . .	Ptolemy Philadelphos, King of Egypt, acc.
280. . . .	Seleukos Nikator, King of Syria, d.; Antiochos Soter, his son, acc.
278 or 277 .	Antigonos Gonatas, King of Macedonia, grandson of Antiochos I, acc.
272. . . .	Alexander, King of Epirus, son of Pyrrhus, and opponent of Antigonos Gonatas, acc.
272. . . .	**Accession of Asoka-vardhana as Emperor of India.**
269. . . .	Coronation (*abhisheka*) of Asoka.
264. . . .	Outbreak of First Punic War.
261. . . .	Conquest of Kalinga by Asoka; Antiochos Theos, King of Syria, son of Antiochos Soter, acc.
259. . . .	Asoka abolished hunting, instituted tours devoted to works of piety, and despatched missionaries.
258. . . .	Magas, King of Cyrene, half-brother of Ptolemy Philadelphos, died; (?) Alexander, King of Epirus, died.
257. . . .	Rock Edicts III and IV of Asoka, who instituted quinquennial official progresses for propagation of Law of Piety (*dharma*), and dedicated cave-dwellings at Barabar for the use of the Ajivikas.
256. . . .	Publication of complete series of Fourteen Rock Edicts, and of the Kalinga Borderers' Edict by Asoka, who appointed Censors of the Law of Piety (*dharmamahamatrah*).
255. . . .	Asoka enlarged for the second time the *stupa* of Konakamana Buddha near Kapilavastu.
?254 . . .	Publication by Asoka of the Kalinga Provincials' Edict.
250. . . .	Dedication by Asoka of a third cave-dwelling at Barabar for the use of the Ajivikas.

YEAR B.C.	EVENT.
249. . . .	Pilgrimage of Asoka to Buddhist holy places; erection of pillars at Lumbini Garden and a *stupa* of Konakamana; (?) his visit to Nepal, and foundation of Lalita Patan; his daughter Charumati becomes a nun.
247. . . .	Ptolemy Philadelphos, King of Egypt, died.
247 or 246 .	Antiochos Theos, King of Syria, grandson of Seleukos Nikator, died; revolt about this time of Diodotos (Theodotos), and separation of Bactria from the Seleukidan empire.
243. . . .	Composition by Asoka of Pillar Edict VI, confirming the Rock Edicts.
242. . . .	Publication by Asoka of complete series of Seven Pillar Edicts.
242 or 239 .	Antigonos Gonatas, King of Macedonia, died.
241. . . .	Close of First Punic War; rise of the kingdom of Pergamum.
?240 . . .	Supplementary Pillar Edicts of Asoka.
?232–231 .	Publication of Minor Rock Edicts and Bhabra Edict; Asoka died; Dasaratha (Kusala, *Vayu P.*), Emperor of India, acc., and dedicated Nagarjuni caves to the Ajivikas; break-up of Maurya empire began.
?224 . . .	Sangata Maurya, king (Bandhupalita, *Vayu P.*).
?216 . . .	Salisuka Maurya, king (Indrapalita, *Vayu P.*).
?206 . . .	Somasarman Maurya, king (Dasavarman, or Devavarman, *Vayu P.*).
?199 . . .	Satadhanwan Maurya, king (Satadhara, *Vayu P.*).
?191 . . .	Brihadratha Maurya, king (Brihadasva, *Vayu P.*).
184. . . .	Pushyamitra Sunga, acc., having slain Brihadratha; final destruction of Maurya empire.

AP[illegible]

CHRONOLOGY OF THE SUNG

No.	King.	Length of Reign. Traditional.	Length of Reign. Assumed.	Accession.	No.	King.	Length of Reign. Traditional.	Length of Reign. Assumed.	Accession.
	Sunga Dynasty.					**Kanva Dynasty.**			
				B.C.					
1	Pushyamitra (*v. l.* Pushpamitra)	60 (*Vayu*); 36 (*Matsya*); 30 (*Jain*)	36	184					
2	Agnimitra	8 (*Brahmanda*, and *Vayu*, sons of P., unnamed)	8	148					
3	Sujyeshtha	7 (*Vayu* and *Matsya*)	7	140					
4	Vasumitra	8 (*Vayu*); 10 (*Matsya*)	8	133					
5	Andraka (*v. l.* Antaka, etc.)	2 (*Vayu* and *Matsya*)	2	125					
6	Pulindaka (*v. l.* Madhunandana, etc.)	3 (*Vayu* and *Matsya*)	3	123					
7	Ghoshavasu (*v. l.* Magha ?)	3 (*Vayu* and *Matsya*)	3	120					
8	Vajramitra (*v. l.* Vikramitra ?)	14 (*Vayu*); 9 (*Matsya*)	9	117					
9	Bhagavata	32 (*Vayu* and *Matsya*)	26	108					
10	Devabhumi (*v. l.* Kshemabhumi, etc.)	10 (*Vayu* and *Matsya*)	10	82					
			112						
									B.C.
	End of Dynasty. .	. . . . . .	. .	72	1	Vasudeva .	9 (*Vayu* and *Matsya*)	9	72
					2	Bhumimitra	14 (ditto) . .	14	63
					3	Narayana .	12 (ditto) . .	12	49
					4	Susarman .	10 (ditto) . .	10	37
							45	45	
						End of	Dynasty . . .	. .	27

Nos 21-25 form a distinct group, with peculiar names, and "bow and arrow" coins. [2] True length of reign of

V

AND ANDHRA DYNASTIES

Andhra Dynasty.

ng.	Length of Reign.		Accession.
	Traditional.	Assumed.	
			B. C.
. *l.* Sisuka,	23 (*Vayu* and *Matsya*)	23	220
. . . .	18 (*Matsya*); ? 10 or 18 (*Vayu*)	18	197
Satakarni	56 (*Vayu*); 18 (*Matsya*)	10	179
ga [omitvasvani or tambhi of R. only]	18 (*Vayu* and *Matsya*)	18	169
rni . . .	56 (*Matsya* and ? *Vayu*)	40 (duration adjusted)	151
a . . .	18 (*Vayu* and *Matsya*)	18	111
(*v. l.* Api-.)	12 (*Vayu* and *Matsya*)	12	93
. *l.* Meghac.)	18 (*Matsya*)	18	81
rni (*v. l.* i)	18 (*Matsya*)	18	63
vati, *i. e* Satakarni	7 (*Matsya*)	7	45
Satakarni	3 (*Matsya*)	3	38
atakarni	8 (*Matsya*)	8	35
karni . .	1 (*Matsya*)	1	27
I (*v. l.* corms)	36 (*Matsya*); 24 (*Vayu*)	32 (duration adjusted)	26
			A. D.
takarni .	38 (*Matsya*)	38	6
Satakarni emikrishna	25 (*Vayu* and *Matsya*)	25	44
. . . .	5 (*Matsya*); 1 (*Vayu*)	5	69

Andhra Dynasty (continued).

No.	King.	Length of Reign.		Accession.
		Traditional.	Assumed.	
				A. D.
18	Mandalaka (*v. l.* Mantalaka, etc.)	5 (*Vayu* and *Matsya*)	5	74
19	Purindrasena (*v. l.* Purishasena, etc.)	5 (*Matsya*); 21 (*Vayu*)	5	79
20	Sundara Satakarni .	1 (*Matsya*); 3 (*Vayu*)	1	84
21	Vilivayakura I (Vasishthiputra = Chakora or Rajada Satakarni)	½ (*Vayu* and *Matsya*)	½	85
22	Sivalakura (Madhariputra Sakasena = Siva Satakarni (-svati)	28 (*Vayu* and *Matsya*)	28	85
23	Vilivayakura II (Gautamiputra Sri Satakarni)	21 (*Vayu* and *Matsya*)	25[1]	113
24	Pulumayi II (Vasishthiputra Sri P. Satakarni)	28 (*Vayu* and *Matsya*)	32	138
25	Siva Sri (Vasishthiputra)	7 (*Matsya*)	7	170
26	Siva Skanda Satakarni	7 (*Matsya*) (*v. l.* 9)	7	177
27	Yajna Sri (Gautamiputra Svami Sri Y. Satakarni)	20 (*Matsya*) (*v. l.* 9); 19 (*Vayu*)	29[1]	184
28	Vijaya (Sri Satakarni)	6 (*Vayu* and *Matsya*)	6	213
29	Vada Sri (Vasishthiputra Sri V. Satakarni)	10 (*Matsya*); 3 (*Vayu*)	10	219
30	Pulumayi III . . .	7 (*Vayu* and *Matsya*)	7	229
	End of Dynasty . .	. . . . . .	456½[2]	236

…etermined approximately by inscriptions. [2] 30 kings, according to Vishnu Purana, reigning for 456½ years.

APPENDIX V

ALPHABETICAL LIST OF BACTRIAN AND INDO-GREEK KINGS AND QUEENS

SERIAL NO.	NAME.	GREEK TITLE OR EPITHET.	REMARKS.
1	Agathokleia .	Theotropos .	Queen, or mother, of Strato I.
2	Agathokles. .	Dikaios . . .	Probably succeeded Pantaleon, No. 28, and contemporary with Euthydemos I or Demetrios.
3	Amyntas . .	Nikator . . .	A little earlier than Hermaios.
4	Antialkidas .	Nikephoros .	Contemporary with early years of Eukratides, *cir.* 170 B. C.
5	Antimachos I .	Theos . . .	Probably succeeded Diodotos II, No. 13, in Kabul.
6	Antimachos II	Nikephoros .	Later than Eukratides, No. 17, or possibly contemporary.
7	Apollodotos .	Soter, Megas, Philopator .	Probably son of Eukratides, and king of entire Indian frontier.
8	Apollophanes .	Soter	Probably contemporary with Strato I or II.
9	Archebios . .	Dikaios, Nikephoros	Probably connected with Heliokles.
10	Artemidoros .	Aniketos . .	Later than Menander.
11	Demetrios . .	Aniketos . .	Son of Euthydemos I, No. 18.
12	Diodotos I . .	——	No coins known.
13	Diodotos II .	Soter. . . .	Son of No. 12.
14	Diomedes . .	Soter. . . .	Apparently connected with Eukratides, No. 17.
15	Dionysios . .	Soter. . . .	Later than Apollodotos.
16	Epander . .	Nikephoros .	Probably later than Eukratides, No. 17.
17	Eukratides . .	Megas . . .	Contemporary with Mithradates I.
18	Euthydemos I .	——	Subsequent to Diodotos II, No. 13.
19	Euthydemos II	——	Probably son of No. 11.
20	Heliokles . .	Dikaios . . .	Son of No. 17; last of Bactrian dynasty.
21	Hermaios . .	Soter. . . .	Last Indo-Greek king.
22	Hippostratos .	Soter, Megas .	Probably succeeded Apollodotos.
23	Kalliope . .	——	Queen of Hermaios.
24	Laodike. . .	——	Mother of Eukratides.
25	Lysias . . .	Aniketos . .	Predecessor of Antialkidas, No. 4.
26	Menander . .	Soter, Dikaios	Later than Eukratides, invaded India about 155 B. C.
27	Nikias . . .	Soter. . . .	Later than Eukratides.
28	Pantaleon . .	——	Contemporary with Euthydemos I or Demetrios, probably preceded Agathokles, No. 2.
29	Peukelaos . .	Dikaios, Soter	Contemporary with Hippostratos (*J. A. S. B.*, 1898, part i, p. 131).
30	Philoxenos. .	Aniketos . .	Probably succeeded Antimachos II, No. 6.

SERIAL NO.	NAME.	GREEK TITLE OR EPITHET.	REMARKS.
31	Plato	Epiphanes . .	165 B. C., contemporary with Eukratides, No. 17.
32	(?) Polyxenos .	Epiphanes, Soter	*Num. Chron.*, 1896, p. 269 : Mr. Rapson doubts the genuineness of the unique coin described.
33	Strato I. . . .	Soter, Epiphanes, Dikaios	Contemporary with Heliokles.
34	Strato II . .	Soter	Son, or grandson, of No. 33.
35	Telephos . .	Euergetes . .	*J. A. S. B.*, 1898, part i, p. 130.
36	Theophilos .	Dikaios . . .	*J. A. S. B.*, 1897, part i, p. 1; connected with Lysias.
37	Zoilos . . .	Soter, Dikaios	Apparently later than Apollodotos.

SYNCHRONISTIC TABLE, 280 B. C. TO 50 A. D.

B. C.	Syria.	Bactria.	Parthia (Persia).	NW. Indian Frontier, Panjab, and Kabul.	Interior India.	Remarks.
280	Antiochos Soter acc.					
261	Antiochos Theos. acc.					
c. 250		Diodotos I acc.				
c. 248			Arsakes I acc.	Maurya dynasty		
246	Seleukos Kallinikos acc. (Antiochos Hierax, rival)					
c. 245		Diodotos II acc.				
c. 232–1					Maurya dynasty.	Death of Asoka.
c. 230		Euthydemos acc.				
223	Antiochos III (the Great)					
c. 208						Recognition of Bactrian independence.
c. 206						Invasion of Kabul by Antiochos the Great.
c. 200				Demetrios — Antimachos — Pantaleon		
c. 190				Euthydemos II — Agathokles		Indian conquests of Demetrios.
187	Seleukos Philopator acc.					
184					Pushyamitra Sunga acc.	
c. 175		Eukratides acc.				
c. 174			Mithradates I acc.			
165		Plato (rival of Eukratides)		Menander (Kabul)		
c. 156		Heliokles		Apollodotos		
c. 155						Invasion of India by Menander.
c. 148					Agnimitra Sunga acc.	
c. 138–130		*End of Bactrian dynasty*		Various Greek princes		Saka Invasion of Bactria, etc.
c. 136			Phraates II acc.			
124			Mithradates II acc.			
c. 120				Strato I — Maues acc. — Satraps of Taxila and Mathura		
c. 90				Strato II — Vonones acc. — Various Greek princes		
c. 72					Vasudeva Kanva acc.	
c. 50				Azes I acc.		
A. D. 21				Gondophares acc. — Hermaios		St. Thomas.
c. 50						Overthrow of Hermaios by Kushans.

APPENDIX VI

APPROXIMATE KUSHAN CHRONOLOGY

DATE.	EVENT.
B. C. 165	Expulsion of main body of Yueh-chi horde from Kan-suh by the Hiung-nu.
c. 163	Nan-tiu-mi, chief of the Wu-sun, killed by the Yueh-chi.
c. 160	Yueh-chi occupation of the Saka territory; Saka migration.
c. 150–140	Saka invasion of India.
c. 140	Expulsion of Yueh-chi from Saka territory by Koen-muo, the young Wu-sun chief, son of Nan-tiu-mi.
c. 138	Reduction of the Ta-hia, both north and south of the Oxus, to vassalage by the Yueh-chi, who begin to settle down.
c. 135	Despatch by Chinese Emperor Wu-ti of Chang-kien as envoy to the Yueh-chi.
c. 125	Arrival of Chang-kien at Yueh-chi headquarters, north of the Oxus.
c. 122	Return of Chang-kien to China.
c. 114	Death of Chang-kien.
c. 70	Extension of Yueh-chi settlements to the lands south of the Oxus; occupation of Ta-hia capital, Lan-sheu, south of the river, probably = Balkh.
c. 65	**Formation of five Yueh-chi principalities, including Kushan and Bamian.**
57	Epoch of the Malava or Vikrama era.
c. 13	Indian embassy to Augustus.
B. C. 2	The Chinese graduate, King-hien, or King-lu, instructed in Buddhist books by a Yueh-chi king.
A. D. 8	Temporary cessation of intercourse between China and the West.
14	Augustus, Roman Emperor, died; Tiberius acc.
c. 24	End of First, or Early Han dynasty of China.
38	Gaius (Caligula), Roman Emperor, acc.
41	Claudius, Roman Emperor, acc.
c. 45	**Kadphises I Kushan (Kieu-tsieu-kio, Kozolakadaphes, etc.) acc.**
c. 45–60	**Consolidation of the five Yueh-chi principalities into Kushan empire under Kadphises I**; conquest by him of Kabul (Kao-fu), ? Bactria (Pota), and ? Kashmir (Ki-pin); Hermaios, Greek king in Kabul and Panjab, contemporary.
54	Nero, Roman Emperor, acc.
c. 64	Buddhist books sent for by Chinese Emperor, Ming-ti.
68, 69	Galba, Otho, and Vitellius, Roman Emperors.
70	Vespasian, Roman Emperor (acc. Dec. 22, 69).
77	Publication of Pliny's *Natural History*.
78	Epoch of the Saka, or Salivahana era.
79	Titus, Roman Emperor, acc.
81	Domitian, Roman Emperor, acc.
c. 85	**Death of Kadphises I, at age of 80; Kadphises II, his son, acc.** (= Yen-kao-ching, Hima Kadphises, etc.); the "Nameless King," *Soter Megas*, contemporary and subordinate.
90	Kadphises II defeated by Chinese general Pan-ch'ao, and compelled to pay tribute to China.
c. 90–100	**Annexation of Northern India, and destruction of Indo-Parthian power in the Panjab by Kadphises II.**
96	Nerva, Roman Emperor, acc.

DATE.	EVENT.
A.D.	
98	Trajan, Roman Emperor, acc.
99	Arrival of Trajan in Rome.
105	Overthrow by the Romans of the Nabataean kingdom of Petra in Arabia; rise of Palmyra; Indian embassy to Trajan about this time.
116	Conquest of Mesopotamia by Trajan.
117	Hadrian, Roman Emperor, acc.; retrocession of Mesopotamia.
123–6	Residence of Hadrian at Athens.
c. 123	**Kanishka Kushan acc.**
c. 125–30	**Conquest by Kanishka of Kashgar, Yarkand, and Khotan; war with King of Pataliputra.**
131–6	War of Hadrian with the Jews.
c. 135	Conversion of Kanishka to Buddhism.
138	Antoninus Pius, Roman Emperor, acc.
c. 140	**Buddhist Council in (?) Kashmir.**
150	Junagarh inscription of Rudradaman, Western satrap.
c. 153	**Huvishka (Hushka) Kushan acc.**
161	Marcus Aurelius Antoninus, Roman Emperor, acc.
162–5	Defeat of Parthian King, Vologeses III, by the Romans.
175	Eastern campaign of Marcus Aurelius.
180	Commodus, Roman Emperor, acc.
c. 185	**Vasudeva Kushan acc.**
192, 193	Pertinax and Julianus, Roman Emperors.
193	Septimius Severus, Roman Emperor, acc.
c. 200	Palmyra created a Roman colony.
211	Caracalla, Roman Emperor, acc.
216	Parthian expedition of Caracalla.
217	Macrinus, Roman Emperor, acc.
218	Elagabalus, Roman Emperor, acc.
222	Alexander Severus, Roman Emperor, acc.
226	Foundation of Sasanian empire of Persia by Ardashir; **the death of Vasudeva, the collapse of the Kushan power in India; and the termination of the Andhra dynasty occurred at nearly the same time.**
260	Defeat of Valerian, Roman Emperor, by Sapor I.
273	Capture of Palmyra by Aurelian.
360	**Successful siege of Amida by Sapor II, with Kushan help.**

APPENDIX VII

CHRONOLOGY OF THE GUPTA PERIOD

DATE A. D.	EVENT.	REMARKS.
cir. 308 . . .	Lichchhavi marriage of Chandragupta I	
320	**Chandragupta I acc. to independent power**	Foundation of Gupta Era, of which year 1 began Feb. 26, 320
cir. 326 . . .	**Samudragupta acc.**	
cir. 330 . . .	Embassy from King Meghavarna of Ceylon	
cir. 326–36 . .	Campaigns in Northern India	
cir. 337–40 . .	Campaign in Southern India	
cir. 341 . . .	Horse-sacrifice	
cir. 375 . . .	**Chandragupta II acc.**	
cir. 395 . . .	Conquest of Western India	
401	Udayagiri inscription	G. E. 82
405–11 . . .	Travels of Fa-hien in Gupta empire	" 86–92
407	Garhwa inscription	" 88
409	Silver coins of western type	" 90
412	Sanchi inscription	" 93
413	**Kumaragupta I acc.**	" 94
415	Bilsar inscription	" 96
417	Garhwa inscription	" 98
432	Mathura inscription	" 113
436	Mandasor inscription	V. S. 493 (= G. E. 117)
440	Silver coins	G. E. 121
443	Silver coins	" 124
447	Silver coins	" 128
448	Silver coins and Mankuwar inscriptions	" 129
449	Silver coins	" 130
cir. 450 . . .	Pushyamitra war	" 131
454	Silver coins	" 135
455	Silver coins	" 136
455	**Skandagupta acc.**; first Hun war	" 136
456	Embankment of lake at Girnar rebuilt	" 137
457	Temple erected there	" 138
460	Kahaon inscription (Gorakhpur District)	" 141
463	Silver coins	" 144
464	Silver coins	" 145
465	Indor inscription (Bulandshahr District)	" 146
467	Silver coins	" 148
cir. 470–80 . .	Second Hun war	" 151–61
477 . . .	Pali inscription (*Ep. Ind.* 2. 363)	" 158
cir. 480 . . .	**Puragupta (? Prakasaditya) acc.**	
cir. 485 . . .	**Narasimhagupta Baladitya acc.**	
cir. 530 . . .	**Kumaragupta II acc.**	
520	Song-Yun visited White Hun King of Gandhara	
cir. 535 to 720 .	**Later Gupta dynasty of Magadha**	
cir. 490 to 770 .	**Dynasty of Valabhi**	
cir. 490 to 510 .	**Toramana**	
cir. 510 to 540 .	**Mihiragula**	Defeat *cir.* 528
cir. 530 to 580 .	**Siladitya of Mo-la-po**	

APPENDIX VIII

CHRONOLOGY OF THE SEVENTH CENTURY

A. D.	EVENT.
cir. 600	Persecution of Buddhism by Sasanka.
cir. 605	Rajya-vardhana, Raja of Thanesar, *acc.*
606	Harsha-vardhana, Raja of Thanesar, *acc.*
606–12	Conquest of Northern India by Harsha.
Oct. 612	Coronation of Harsha as Lord Paramount of N. India.
618	Tang dynasty of China *acc.*
619–20	Ganjam inscription of Sasanka.
620	Defeat of Harsha by Pulikesin II Chalukya.
627–8	Banskhera inscription of Harsha.
629	Hiuen Tsang, Chinese pilgrim, began his travels.
630–1	Madhuban inscription of Harsha.
639	Reception by Harsha of A-lo-pen and other Syrian Christians, who introduced Nestorianism into China in 635 A. D.
643	Expedition of Harsha to Ganjam (Kongoda); his meeting with Hiuen Tsang; Chinese mission of Li-I-piao and Wang-hiuen-tse.
644	Harsha's assemblies at Kanauj and Prayaga; Hiuen Tsang started on return journey.
646	Second mission of Wang-hiuen-tse despatched; arrival of Hiuen Tsang in China.
647–8	Death of Harsha; usurpation of Arjuna (A-lo-na-shoen, or O-lo-na-shoen); attack on Chinese mission; defeat of Arjuna by Wang-hiuen-tse with aid of Nepalese and Tibetans.
657	Third mission of Wang-hiuen-tse.
671	I-tsing, Chinese pilgrim, began his travels.
675–85	Residence of I-tsing at Nalanda monastery.
691–2	Composition of I-tsing's *Record*
695	Return of I-tsing to China.

INDEX

B

I

J

K

L

M

N